Ortwin Renn | A. Reichel | J. Bauer (Eds.)

Civil Society for Sustainability

A Guidebook for Connecting Science and Society

Renn, Ortwin; Reichel, A.; Bauer, J. (Eds.)
Civil Society for Sustainability
A Guidebook for Connecting Science and Society

ISBN/EAN: 978-3-86741-761-7
First published in 2012 by Europaeischer Hochschulverlag GmbH & Co KG, Bremen, Germany.

© Europaeischer Hochschulverlag GmbH & Co KG, Fahrenheitstr. 1, D-28359 Bremen (www.eh-verlag.de). All rights reserved.

No part of this publication may be reproduced or transmitted, in any form or by any means, electronic, mechanical, photocopying, recording or otherwise, or stored in any retrieval system of nay nature, without the written permission of the copyright holder and the publisher, application for which shall be made to the publisher.

Ortwin Renn | A. Reichel | J. Bauer (Eds.)
Civil Society for Sustainability

Contents

Editorial 1

A. Challenges for Civil Society and Science in Theory and Practice 5

NGOs between influence and participation overkill: The Merits, Strengths and Weaknesses of Environmental Civil Society Organisations 5
Joachim H. Spangenberg

Sustainability: The need for societal discourse 18
Ortwin Renn

The Knowledge of Civil Society 37
Nico Stehr

B. Theory and Concepts of Civil Society 56

Civil Society as a System 56
André Reichel

Bases of Power and Effective Participation of Civil Society Organisations in Development Partnerships - The Need for Governance? 73
Annekathrin Ellersiek

Cooperatives and Climate Protection 107
Christine von Blanckenburg

C. Cases in Collaboration between Civil Society and Science 126

Democratic culture for sustainable development in Slovenia: Outcome of a European action research project involving CSOs and researchers for sustainability 126
Milena Marega, Andrej Klemenc, Mateja Sepec, Gilles Heriard Dubreuil, Stephane Baudé, Matthieu Ollagnon

Participatory Action Research for Local Human Rights – The Case of Roma Minority in Szeged, South-Hungary 149
György Málovics, Barbara Mihók, István Szentistványi, Bálint Balázs, György Pataki

Participation-Action-Research: a Hungarian Case Study 171
Vári Anna, Ferencz Zoltán, Bozso Brigitta

The CSS-Project – new strategies for an established CSO supported by Social Science - A learning process with Dialogik gGmbH and unw e. V. 191
Joa Bauer, unw, Ulm, Germany and Dialogik, Stuttgart, Germany

Civil Society Involvement towards Sustainable Energy Development in Africa: Expectations, Challenges and Perspectives 211
Angela Meyer, Gregor Giersch

Social Acceptance in Quantitative Low Carbon Scenarios 232
Eva Schmid, Brigitte Knopf, Stéphane La Branche, Meike Fink

Author Information 252

EDITORIAL

Civil society and its organisations play a vital role in the implementation of sustainable development. Civil society actors exhibit special features: they are to a large degree driven by visions and ideals; they place a focus on common action thus balancing individual and collective goals; they participate in and initiate discourses on sustainable development in society; they enhance social capital and share a non-economic, non-efficiency driven world view.

Given these characteristics, organisations of civil society show some specific shortcomings: their non-economic worldview leads to less efficient pursuit of sustainability goals, endangering possibilities for representation in decision processes in politics and business; initiating discourses aimed at direct action often excludes evidence-based thinking, surrendering opportunities for increased self-reflexivity and learning; a general lack of institutionalisation within existing frameworks of governance do not provide enough leverage to influence policy-making in administrative and legislative processes. Apart from these more general shortcomings, there are numerous specific and context-related issues that would need to be researched into and reflected on in order to increase the contribution of civil society and its organisations to a sustainable development.

In order to make civil society truly deliver the promise of a more sustainable society, stronger connections between sustainability research and activists "on the ground" need to be fostered. These collaborative networks between science and civil society are in themselves a critical research object for successfully implementing sustainable development.

This volume is the result of a research project called "Civil Society for Sustainability (CSS)", funded under the Seventh Research Framework Programme of the European Union, addressing all these questions. Together with contributions from different European countries that were presented at the "International Conference on Connecting Civil Society and Science — A Key Challenge for Change towards Sustainable Development" [1] held in October 2011 in Stuttgart, Germany, it provides a guidebook for civil society organisations and research to help them navigate through the stormy waters of collaboration for sustainable development. The structure follows the grand themes of this conference.

In **Part A "Challenges for Civil Society and Science in Theory and Practice"** the greater view on the complex interaction between science and civil society, between politics and knowledge, between implementation and

---

[1] URL: www.tinyurl.com/css-conference.

frustration is analysed. *Joachim Spangenberg* opens the discussion on "NGOs between influence and participation overkill", giving an overview of the emergence of civil society as a key actor in sustainable development. In "Sustainability – the need for societal discourse", *Ortwin Renn* develops a normative-functional concept of sustainability and its indicators from which he derives a deliberative approach for generic sustainability strategies. In a critical reflection on "The Knowledge of Civil Society", *Nico Stehr* rounds up the discussion in questioning the role of expert knowledge in societal decision making processes.

Part B on "Theory and Concepts of Civil Society" focuses on different theoretical aspects of civil society and its organisations. *André Reichel* starts with developing a system-theoretical perspective on "Civil Society as a System", shedding light on civil society's role in society and a possible outlook on its future significance in the transition to a sustainable society. The often-overlooked issue of power in relations between civil society and other actors is the main topic in "Bases of Power and Effective Participation of Civil Society Organisations in Development Partnerships" by *Annekathrin Ellersiek*. "Cooperatives and Climate Protection" by *Christine von Blankenburg* focuses on cooperatives as a suitable organisational form for civil society organisations and how their specific rules of governance can contribute to sustainable development.

Part C "Cases in Collaboration between Civil Society and Science", which is the heart of this volume, deals with the complex relations between civil society activism and sustainability research when joined in participatory action research. One of the research tandems in the CSS project begins this part with *Milena Marega*, *Andrej Klemenc*, Mateja Sepec, *Gilles Heriard Dubreuil*, *Stephane Baudé*, and *Matthieu Ollagnon* discussing steps in building a "Democratic Culture for Sustainable Development in Slovenia" with a special emphasis on how civil society organisations can build credibility in political decision making processes. Regarding the issue of empowerment and collaboration, "Participatory Action Research for Local Human Rights" deals with human rights of ethnic minorities in a joint research project by *György Málovics*, *Barbara Mihók*, *László Jakab*, *Elizabeth Lakatos*, *István Szentistványi*, *Bálint Balázs*, and *György Pataki*. Another research tandem from the CSS project, constituted by *Anna Vári*, *Zoltán Ferencz*, and *Brigitta Bozsó*, deals with an organisational change project of a Hungarian civil society organisation in "Civil Society Organisations and Researchers for Sustainability". *Joa Bauer* presents the German case of the CSS project in "The CSS-Project – New strategies for an established CSO supported by Social Science" focusing on the critical issue of how to involve concerned citizens in civil society action. Turning away from a European perspective,

Angela Meyer and *Gregor Giersch* take on the challenge of how to involve civil society in building renewable energy infrastructures in developing countries in their paper on "Potential contributions and challenges of civil society organisations for sustainable energy development in Africa". Continuing with issues of energy and climate, *Stéphane La Branche, Eva Schmid,* and *Meike Fink* take on collaboration of civil society and science in "Social Acceptance in Quantitative Low Carbon Scenarios".

Summing up the conference discussions the following findings condense the overall impression from the fields of reflection. Regarding the roles of civil society organisations, advocacy, collective learning, raising awareness, connection to and also influencing the media landscape are crucial. From the experience of field and action research, the involvement of civil society improves political processes by broadening perspectives of decision makers and involving different stakeholder groups, with civil society organisations being held as a "trusted broker". Additionally, one significant role for civil society is the translation of expert and political knowledge into "lay language" and the infusion of non-expert knowledge into political processes, thus often providing critical thinking about the existing order and power structures that underlie governance processes.

The results from action research and collaboration of science with civil society showed all the differences and difficulties accompanying this type of knowledge generation. Scientists often have to abandon scientific language in order to communicate their findings and this is seen not only as challenging but also as endangering the content of these findings. The action orientation of civil society organisations implies an increased interest in applicable knowledge which, for scientists, is a mere by-product. The challenge is to overcome pre-existing stereotypes and the "us versus them" logic. All presented case studies, which consisted largely of collaboration and action research show, that openness, flexibility, and some sufficient knowledge about "the other side" are critical success factors. Living a double culture of science and activism can help to bridge the divide between these differing rationalities. Scientists who engage in civil society organisations as well as civil society activists who were or turn into academics are in a better position to translate knowledge and overcoming the gap between the two cultures.

The benefits of this kind of collaboration are multifold. Scientists bring in a form of reflectivity and second-order thinking that is hard to create from an activist's point of view, where time is an ultimate constraint. This provision of a "third room" by science, which accompanies collaborative research projects, but enables discussion beyond the daily business of project work, helps activists to facilitate strategic discussions on the broader implications and underlying motives of their actions. Activists, on the other hand, provide a critical edge to scientific reasoning as regards applicability and implementation, and challenge established research questions and procedures. This enables scientists to reassess theories and methods from an action perspective. Both types of reflection, theoretical reasoning and second-order thinking, as well as action reasoning and implementation orientation are crucial in pursuing sustainable development.

With this Guidebook we hope to spark discussions on collaborations between science and civil society for a more sustainable society. We also wish to encourage both activists and scientists to engage in this type of collaborative action research and experience the great learning processes we encountered in so many of the cases detailed in here. Sustainable development demands a broad view and an inclusion of heterogeneous and often conflicting knowledge, from grassroots to policy level. The path sketched in this Guidebook appears to be a path well worth taking to truly deliver what is needed to transform our societies towards sustainability.

A. CHALLENGES FOR CIVIL SOCIETY AND SCIENCE IN THEORY AND PRACTICE

NGOs between influence and participation overkill: The Merits, Strengths and Weaknesses of Environmental Civil Society Organisations[2]

Joachim H. Spangenberg

In order to understand the functions of NGOs, their possible role in governance and their inherent, systemic limitations, it is helpful to take a look at how and why they emerged. This provides insight into their support base, which constitutes their political strength, but at the same time limits their room for manoeuvring.

A civil society (i.e. institutions within a society – organisations and processes, formal and informal – beyond formal government and market) is neither initiated nor founded. It is commonplace in all societies as an emergent property of any society with more than a minimum level of complexity and space for individualism. Humans with similar interests get together, organise and become active to promote their common interest. This definition includes human rights movements as well as organised crime; civil society is not a priori a beneficial institution.[3] A choice has to be made; this contribution deals exclusively with civil society organisations acting (in their own understanding) for the public good. Although some of the facts presented in this chapter, and the line of argumentation are similar for all of civil society groups, for instance for feminist, solidarity, justice, developmental and environmental NGOs, the focus here is on the latter group, and in particular on formal organisations for conservation and environment protection, as this is the domain the author can best describe from his own experience.

Why did a civil society emerge?

Although all modern societies always have a civil society as a part of the self-organisation mechanisms in every complex system, the occasions or

---

[2] This paper is based on a presentation at the International Conference "Connecting Civil Society and Science – A Key Challenge for Change Towards Sustainable Development", October 20th, 2011, Conference Venue, University of Stuttgart.

[3] This makes a description as "social capital" questionable: the capital metaphor rules out accounting for qualities (there is no negative and positive capital); thus this economistic terminology is avoided here. The situation is different for social sustainability; different elements of "social capital" can be valued as positive or negative.

crystallisation points, triggering the development of new social movements from a critical mass of people ready to act, vary over time and between societies. Such a situation was given in Germany in the early 1970s, when the '68 movement had sensitised many beyond its own circles on the need for broader democratic change, leading to a widely spread perception that change was not only necessary but indeed desirable and possible. This public mood calling for change, for a reform era, was not satisfied with what politics had to offer. An alternative to the prevailing closed shop political corporatism ("concerted action" of politics, business and trade unions) was sought, as this mode of governance was experienced as not offering sufficient opportunity to express the needs and concerns, and to harbour the visions which environmentally concerned citizens considered urgent.

Such concerns were abounding, from the traditional conservation organisations and environmental action groups (existing since the 1950s), to those sensitised by the "Limits to Growth" report to the Club of Rome, and those mobilised by the government's ambitious plans for new nuclear power plants. Thus, problems not solvable within the existing institutional structures called for an independent opposition force, as a means to break up the closed shop of politics (once that was achieved, agents took different routes, remaining opposition, becoming administrators, becoming politicians or lobbyists, using the extended range of stakeholders accepted as relevant voices in the policy process).

All over continental Europe, the main addressee of demands for change was the government, with business perceived (only a part of the 1968 heritage, but also based on evidence) as the main culprit for environmental damage causation. The state / politics was seen to be in charge of balancing the diverse interests in society, an intellectual tradition that goes back to Kant and the enlightenment period.[4]

It was a period of change, which provided a seedbed for the modern civil society. Consequently it is not surprising that civil society organisations of all kinds were established, the feminist movement had a peak of influence, and trade unions began to question their past dedication to economic growth and began discussing the quality of life. Forty years later, many of the

---

[4] Unlike the anti-etatist US tradition, which – together with the perceived or experienced unwillingness of government to make the "green cause", and its dependency on big money at least from 1980 on – led US NGOs to oppose the state more and seek collaboration with business. Thus it is important to distinguish between the Anglo-Saxon and the continental European situation when analysing civil society development: US studies are usually not replicable, and their conclusions not applicable in Europe.

current social and technological developments (low carbon technologies, sustainable consumption, etc.) can be traced back to this period. The French ban on shale gas exploration, the German nuclear energy phase out, the EU-wide waste recycling policies, fair trade and organic food would be hard to imagine without that period. In retrospect, 40 years of the environmental movement have been a success – although it is much less success than its activist members consider necessary, not least based on scientific information.

Resources for NGOs – support under permanent scrutiny

What makes the strength of current environmental NGOs? First of all, their broad support base includes people of all ages and professions. The majority of members are women, with the stronghold being in middle aged, middle class population groups. Proportionally, more are in the public service than in the industry and they are more educated than the average citizen. Despite these deviations from the "average citizen", the membership of NGOs is more representative of the German society than that of any political party, which contributes to the credibility of the respective organisations. These people contribute not only money but also their knowledge and leisure time. Millions of them participate actively in NGO work, or make the work possible through their donations. They provide the following resources on which environmental NGOs thrive:

- Credibility through economic and political independence thanks to income from membership fees and donations.
- Scientific excellence and argumentative strength through fact-based reasoning, building upon internal and external expertise[5]. This includes a non-economic world view, a different view on the economy based on physical resources ("the really real economy", Martinez-Alier). Policy concepts like capping and tradable permits (less so eco-taxes) are a result of this way of thinking.

---

[5] Some NGOs rely on the "green research institutes" as the main source of knowledge, others draw on mainstream science, again others have been building up own capacities. In the latter case, research was usually outsourced, and used in campaigns by scientifically qualified staff. This qualification was initially focussed on science and engineering, then complemented by legal expertise. Only later some NGOs built up capacity in economics, less so in other social sciences, and little in humanities. These have built a capacity as transdisciplinary, independent think tanks, providing public science.

- Highly efficient professional organisation of campaigns, including media and communication skills, supported by unpaid work by volunteers from all walks of life.

The gifts are free, but they come with strings attached. Donors and members want to see their contributions used for the "right" purposes. Otherwise volunteering can stop, and donations can end overnight. The sources of NGOs' resources are more fragile than those of states (taxes) and businesses (profits). Marketing NGO activities is a challenge that is at least as big as marketing a business, but with no material goods to sell. However, while a part of the credibility of environmental organisations, the social capital on which their income and impact are based, is a collective good, which is a common property of the environmental movement (implying that by violating the unwritten standards, any major NGO can put much of the movement at risk), a significant part is earned by the individual NGO and is based on diverse expectations of their respective constituencies.

Different knowledge – better knowledge?

The supply of intellectual resources and the initial situation of opposing solutions rubberstamped by representatives of the scientific establishment have influenced the position of NGOs towards science and the scientific community (for instance the safety analyses for nuclear power plants were debunked by "alternative" scientists closely working with NGOs). Since the outset, NGOs looked for alternatives beyond established knowledge, with a focus on stakeholders' knowledge. This rejection of the hegemonial technology fix attitude resulted in the promotion of alternative lifestyles and consumption patterns and on social innovations including going beyond technological fixes. The result of viewing the environment in a social context was a dedication to public science, for NGOs, unions and civil society at large, long rejected by politics and the science system.

Today, although not homogenous in their approach to knowledge, be it new or established, critical/alternative or mainstream, some commonalities amongst environmental NGOs have emerged. They tend to favour a new approach characterised by transdisciplinarity, by the combination of visions and normative stances (sustainability is a normative concept) with openness and willingness to experiment to find problem-solving innovative approaches, by offering a long-term perspectives in politics, economics and technology, and of course by focussing on stakeholder participation. Such approaches have resonated with parts of the scientific system; methods like discourse based solution framing or post-normal science draw heavily on impulses from the environmental movement.

Choosing strategies, choosing identities

What does that imply for NGO strategies? NGOs are assessed on two accounts: their success in getting change implemented, and the moral/ethical standard of their performance. This requires a permanent balancing act, live on stage, with donors as careful observers. Each wrong move can be fatal. While this is positive in terms of democracy (enforcement of transparent responsible behaviour), this situation also limits the possibilities of NGOs as political actors, as compared to those of other interest groups under less permanent public scrutiny. The duality of expectations regarding implementation success and a clear moral stance requires delicate compromises. Effective change can be achieved by different means in different policy domains (conservation vs. energy policy, for instance), and by a wide range of strategies from confrontation to cooperation, depending on the ideology and moral stance of the respective organisation. Both parameters are not independent. Advocating change requires getting involved with existing policy structures, although getting too deeply involved may compromise the moral stance.

This dilemma has led to specialisation, either in themes dealt with, or in methods considered legitimate and appropriate, according to ideological / moral stance, always with an eye on the preferences of the respective organisation's supporters. E.g., for some NGOs, such as the WWF, conservation is at the core of their efforts. Social impacts are regarded as of secondary importance (if considered at all), and business cooperation is considered less problematic. Others such as Friends of the Earth cultivate a spirit of radicalism, in the sense of asking for the "radix", i.e. the root of the problems, and pride themselves with respect to their habit of plain speech, social sensibility, economic competence, disregard for populism and opportunism. The basis for this attitude is a strong membership base (1/2 million in Germany – more than almost all political parties) and the resulting financial independence. The hands-on work on environment and conservation issues of the more than 2500 local BUND/FoE Germany groups underpins this strength. Frustrated with the outcome of the Rio+20 summit, Greenpeace International even announced a turn to "war footage" and a global strategy of civil disobeyance.

Donors with a more subjective motivation (some expecting exculpation from the guilt they feel in their everyday work, others just wanting to be good citizens, supporting those who explicitly advocate the public good) tend to support both kinds of organisations on a case-by-case basis, while those with a strong ideological or ethical orientation give to an organisation with the corresponding moral stance (business friendly – WWF; viewing the environment in a social context, questioning power relations and justice deficits, being sceptical against business – Friends of the Earth/BUND). The latter group of donors (often described as postmodernists, with post-material values) plays a major role as a NGO constituency and reference group. Responding to their wish to see their non-economic world views and values brought to the attention of decision makers of all kinds is an imperative and a condition for survival for many environmental NGOs. Their demands for new lifestyles are practiced as part of the corporate culture of responsive NGOs. This may range from the absence of a car park and avoiding air transport to provision of organic food at all major meetings.

Skills and limits: what to do?

One activity almost all environmental NGOs are involved in is education and information dissemination. This general term covers a wide range of activities. The WWF uses pictures of iconic species to point to their risk of extinction and claims that donating of three or five Euros to WWF would save them. Greenpeace pursues sensitising through spectacular action. The Nature Protection Society – Birdwatch Germany (Naturschutzbund NaBu) organises excursions, manages protected areas and trains citizens in species recognition and monitoring.[6] Friends of the Earth Germany/BUND does that as well, but covers a wider spectrum of issues and is more critical of government policy. According to their thematic focus and moral stance, NGOs chose different target groups to concentrate on, albeit with overlaps (there are no fixed claims, but permanent competition prevails). Almost all address consumers, e.g. about sustainable consumption or green mobility, and politics, e.g. about upcoming risks, necessary policy priorities, new policy instruments (from green taxes to tradable permits) and the resistance they have to expect in case specific decisions are taken (the latter borders to lobbying, pressure group action and campaigning). The differences between different NGOs become more visible when it comes to education and collaboration with other civil society groups. Some prefer to go it alone, like Greenpeace, or work only withother NGOs, but FoE Germany also cultivates their cooperation with trade unions and consumer organisations. Others prefer to work with businesses, e.g. on greening the supply chain.

In the German legal system, recognised environmental NGOs ("anerkannte Naturschutzverbände") have to be heard when environmentally sensitive planning is done by public or private actors. Due to the Aarhus

---

[6] Since some years, they are extending their portfolio of themes; the latest add-on is resource efficiency policy.

Convention they have data access (limited) and last but not least the possibility to take the culprits to court on the basis of national or EU law.[7] They can thus act as watchdogs, monitoring environmental law compliance, safety standards violations etc., mobilise supervising bodies and in case of a problem, bring violations to court and/or to the media. Here Friends of the Earth/BUND and Birdwatch/NaBu are the dominating organisations at national level, complemented by a variety of local organisations. Locally they most often work hand in hand, but the different stance is reflected in how outgoing they are, how ready they are to go to court, etc. For groups focussed on monitoring, compliance control is their way of participation (such legal conflicts turn them into a part of the governance system).

Between environmental NGOs, both the readiness to go public, and the means of doing so differ significantly. For the more "radical" NGOs, with their strength based upon a large membership with critical supporters, a key means of getting change implemented is by mobilising public support through campaigns, in order to pressurise policy to "*do better things!*" Such campaigns can but need not include cultural events, in traditional and new forms. They include all kinds of mobilisation, traditional and innovative forms, direct action and the use of new technologies. The locations for actions vary and can be combined; they include

- the streets: from flash mobs in the streets to mobilising big demonstrations;
- the media: from press conferences via public events to boycotts/buycotts;
- the internet: from mass signatures to appeals to spam jams.

The less radical, closer-to-business NGOs use these tools only to a very limited degree, often combining media work and internet presence not with political demands but with fundraising. While their focus is on sensitisation and information provision, they join the more ambitious groups when it comes to lobbying, e.g. at international conferences or regarding certain pieces of legislation (although the diverging level of closeness to business interests is making copperation increasingly difficult as it bthretens to undermine the moral credibility). For such lobbying NGOs, working behind closed doors, policy participation at the expense of transparency is part of their business model. One specificity of any lobbying is that it is only successful if based on a detailed knowledge of the on-going discussions and negotiations, and the drafts of bills or treaties. Then lobbyists can come with

---

[7] This right has been systematically dismantled by the German Federal Government over the last 10 years.

suggested phrasing for specific aspects ("*do things better!*"), and have a chance of convincing decision makers to follow their suggestions. Lobbying (as opposed to policy advocacy) is not there to change the direction of politics, but to modify the chosen course.

Most significant is the differentiation of environmental NGOs when it comes to business collaboration. The more ethically oriented ones like Greenpeace or Friends of the Earth prefer short term, product related cooperation with carefully selected companies to "make good alternatives known" (which does not rule out campaigning against the same company on other aspects of its performance),[8] while others enter in long term, strategic partnerships with businesses ("make things better and better known"). As credibility is the main social capital of NGOs, and not loosing it a matter of survival, the scepticism of the respective members and supporters is strongly reflected in the attitude towards business cooperation. In all cases, certain business sectors, for instance nuclear industry and weapons industry are unanimously considered a clear cooperation no-go zone. On the other hand, other former key target industries like the chemical industry (Ökoinstitut), car industry (Greenpeace), food industry (Birdwatch-NaBu), or retailers (FoE-BUND), have managed to enter into cooperations. As former conflicts fade and new constellations emerge, what remain indispensible essentials of NGO success and effectiveness? Five imperatives for success can be highlighted:

- Independence (don't be too close to business, with varying definitions of "too close") as a condition for credibility.
- Emphasising non-monetary values as a condition for public resonance and support, in order to maintain legitimation in the eyes of the public, overwhelmingly refusing a one-sided economic world view. This requires understanding economics (neoclassical and heterodox), without adopting an economic world view.
- "*The Vision Thing*"; Reflecting about the chosen path, imagining alternative worlds, incorporating new, upcoming issues and/or revitalising old ones (e.g. degrowth) as a condition for long-term supporter motivation.
- Safeguarding volunteer support as a condition for performance efficiency that has been proven to be superior to business campaigns.

---

[8] Of course business is not happy with partners which can at the same time collaborate and buycott – NGOs, in particularly the stronger ethically motivated ones, are necessarily ambivalent, a stance hard to swallow for most businesses.

- Maintaining the combination of value discourses, science based arguments, fact based arguments and inspiring storylines („zählen und erzählen").

In a nutshell, the role of NGOs is a multiple one: they are policy advocates, lobbyists, confronting and cooperating with politics and business. They educate and sensitise the public, and they are networking think tanks. NGOs gain influence through credibility. Their influence is based on their public resonance, resulting from their pursuit of public good and their independence. They are only influential if the public feels represented by their work (in hearings, studies, discussions, court cases), supports them through opinion, volunteering and donations.

Summary and Outlook

NGOs started as an independent opposition force, fundamentally questioning "the system", i.e. the prevailing close cooperation of business and politics, with limited influence of citizens on decisions affecting them directly. Their call for different policies was a cultural revolution, promoting a more open and diverse society. They advocated new, alternative, environmentally sensible production and consumption patterns, and tried to demonstrate the viability of alternative lifestyles in their everyday practice. Much of that was illusionary, at least in the current system of a market driven society, and the organisations built upon these new principles more often than not either failed and collapsed, or became viable by introducing rather conventional management structures. Nonetheless, some of their ideas made it into mainstream politics (the unanimous support of politics for a nuclear phase out being maybe the most obvious example). Thus the emerging environmental movement was also an innovation force and the breeding ground for a new elite; even the younger members of the conservative parties are significantly influenced by this cultural innovations (hence the occasional coalitions between conservatives and greens in German Federal States).

This testifies that their ideas have reached the mainstream; the NGOs as such are now an integrated part of the governance system, playing an important role as a pressure group for the common good. Given their resource constraints, they are forced to react instantly to the mood of their supporters, which on the one hand makes them a somehow erratic cooperation partner, but on the other hand has enhanced the credibility gains other agents can draw from cooperation. As innovation agencies and think tanks (with network character), they are defending the public goods in a way no other societal agent is capable of. They do so by:

- providing monitoring and feedback on implementation of legislation, based on their tens of thousands of local activists' groups;
- claiming transparency and thus exposing corruption, in particular at the local and regional level, not least due to their usually good media contacts and their own high credibility;
- offering systematic and in this sense, non-chaotic ways of integrating discontent into decision making, by organising protest. This offers a better chance to receive an adequate response from the political agents; thus strengthening cohesion and stabilising democracy;
- enhancing political diversity by putting new issues on the agenda of the *classé politique* (and before that, into the public domain for scrutiny). As much as it is true that politicians pick up new issues once they have been weathering the first storm in good shape, it is mainly the NGO's role to start the debate and stand the first storm of disagreement and disbelief;
- being partners in governance, providing expertise and information the government does not have, directly in advisory boards or public and parliamentary hearings, and indirectly via the media and a broader public, thus building a bridge between administration and the public at large.

What about the future? The role, the political targets and the line of argumentation may have to change significantly in the foreseeable future, due to a change in the general orientation of society and its agents. More specifically, there are indications that the majority in the German business sector have now moved to endorse "green growth" as the most desirable future option[9]; with eco-technologies as the basis for a new, again decade-long growth period, such as the one based on IT (and unlike the biotechnology economy, which has not materialised, despite the on-going massive subsidies from the research and development budgets). If this trend continues, NGOs cannot any longer accuse business of "greenwashing" – companies would seriously promote going green, not for image but for future profit and share value reasons. What then should be the role of NGOs, except for pointing at the laggards? Probably questions about economic growth, resource consumption on the macro level, global environmental

---

[9] While Green Growth is the new OECD mantra, and the Green economy is promoted by the EU and UNEP alike, theRio+20 summit even gave up the "sustainable growth" terminology, promoting instead "sustained growth", thus falling back behind the 1987 Brundtland Commission report and the UN General Assembly decision setting up the Commission in 1984.

impact, corporate responsibility (much more than CSR!) on a global scale (a FoE campaign at the 2002 Jo'burg Sustainability Summit, blocked in Rio 2012 by the G77 and China), technology assessment, risk assessment plus responsibility criteria (as in the past discussion on nuclear energy or genetic engineering and in the upcoming ones on nanotechnology and geo-engineering), the ethical questions of valuing nature in monetary terms, i.e. the on-going commodification of nature vs. protection of public goods (public property, allmende), the regulation mechanisms and owner/stewardship structures related to this may be future issues. However, this would require building up new capacities in social sciences and economics, sufficient to be not only competent, but also represented in the relevant decision bodies of university boards', economic planning committees, etc. (the past work on tradable permits, eco-taxes, law enforcement, and technology assessment provides suitable starting points, but also illustrate the need for new resources capacities). In spring 2012, BUND/FoE Germany was the first NGO to publish a science policy position, after a call for degrowth policy in late 2011.

Others may choose to join business in their quest for "getting greener"; focussing on eco-technical performance improvements, but less so on social aspects or on absolute limits to resource consumption. Building up the necessary additional consulting capacities would be close to impossible, were it not for businesses ready to be the paymasters in such situations – a serious temptation for cash-strapped NGOs. This might easily lead to a split of the environmental movement which could no longer – as it is currently the case – be hidden behind a smokescreen of compromise formulations and polite silence in case of discrepancies which cannot be papered over. Such a split could put the credibility of all environmental NGOs into question, as part of their *credibility is a collective achievement.*

All these possibilities represent major challenges to the environmental movement as a whole, and to each individual NGO. This is a new situation for which no contingency plans exist – so far not even the discussion analysing such developments has seriously started.

Participation overkill

Despite all their calls for participation, NGOs are already facing problems to fill all the participation opportunities with qualified representatives (staff or volunteers). Whenever capacity use for participation procedures conflicts with alternative uses of the same resources, the participation overkill is a threat to be taken into account; the opportunity cost of participation may simply be too high. The tension between participation, lobbying and campaigning is not new. For instance:

- a major NGO like Friends of the Earth Germany – BUND could have run a one year, fully fledged national campaign on any environmental issue using the resources they used to participate in the preparation of the 1992 Rio conference, and the conference itself. What would have been the most efficient use of donors' gifts?
- How much money and working capacity should be spent on presence in standardising commissions, regulatory bodies, radio TV supervisory boards, in parliamentary commissions and for writing comments on draft legislation (as long as the input is mostly ignored)?

In future, the fact that investments in new capacities to meet new challenges cannot (or most probably at least not exclusively) be financed from growing revenues, will require either additional resources (which, if not from the own membership, could compromise credibility, the core capital, e.g. charging consultancy fees for participation) or a refocusing and reprioritisation of issues and activities. This in turns risks frustrating members who have so far been active in these fields such as volunteers (they cannot be reallocated and retrained like staff members can be), and to alienating more traditional donors and supporters.

Furthermore, supporters want results which can often best be achieved by participating in decision preparation bodies, but they also demand NGOs to be an independent voice, which is not necessarily possible in bodies where confidential information are presented. Another mechanism weakening NGO influence is that they cannot take a seat in decision making bodies, as they cannot make compromises or contracts, promising to stop critique of the compromise – their members and supporters would not accept them endorsing certain decisions for all time, regardless of their members' and supporters' changing and yet unknown future point of view. In this sense, NGOs tend to be structurally unreliable partners.

Nonetheless, capacity building is indispensible. One more reason for it is the changed institutional setting. NGOs are not alone in pursuing environmental (and increasingly, sustainability) issues. There is a whole network of institutions, from the ministries of the environment, of development cooperation and partly of research, of health, of family, Federal Agencies for the environment, for nature protection, for nuclear safety etc., to the respective parliamentary committees, three advisory boards with members nominated by the government, green business groups, and so on. Within these circles there is still significant competition between different NGOs, but no need to argue about environmental consciousness and NGO participation. However, there is another world, including the ministries of economics and finance, foreign relations etc. which are only slowly opening up to environmental challenges (the environment ministry even occasionally asks NGOs for support with these). To expand their political niche, NGOs must be able to express their arguments in ways that such institutions recognise the relevance (i.e. teaching the institutions), while they themselves learn to take economic and social arguments into account, but at no cost give up their value-based, non–economic world view. Given the importance of NGOs for the governance of modern societies, these are developments are challenges not only for NGOs, but for (civil) society as a whole. Discussing them is overdue and urgent.

Sustainability: The need for societal discourse

Ortwin Renn

The Problem: Sustainability

Many textbooks state that sustainable development characterizes an economy in which humans can live on the interest of natural capital without depleting the capital itself (see review in Ott & Döring 2004). This highly attractive requirement is an illusion regarding today's population density. To supply six billion people with energy on the basis of solar radiation alone, to abolish the use of all non-renewable raw materials, to reverse the process of transforming nature into productive environments and further measures of returning to a more natural world would cause a social disaster which would go beyond any catastrophe in the history of humankind. This would not be justified by any benefits reserved for future generations.

Our future does not depend on the preservation of original nature, but on the preservation of anthropogenic ecosystems. An intact and productive environment is an indispensible requirement for human existence and culture. The anthropogenic ecosystems we live on need a constant supply of energy and constant constructive interventions. Otherwise they will not provide the services and goods that humans expect from them. Nothing in today's world regulates itself to serve the benefit of humankind. Humans are forced to intervene constantly to make the environment a productive resource. Therefore, reliable knowledge about the ecological basics of our life is so important, and the creative application of this knowledge is a requirement for further existence of the human species (Mohr 1995).

The carrying capacity of the environment for human purposes is flexible within limits that are set by natural constraints. The extent, to which economies can grow within those limits, depends on the production conditions, i.e. the quality of the resources and the technology and organizational skills to use them efficiently. Twelve thousand years ago, about five million people lived on this planet and the maximum carrying capacity under those production conditions – gatherers and hunters – had been reached according to our knowledge. The agrarian-preindustrial culture, too, suffered the limits of expansion around the year 1750 with approximately 750 million people on the globe. The new era of industrial production conditions expanded the carrying capacity to another high of several billion global inhabitants. Promoters for these advances of human culture are the five "Promethean innovations": control of fire, invention of agriculture, transformation of fossil heat into mechanical energy, industrial production, and substitution of matter for information (Renn 2004).

The success of the human race to amplify its population and its share of natural resources over its brief history may lead us to believe that new innovations and production conditions will evolve over time and will enable us to continue on the road of economic growth and to ensure a constant increase of welfare. However, such optimism about the ingenuity of the human mind to provide new conditions for ever-lasting economic growth may not be justified. Today's population density in connection with the present consumption level of the rich required already the complete transformation of nature into a productive environment. About 95 per cent of fertile land worldwide is used for human purposes, such as agriculture, forestry, settlements, and infrastructure facilities. There is not much room for further expansion. Furthermore, the present generation relies on the strictly limited fossil resources of energy and raw materials, and on the exploitation of renewable resources beyond their regenerative capability. Humans deplete the natural capital faster than potential substitutes can be generated. Although living from the interests of the natural capital alone will not suffice to feed 6 billion people, the rate by which we deplete this capital is alarming and destroys the potential for future generations to use the environment for their needs. We may not be able to perpetuate the natural resource base, but at least we can stretch them.

From an economic point of view, stretching of resources may buy us enough time to steadily increase the productivity of natural resources and to develop and introduce substitutes when natural resources become scarce. This implies that substitutes from artificial capital stock can partly (that is, within limits) help satisfy needs which would have otherwise demanded utilization of elements from the natural capital. The main focus of a sustainable economy is therefore to increase and enhance the efficiency of using natural resources. At the same time, however, the carrying capacity and hence the extent to which the environment can be used more efficiently are limited. In areas where these limits are met or even overstepped, decrease of human consumption is the only viable response.

Perspectives on Sustainable Development

The term "sustainable development" is a prophetic combination of two terms which unites both aspects – co-evolution with nature and long-term quality of life – in one vision. This vision of an economic structure that meets all demands of this generation without restricting the demands of future generations is highly attractive, as it interlocks the terms "economy" and "ecology" – often seen as opposites – and postulates a generally acceptable distribution rule between the generations. The attraction of this concept is, of course, compensated by the fuzziness of the meaning associated with this concept and its implications for practical action.

In addition to different images that sustainability evokes in individuals, groups and cultures, the basic discipline or research tradition to which analysts of sustainability adhere plays a major role in their attempt to define the concept of sustainability. These differences come from (Renn 2004):

- Economics: Sustainability describes an economic system in which future generations will enjoy at least the same level of welfare as the present generation. Welfare can include non-marketable (public) goods such as social and political stability, social harmony, resilience, or the immaterial conditions for subjective well-being. Such a broad definition of welfare could also captured by the term "quality of life" (individual and collective). Central tenet in the economic view is that the welfare level is determined by some aggregate measure of individual utilities, no matter what elements individuals include in such a utility assessment. Consequently, economists assume that manifold substitution possibilities exist between the variety of elements stemming from the natural capital (resources for production and the environment as repository for waste) and those of artificial capital (like machines, production processes). If such substitution mechanisms are taken for granted, sustainability implies the necessity of preserving the natural capital only within the limits of available substitutes, i.e. if elements of the natural capital stock cannot be exchanged for elements of the other. The main evaluative criterion for assessing sustainability is the level of aggregate social utility over time. This aggregate level should not decrease over time assuming that non-renewable resources can be substituted by artificial capital, at least in principle and to a certain degree.

- Ecology: Sustainability means the use of natural resources for human purposes to the extent that the carrying capacity of the corresponding ecosystem is not endangered. It is essential for the ecological perspective not to focus on a single resource as a production input or waste repository, but to include the interaction of related resources within one ecosystem. The system may be disturbed by human interventions as long as the functionality and regenerative capability of the system is not jeopardized. Within the field of ecology, there are different methods to measure the degree of anthropogenic influence on ecosystems. Especially meaningful is the degree to which the net primary production is used for human purposes.

- <u>Physics (and other natural sciences):</u> Sustainability is the ability of biological systems to create permanent order (negentropy) using solar energy. The potential and time scale to sustain a well-ordered world is only limited by the sun's life cycle. Since any transformation of energy increases entropy (which is disorder), all physical processes are accompanied by an increase in disorder and diffusion. Biological systems, however, have the ability to create order on a limited scale by using solar energy and to keep the necessarily produced entropy outside of their system. The practice of human societies to transform more energy than the sun offers on a continuous basis by using fossil fuel, and to produce order by shaping and transforming anthropogenic ecosystems for increased production and consumption decreases the biological systems' ability for survival and regeneration. Central issue in connection with sustainable development is therefore the permanent preservation of the biological systems' potential to create negentropy.

- <u>Chemistry:</u> Sustainability means closing anthropogenic material cycles. All resources used by humans (as production factors or waste repositories) have to be integrated in a closed material cycle. Waste should provide useful residues for oneself or others (humans, plants, animals) within the limits of the second law of thermodynamics. Applied to human economies, production has to be organized in a way that all wastes can be reused as energy carriers or useful material for new products or services. If that is not possible, it should biologically degrade into non-toxic substances.

- <u>Social sciences:</u> Sustainability means compatibility of human interventions with the dominant images and concepts of nature (and or environment) that are socially and culturally constructed by different groups within societies. It does not matter whether the environmental crisis is real in the sense of facts proven by the natural sciences. The social science perspective starts with the observation of social perceptions of nature and the social evaluation of scientific expertise by different individuals and groups. Such a perception and evaluation process is always selective and suggests certain (culturally shaped) assessment patterns. How people perceive and evaluate sustainability is therefore this generation's expression of preferences with respect to the perceived quality of environment and life that people want to grant to themselves and to future generations. Mental constructions of distributional equity and social justice dominate the social visions of sustainability rather than ecological findings or physical laws.

These differences in disciplines are not only semantic. The economic understanding of sustainability, for example, places sustainability in the context of scarcity. The goal of sustainable development is to express the relative scarcity of the resource "environment" compared to other goods. According to the natural science perspectives, societies have the obligations to make sure that the absolute limits of the carrying capacity are not exceeded and that such environmental products are taken from the market rather than integrated into the market system. The social scientists, on the other hand, emphasize the constructive character of the concept "sustainability" and focus on equity conflicts, which can be solved neither by incentives nor by regulations, but demand specific political measures of redistribution or communication (legitimization).

Despite the variety of approaches to, and perspectives on, sustainability that exist, the particular challenge is to develop a basic concept of sustainability that is acceptable to most authors and practitioners, and then to integrate the particular strengths of each perspective into it. In the following two sections we will describe the requirements for an integrative concept of sustainability, and then develop from that analysis the requirements for discursive approaches to sustainability.

A normative-functional concept of sustainability and its indicators

Arguing for a normative-functional understanding of sustainability

We believe that a normative-functional concept is most appropriate for an integrative understanding of sustainability (Renn et al. 2009). By combing normative standards and functional statements, it aims at concrete, time and place specific dimensions, criteria and indicators for sustainable development. In the following, norms are defined as behavioural principles that are established by a broad consensus within society. A concept of sustainability based on norms, in this sense, refers to an approach that is guided by socially established moral ideals and formulates directives how to translate these ideals in concrete plans for action. In general, normative approaches combine ethical and analytical ideas and result in sets of rules that incorporate what is desirable and what ought to happen.

Other than normative approaches, functional ones are building on the idea that phenomena and institutions do have particular functions within a societal or ecological system. Concrete institutions can therefore be placed in the overall context and evaluated as beneficial, i.e. functional, or harmful, i.e. dysfunctional, in regard to the system. In addition, they can be replaced by functional equivalents which can substitute all or most of the functions of the earlier phenomena (Merton 1973).

Combining both normative and functional approaches prevents the excessive application of one of these principles. In this way, a normative-functional concept establishes socially accepted principles of action in accordance with the given functional reality of societal or ecological systems. The combination of normative and functional perspectives does offer several advantages:

- Norms, as the very base of the idea of sustainability, become clearly visible and lead to more transparent decision making processes
- Functional aspects ensure that basic conditions of human existence are taken into account
- The approach offers the potential to formulate central, relevant dimensions of sustainability and to deduce adequate criteria and indicators leading to a coherent understanding of sustainability
- When systems develop further and societal definition of values change, no completely new conceptual components have to be introduced but can be incorporated and constructively combined with already existing ideas

How to establish the basic dimensions of a normative-functional concept of sustainability? When looking at the literature of concepts of sustainability three norms appear to be of special importance: Firstly, to ensure the continuity of ecological systems, secondly, to act in accordance with inter- and intragenerational justice and, thirdly, to ensure an optimal level of quality of life (Renn et al. 2009). Historically, these three centres of the debate can be assigned to three particular scientific communities and interests groups: ecologists and ecological oriented NGOs; developmental NGOS, unions and churches; and classical and neoclassical economics (see section 2). However, the importance of these three aspects of sustainability can not only be induced from the general debates on sustainability but they can also be argued for as functional the basis of sustainable development from the very importance of e.g. necessary ecological resources of human existence, from the just distribution of goods over and within generations that ensures a peaceful coexistence and from the state of quality of life that each individual strives for. Whereas the groups mentioned above mostly try to establish their field of interest at the centre of the debates and to narrow the scope of sustainability, we argue that is it possible to combine the normative assumptions underlying these three perspectives and to integrate them – at least partially – at the level of more concrete goals of sustainable behaviour. The three normative principles that we identify hereby are: the integrity of systems – both ecological and social –, the observance of general codes of justice, and the maintenance of quality of life. In brief these norms will be referred to as systems integrity, justice and quality of life. The concept as described in the following paragraphs is based on these very three normative-functional principles.

Before elaborating the three basic categories of the normative-functional concept, it has to be added that sustainability is to be seen as a continuous process of social definition of norms and integration of different perspectives. For this process, the communication structure and conflict management within a society is of major importance, as well as the evaluation of hitherto achieved progress. Sustainability as an iterative social process builds on a value based socialization on the macro level and on individual's convictions on the micro level. To negotiate the goal conflict between these two levels is a central aspect of the dynamic establishment of a society that acts in accordance with the principles of sustainability.

Dimension A: Systems integrity

Systems integrity means the continuity and endurance of human social systems as well as ecological systems that are relevant, instrumental and/or meaningful to humans. The notion of system denotes phenomena which consist of interrelated parts that constitute a whole. In connection to the idea of ultra-stability in cognitive science and ecological theory (Cadwallader 1979), the notion of systems integrity refers to a state of dynamic change leading to continuity of systems without uncontrolled disruptions. It therefore does not aim at conservation or rigid states of equilibrium but on change and the ability to develop.

For the following analysis, social and ecological systems will be treated independently. This results from basic differences in regard to their composition, individual parts and development processes which render an identical analysis procedure impossible. This does not mean that these levels of analysis cannot be combined; in fact, they will have to be brought together when turning to human interference into ecological systems.

In terms of function, ecological and social systems integrity is directed at the continuity of mankind and its stable utilization of social and ecological systems. Integrity is a constitutive characteristic of human societies even though its degree might vary from society to society (Merton 1973, p.189). It is also a basic evolutionary aspect of ecological systems. The difference between social and ecological systems in regard to function is that social systems define their function themselves. Ecological systems, however, are attributed its function by humans benefiting from it or relating to it.

Social systems integrity

Social systems are constituted by the interaction of a minimum of two persons, of a defined group or of whole societies. Change and stability are central ideas to describe these structures and are part of the debates on political, economic or social-integrative issues. However, when looking at the contemporary social sciences it is not possible to identify a standardised idea of continuity or change. Political sciences, at least, makes use of comprehensive notions of change and stability to describe states in upheaval. When it turns to more stable societies, though, it uses single, case specific aspects of political reality to describe change and stability.

Given this state of social science knowledge, we do not try and define an all-embracing, monolithic concept of systems integrity. Instead, we identify aspects of major importance for the development of the social system in modern industrial countries such as Germany. For this, we will introduce selected areas and subareas of focus. In accordance with standards of measurement they will be referred to as criteria and sub-criteria. The criteria of social systems integrity are: Demographic transition, integrity of the economic system, social integration, integrity of the political system (Renn et al. 2009).

Ecosystems Integrity

Ecosystems denote the interrelations of creatures of different species and their habitat. Comparable with social systems, ecosystems are mostly open structures. In their normal states, matter cycles of ecosystems are balanced and form a dynamic equilibrium. By changing single components or subsystems it is possible to disrupt this balance. This mostly leads to the disturbance of neighbouring or interrelated ecological systems as well.

In the following, the term integrity is used instead of stability to emphasis the dynamic character of the processes at stake. This is very much true for ecosystems as can be seen in a quote from Fridolin Brand: "Ecosystems cannot be seen as static entities; rather, they represent always changing, fluctuating, dynamic systems. There is no balance of nature; rather endless change and the on-going creation of novelty are the rule" (Brand 2005, p.42).

In recent debates our understanding of ecosystem integrity has been described with term such as persistence, resistance, elasticity and resilience (Drossel & Scheu 2004, p.49; Brand 2005, p.30ff.). However, ecosystems integrity cannot be assessed merely by "factual", i.e. physical of biological, evidence. It always refers to the social negotiation of what is a functional or dysfunctional state of nature and how humans want to benefit from it.

As for social systems stability, it is not possible to identify all-embracing criteria. Instead the most critical aspects of the ecosystems relevant for the case of modern industrialized countries have been selected as following: Climate change, ensuring air quality, stability of the biosphere, ensuring energy supply, waste and ensuring biodiversity (Renn et al. 2009).

Dimension B: Justice

Social justice represents deep desire f which people in all cultures and epochs have in common. Justice is the strongest normative principle of social order (Höffe 2001, p.29; Kersting 2004, p.37). The continuation of a community or society could be called into question, if its members perceive the public order as unjust. This leads to the conclusion that justice and sustainability are closely linked (Grunwald & Kopfmueller 2006 p.1; Ott &Döring 2004, p.41). However, it is not clear what is meant when we talk about the principle of justice. And more specifically: Which (just) order is likely to support a sustainable development?

The offer on the market of theories of justice is abundant. The concept of justice is surrounded by different culture- and time-shaped ideas and judgements. There is has never been the one and only theory. The market leaders are utilitarianism, communitarianism and liberalism. The choice is contingent on personal preferences and the definition of collective goals. Is there a concept of justice that is specifically linked to sustainable development? The result of our evaluations is that the reference point we are looking for is given within the written constitution of the Federal Republic of Germany and the social market economy based on liberal principles (Renn et al. 2009). Our argument is that this constitution and economic system is a matured and well considered synthesis of philosophical ideas, historical developments and experiences of everyday life. From a theoretical view a social system has been accomplished that stands between egalitarianism and liberalism. By including a section on human rights it contains a doctrine of natural law as well as a doctrine of legal positivism which is given by the order of the constitutional state. The responsibility for all people has been confirmed in the preamble. There are four principles of justice which found their way into the constitution: Equality of chances, justice of achievement

(Leistungsgerechtigkeit), justice to needs (Bedürfnisgerechtigkeit) and justice between generations. The postulate of equality is the default-option. Deviations from equity solutions require an intersubjectively valid justification.

Linking the four principle of justice to the constitution should not lead to the thought that the realization of social justice is only an administrative task. The constitution stipulates that it is the task of every member of society to practise justice. However, the motivation to serve this obligation cannot arise only by rational considerations, but requires further ethical foundations. One must abstain from actions that provide personal benefits if this action results in injustice towards others. Empathy and compassion with the present and future generation can be such an ethical foundation. Discursive procedures between and among all social and public levels can help to guarantee the combinational of rational and ethical drivers for a fair conversion of the four principles of justice. Similar to the discussion on systems integrity, criteria can be defined in accordance with the four principles of justice. These are equality of opportunities, justice of achievement, justice to needs and intergenerational justice.

Dimension C: Quality of life

A serious problem which underlies every concept of sustainability is public acceptance. We assume that the probability to reach public acceptance is high if people perceive that the measures of sustainability improve their personal well-being. We distinguish therefore the objective conditions of life on the one hand and the subjective well-being on the other. The relation between both is interdependent: Well-being is a value that is understandable to all people all over the world and the objective conditions of living should promote it. On the base of subjective well-being one may infer that the measures of sustainability lead to a good life for one self and everyone else, and vice versa (Birnbacher and Schicha 1996, p.146). So the acceptance for a sustainability-strategy could be spread all over the world by arguing in favour of personal well beings.

First we think that the quality of life is one of the meaningful values and ends of the human existence which is communicable to every culture at any time. Second it could therefore be a cross-cultural door opener for transmitting the principles of sustainability. Behind this function stands the so called Golden Rule. According to the philosopher of religion, Hans Kueng (1996), the Golden Rule can become the foundation of a cross-cultural ethos for sustainability because of its universal comprehensibility. Combined with the fundamental meaning of personal well-being, the Golden Rule constitutes a mutually dependent order of personal and social welfare. The rule itself does not say anything about the building bricks of good life, that's the task of the quality of life-concept. However, even without knowing the bricks of the house of good life, we can draw from its blueprint: Sustainability should promote the well-being of the present as well as the future generations. Like sustainability our quality of life concept is a normative model –everyone should have access to it. We summarize objective conditions of living and subjective well-being under the concept of sustainable quality of life (Renn et al. 2009). Which principles follow this concept and what are the building blocks?

Immediate associations of well-being refer to material wealth and solidarity for people in need (social security systems). Hardly anybody would deny that solidarity and material prosperity have both improved the living conditions of people in the modern industrialized countries for almost two centuries. Changes in the conditions of living (social legislation, economic system) improved the well-being on the individual and collective level. It is questionable whether a sustainability strategy would be accepted if it were to fall behind these two achievements. However, since at least three decades there are critical comments especially about negative consequences of the concept of material prosperity. This concept does not seem to match the requirements of sustainability. At the same time, the social security system that guarantees solidarity in societies is called into question too because of its costs. However, we believe it is possible to work out a concept of quality of life which does fall behind the achievements of the past and which is sustainable at the same time.

In the 1990s the concept of qualitative growth was introduced to the sustainability literature (Majer 1984 & 1998; Mohr 1995). This concept criticized the traditional model of quantitative growth and came up with an alternative growth model based on qualitative developments. Qualitative growth in our context means that resource productivity is constantly increased in this value-creation process (Renn 2004). All increases in the performance of a national economy for reasons of growth have to be realized by decreasing preliminary work for non-renewable resources and environmental damage. At the same time it has to be taken care of that all renewable resources are only used as much as they can regenerate themselves under the conditions of cultivated land and productive land or as much as can be substituted by equivalent use of artificial capital. Every unit of nature should become more productive in such a way that we need less of nature in total. The objective would be to create a parallel event to the historic achievement of the enormous increase in working productivity per hour, and to initiate a new era of rising natural productivity (per unit of energy or raw materials). Qualitative growth is characterized by a further increase in gross national product, although use of resources and environmental damages decrease (Weizsäcker et al. 1995). This is possible because material resources and manual work is substituted by intellectual work: structured work and software substitute raw materials, energy and time. We can make a distinction between three stages:

- In phase I qualitative growth means a permanent decrease in the intensity of resources per unit of gross national product. Every product shall be less intensive in resources than the one before. This also goes for utilizing the environment as waste repository for waste no longer needed. Most industrialized countries have reached his first phase of qualitative growth for most industrial goods.
- In phase II qualitative growth means the permanent decrease of resource intensity per capita. Here we also have to take into consideration that saving effects by better use of the environment have to be higher than the additional use of resources according to increase in production and consumption. Only branches promising an over-proportional net product along with a little use of environment will grow in phase II. This second phase of qualitative growth has been fulfilled only in some product branches so far.
- In phase III qualitative growth means decrease of resource intensity per national economy and therefore indirectly global. This third phase has been especially designed for countries with population growth. There the economic structural changes need not only compensate the higher consumption demands of every single individual but the collective demands caused by population growth as well. This third phase of qualitative growth therefore is a part of the future and will be the hardest part to realize. Success will only be possible, if measures for controlling the population growth are enforced in parallel to structural changes.

Qualitative growth is no illusion. We have learned a long time ago to get out more of little input by using structured knowledge. Net product by software and know-how opens a new dimension of qualitative growth. With these innovations we have to lay the foundation so the requirements for the realization of phase II of qualitative growth will adjust in all areas.

A deliberative approach to generate strategies for sustainability

The crucial part missing in our approach to sustainability is the design of strategies to accomplish the goals that are linked to our three components:

system integrity, justice and quality of life. We are convinced that the task of designing strategies cannot be delegated to an institution or a committee of experts but requires a broad societal discourse. Inviting the public to be part of the decision making process for defining the targets of sustainable development and facilitate the implementation of sustainable policies has been a major objective in most environmental policy circles. As one prominent example, the US-National Academy of Sciences encourages environmental protection agencies to foster citizen participation and public involvement for making environmental policy making guided by the goal of sustainable development more effective and democratic (Stern & Fineberg 1996; US-National Research Council 2008). The report emphasizes the need for a combination of assessment and dialogue which the authors have framed the "analytic-deliberative" approach.

The term deliberation refers to the style and procedure of decision making without specifying which participants are invited to deliberate (Stern & Fineberg 1996; Rossi 1997). For a discussion to be called deliberative it is essential that it relies on mutual exchange of arguments and reflections rather than decision-making based on the status of the participants, sublime strategies of persuasion, or social-political pressure. Deliberative processes should include a debate about the relative weight of each argument and a transparent procedure for balancing pros and cons (Tuler & Webler 1999). In addition, deliberative processes should be governed by the established rules of a rational discourse. In the theory of communicative action developed by the German philosopher Juergen Habermas, the term discourse denotes a special form of a dialogue, in which all affected parties have equal rights and duties to present claims and test their validity in a context free of social or political domination (Habermas, 1970 & 1987; Renn &Schweizer 2009).

The rules of deliberation do not necessarily include the demand for stakeholder or public involvement. Deliberation can be organized in closed circles (such as conferences of catholic bishops, where the term has indeed been used since the Council of Nicosea) as well as in public forums. We suggest to use the term "deliberative democracy" when one refers to the combination of deliberation and third party involvement (Renn 2008, p. 294).

What needs to be deliberated? First, deliberative processes are needed to define the role and relevance of systematic and anecdotal knowledge for making far-reaching choices. Second, deliberation is needed to find the most appropriate way to deal with uncertainty and plurality in environmental decision making and to set efficient and fair trade-offs between the three major goals of sustainability: system integrity, justice and quality of life.

Third, deliberation needs to address the wider concerns of the affected groups and the public at large when these goals are translated into strategies and concrete measures.

Why do we expect that deliberative processes are better suited to deal with these three challenges than using expert judgment, political majority votes or relying on public survey data (Renn 2008, p.304 ff.)?

- Deliberation can produce common understanding of the issues or the problems based on the joint learning experience of the participants with respect to systematic and anecdotal knowledge.
- Deliberation can produce a common understanding of each party's position and argumentation and thus assist in a mental reconstruction of each actor's argumentation. The main driver for gaining mutual understanding is empathy. The theory of communicative action provides further insights in how to mobilize empathy and how to use the mechanisms of empathy and normative reasoning to explore and generate common moral grounds.
- Deliberation can produce new options and novel solutions to a problem. This creative process can either be mobilized by finding win-win solutions or by discovering identical moral grounds on which new options can grow.
- Deliberation has the potential to show and document the full scope of ambiguity associated with complex problems. Deliberation helps to make a society aware of the options, interpretations, and potential actions that are connected with the issue under investigation. Each position within a deliberative discourse can only survive the crossfire of arguments and counter-arguments if it demonstrates internal consistency, compatibility with the legitimate range of knowledge claims and correspondence with the widely accepted norms and values of society. Deliberation clarifies the problem, makes people aware of framing effects, and determines the limits of what could be called reasonable within the plurality of interpretations.
- Deliberations can also produce agreements. The minimal agreement may a consensus about dissent. If all arguments are exchanged, participants know why they disagree. They may not be convinced that the arguments of the other side are true or morally strong enough to change their own position; but they understand the reasons why the opponents came to their conclusion. At the end the deliberative process produces several consistent and – in their own domain – optimized positions that can be offered as package options to legal

decision-makers or the public. Once these options have been subjected to public discourse and debate, political bodies such as agencies or parliaments can make the final selection in accordance with the legitimate rules and institutional arrangements such a majority vote or executive order. Final selections could also be performed by popular vote or referendum.

- Deliberation may result in consensus. Often deliberative processes are used synonymously with consensus seeking activities. This is a major misunderstanding. Consensus is a possible outcome of deliberation but not a mandatory requirement. If all participants find a new option that they all value more than the one option that they preferred when entering the deliberation, a "true" consensus is reached. It is clear that finding such a consensus is the exception rather than the rule. Consensus is either based on a win-win solution or a solution that serves the „common good" and each participant's interests and values better than any other solution. Less stringent is the requirement of a tolerated consensus. Such a consensus rests on the recognition that the selected decision option might serve the "common good" best but on the expense of some interest violations or additional costs. In a tolerated consensus some participants voluntarily accept personal or group-specific losses in exchange for providing benefits to all of society.

In summary many desirable products and accomplishments are associated with deliberation (Chess et al. 1998). Depending on the structure of the discourse and the underlying rationale deliberative processes can:

- enhance understanding,
- generate new options,
- decrease hostility and aggressive attitudes among the participants,
- explore new problem framing,
- enlighten legal policy makers,
- produce competent, fair and optimized solution packages and
- facilitate consensus, tolerated consensus and compromise.

The applications of deliberative methods for designing and implementing policies towards sustainability provide some evidence and reconfirmation that the theoretical expectations linked to this approach can be met on the local, regional and also the national level. It is a valid approach to elicit preferences and educated responses of citizens in a rather short time period.

Evaluation studies by independent scholars confirmed that the objectives of reaching consensus or at least more clarity about concrete strategies to implement sustainability could be met (Vorwerk & Kämper 1997; Roch 1997).

Conclusions

The term "sustainable development" is a prophetic combination of two words which unites both aspects – economic progress and avoiding environmental damages – in one vision. This vision of an economic and institutional structure that meets all demands of this generation without restricting the demands of future generations is highly attractive, as it interlocks the terms "economy", "society" and "ecology" and postulates a generally acceptable distribution rule between the generations. It is unclear, however, whether the combination of ecological stability, economic development and social compatibility can be accomplished. At least the possibility of conflict exists between these objectives making trade-offs that are often disguised by the euphemistic use of the term necessary.

Given this confusion, we decided to define sustainability as a normative-functional term divided into three major components: system integrity, justice and quality of life. We also envisioned a hierarchy between these three components. Prima facie system integrity takes the highest priority, followed by justice and quality of life. Sustainability should be a condition or constraint based on criteria of system integrity and justice under which economic development can occur in its own rights for improving quality of life over time.

The objective of this paper was to address and discuss the implications of this concept of sustainability and to generate participatory strategies to implement them. Such an ambitious program requires participatory processes in democratic and pluralist societies. Organizing and structuring discourses environmental policies goes beyond the good intention to have the public involved in decision making. Discursive processes need a structure that assures the integration of expertise, interests, and public values. These different inputs should be combined in such a fashion that they contribute to the deliberation process the type of input that can claim legitimacy within a rational decision making procedure.

An organizational model is needed that assigns specific roles to each contributor but makes sure, at the same time, that each contribution is embedded in a dialogue setting that guarantees mutual exchange of arguments and information, provides all participants with opportunities to insert and challenge claims, and to create active understanding among all participants. Far from being an established tool for making sustainability work, it promises to provide the type of holistic judgments and policies that are needed to progress on the route of sustainable development.

References

Birnbacher, D. & Schicha, C. 1996, ‚Vorsorge statt Nachhaltigkeit – Ethische Grundlagen der Zukunftsverantwortung', in: Kastenholz H; Erdmann, G. & Wolff, M. (Eds.): Nachhaltige Entwicklung. Zukunftschancen für Mensch und Umwelt. Springer, Berlin, pp. 141–156.

Brand, F. 2005, Ecological resilience and its relevance within a theory of sustainable development. UFZ-Report 03/2005. UFZ Centre for Environmental Research, Leipzig.

Cadwallader, M.L. 1979, ‚Die kybernetische Analyse des Wandels', in: Zapf W (Ed.) Theorien des sozialen Wandels. Verlagsgruppe Athenäum, Hain, Scriptor, Hanstein, Regensburg, pp.141–147.

Chess, C.; Dietz, T. and Shannon M 1998, 'Who should deliberate when?' Human Ecology Review, vol. 5, no. 1, pp.60–68.

Drossel, S. & Scheu, B. 2004, ‚Komplexität und Stabilität von Ökosystemen: Forschungsstand und offene Fragen', in: Ipsen D & Schmidt J (Eds.): Dynamiken der Nachhaltigkeit. Metropolis-Verlag, Marburg, pp.1–60.

Grunwald, A. & Kopfmueller, J. 2006, Nachhaltigkeit. Campus, Frankfurt am Main.

Habermas, J. 1970, 'Towards a theory of communicative competence', Inquiry, vol. 13, pp. 363–372.

Habermas, J. 1987, Theory of communicative action. Vol. II: Reason and the rationalization of society. Beacon Press, Boston.

Hayek, F.A. von 1991, Die Verfassung der Freiheit, 3. Edition. Mohr, Tübingen.

Hayek, F.A. von 2003, Recht, Gesetz und Freiheit. Eine Neufassung der liberalen Grundsätze der Gerechtigkeit und der politischen Ökonomie. Mohr, Tübingen.

Hoeffe, O. 2001, Gerechtigkeit. Eine philosophische Einführung. Beck, München.

Kersting, W. 2004, John Rawls zur Einführung. 2nd edition. Junius, Hamburg.

Küng, H. 1996, ‚Das eine Ethos in der einen Welt – Ethische Begründung einer nachhaltigen Entwicklung', in: Kastenholz H;Erdmann G &Wolff M (Eds.) Nachhaltige Entwicklung. Zukunftschancen für Mensch und Umwelt. Springer, Berlin, pp.235–253.

Majer, H. 1984, ‚Qualitatives Wachstum und Lebensqualität: definitorische und analytische Zusammenhänge', in: Majer H (Ed.): Qualitatives Wachstum. Einführung in Konzeptionen der Lebensqualität. Campus, Frankfurt am Main, pp.32–50.

Majer, H. 1998, Wirtschaftswachstum und nachhaltige Entwicklung. Oldenbourg, München.

Mohr ,H. 1995, Qualitatives Wachstum. Losung für die Zukunft. Weitbrecht, Stuttgart.

Merton, R.K. 1973, ‚Funktionale Analyse', in: Hartmann G (Ed.):Moderne amerikanische Soziologie. Ferdinand Enke Verlag, Stuttgart, pp.169–214.

Ott, K. & Döring, R. 2004, Theorie und Praxis starker Nachhaltigkeit. Metropolis, Marburg.

Rawls, J. 1975, Eine Theorie der Gerechtigkeit. Suhrkamp, Frankfurt am Main.

Renn, O. 2004, 'Sustainable development. Exploring the cross-cultural dimension', in: Wilderer PA; Schroeder ED & Kopp H (Eds.): Global sustainability. A new perspective for science and engineering, economics and politics. Wiley, Weinheim, pp. 21–42.

Renn, O. 2008, Risk governance: Coping with uncertainty in a complex world. Earthscan, London.

Renn, O. &.Schweizer, P.-J. 2009, 'Inclusive risk governance: Concepts and applications to environmental policy making', Environmental Policy and Governance, vol. 19, pp. 174–185

Renn, O.; Jaeger, A.; Deuschle, J. & Weimer-Jehle, W. 2009, 'A normative-functional concept of sustainability and its indicators', *Int. J. Global Environmental Issues,* vol. 9, no. 4, pp. 291–317.

Roch, I. 1997, Evaluation der 3. Phase des Bürgerbeteiligungsverfahrens in der Region Nordschwarzwald. Research Report No. 71, Akademie für Technikfolgenabschätzung, Stuttgart.

Rossi, J. 1997, 'Participation run amok: The costs of mass participation for deliberative agency decision-making', Northwestern University Law Review, vol. 92, pp.173.249.

Stern, P.C. & Fineberg, V. 1996, Understanding risk: Informing decisions in a democratic society. National Research Council, Committee on Risk Characterization, National Academy Press, Washington, D.C.

Tuler, S. & Weblerm T. 1999, 'Designing an analytic deliberative process for environmental health policy making in the U.S. nuclear weapons complex', Risk: Health, Safety & Environment, vol. 65, no.10, pp.65–87.

US-National Research Council of the National Academies 2008, Public participation in environmental assessment and decision making. The National Academies Press, Washington, D.C.

Vorwerk, V. & Kämper, E. 1997, Evaluation der 3. Phase des Bürgerbeteiligungsverfahrens in der Region Nordschwarzwald. Report No. 70, Akademie für Technikfolgenabschätzung, Stuttgart.

Weizsäcker, E.U. von: Lovins, A.B. & Lovins, L.H. 1995, Faktor vier. Doppelter Wohlstand – halbierter Naturverbrauch. Droemer Knaur, München.

The Knowledge of Civil Society [10]

Nico Stehr

> ... my own experience and everyday knowledge illustrate that comfort and ignorance are the biggest flaws of human character. This is a potentially deadly mix.
>
> Hans Joachim Schellnhuber (2011)[11]

In the context of the questions about the knowledge of civil society, we tend to encounter, as far as I can see, a liberal mix of four arguments: (1) Not only is knowledge power but the powerful are knowledgeable, (2) the public is ignorant, (3) the exercise of power is cemented through the control of relevant scientific findings by the powerful, and (4) the effective political participation of the citizens is therefore seriously damaged.

These arguments are not easily separated. I immediately confess, as I will explain in detail that I do not share the discouraging thesis about the inevitable enslavement of the modern individual. [12]

Let me first sum up my criticism of this melange of ideas on the convergence of knowledge and power and say a few words about the central notion of this discussion, knowledge:

A critique

1. The thesis that scientific knowledge accrues more or less automatically to the politically powerful and can therefore easily be monopolized by them is mistaken.

2. Is it possible to reconcile democracy and expertise? The thesis of the convergence of power and knowledge is misleading insofar as it raises the expectation of a policy or practice-relevant influence of scientific findings that is immediate and direct. It is not possible to directly

---

[10] I am grateful to Reiner Grundmann and Scott McNall for his critical comments on an earlier version of the lecture manuscript.

[11] The climate scientist Hans Joachim Schellnhuber in an interview with *DER SPIEGEL* (Issue 12, 21. March 2010, p. 29,) in response to the question on why the messages of science do not reach society.

[12] My own response to the enslavement assertion is last but not least based on the Kantian principle of individual moral autonomy: "We must not accept the command of an authority ... as the basis of ethics" (Popper, [1960] 1968:26).

derive instructions for action from scientific knowledge. Scientific judgements are always preliminary and tentative. Choosing between options is never a purely scientific matter. There has always been and continues to be in public discourse a mix of scientific and political reasoning including the politicization of the language of science.

3. The authority of expertise or influence of rational reasoning aided by scientific findings or so-called facts known/available in the context political decision-making is overestimated and

4. The lack of scientific and technical knowledge is constitutive of many facets of everyday life in modern society and therefore loses much of its alleged danger. Science does not de-politicize public issues.[13] Civil society is as a result not disqualified a priori from participation in discussions and decisions about the handling of scientific knowledge and technical developments. Varied "publics" possess their own intellectual capacities and epistemic cultures. In order to challenge expertise, one does not have to "know" as much as the experts (see Nelkin, 1975: 49–54).[14] Public issues remain political issues.

5. And in a final point of criticism to which I will return in my summary in greater detail: Is it the case – as Joseph Schumpeter for example suggests – that the political decision calculus of knowledgeable and ignorant individuals different? [15]

Knowledge may be defined as a *capacity for action*. My use of the term "knowledge" as a capacity for action is derived from Francis Bacon's famous metaphor that knowledge is power (*scientia est potentia*). Bacon suggests that knowledge derives its utility from the capacity to set something in motion; for example, using modern examples, new communicative devices, new forms of power, new regulatory regimes, new chemical substances, new political organizations, new financial instruments or new illnesses. To refer to one concrete instance of knowledge as a capacity for action: In 1948,

---

[13] Of course, the statement does not put into question the practice by policy makers to define issues as technical rather than political issues.

[14] Dorothy Nelkin (1975:53–54) summing up her case study of two controversial large-scale construction plans, the building of a power plant and the construction of a new runway of an international airport, concludes, "those opposing a decision need not muster equal evidence. It is sufficient to raise questions that will undermine the expertise of a developer whose power and legitimacy rests on his monopoly of knowledge or claims of special competence."

[15] A study of the voting behaviour of the American electorate in the 1992–2004 presidential elections indicates that the "primary effect of increasing voter knowledge is to raise turnout levels and solidify pre-existing vote tendencies" (Dow, 2011:381).

Claude Shannon (1948) published a small paper entitled *The Mathematical Theory of Communication*.[16] In it he explained how words, sound and images could be converted into blips and sent electronically. Shannon foretold the digital revolution in communications. With respect to science, my definition of knowledge implies that science is not only interested in a representation of reality but also in how something may be realized. As a result, knowledge is always also a **model for reality**.

It would be erroneous to underestimate *a priori* the ability of many segments of the public to mobilize knowledge in efforts to challenge powerful social actors. As recent events in this city demonstrate, political activity that challenges elites and elite knowledge is by no means absent or declining in modern society.

The knowledge of civil society and the scientific community

The influence and impact of some social institutions and some social roles within these institutions, especially the economy and science but also more generally the role of the expert – contrary to the theory of functional differentiation within modern societies, often extend well beyond their own institutional boundaries. The social consequences these institutions have are controversial. For example, the number of social scientists and humanists who alert us to the supposedly overwhelming societal power of the markets and call for our resistance against surreptitious and mysterious market forces are legion (for example Bourdieu, 1998).

However, the number of humanists and social scientists who mobilize against the extraordinary societal power of scientific knowledge and scientific expertise that are seen for example to undermine the very foundations of democratic governance is rather modest. *Scientists* almost unanimously agree that science occupies an extraordinary, perhaps the pole position within modern society. But they also concur that the knowledge held by members of civil society, that is, the scientific knowledge of civil society is best described as one of complete ignorance. There is also

---

[16] As Freeman Dyson explains in a review in the *New York Review of Books* (March 10, 2011): "In 1945 Shannon wrote a paper, "A Mathematical Theory of Cryptography," which was stamped SECRET and never saw the light of day. He published in 1948 an expurgated version of the 1945 paper with the title "A Mathematical Theory of Communication." The 1948 version appeared in the *Bell System Technical Journal*, the house journal of the Bell Telephone Laboratories, and became an instant classic. It is the founding document for the modern science of information. After Shannon, the technology of information raced ahead, with electronic computers, digital cameras, the Internet, and the World Wide Web."

considerable agreement among many observers, that our ignorance has rather detrimental political if not many other undesirable consequences.

Here are some voices that substantiate our claim. In an essay in the *New York Review of Books* (November 18, 2004, p. 38), the molecular biologist Richard Lewontin maintains that, "the knowledge required for political rationality, once available to the masses, is now in the possession of a specially educated elite, a situation that creates a series of tensions and contradictions in the operation of representative democracy."

A prominent social scientist, Immanuel Wallerstein (2004:8) agrees and specifies that the ever increasing *specialization* of the production of scientific knowledge restricts to but a few individuals, the ability to form a separate, rational assessment of the quality of the evidence or the cogency of theoretical thought. The "harder" science is, the more this applies.

The historian of science, Gerald Holton, expresses the same case, in an even more drastic fashion. For Holton the citizens of modern societies are slaves.[17] The citizens are unable to act in a self-determined manner. The slave mentality of modern citizens, one is able to add, produces and manifests itself not only in **"power-without-corresponding-representation"** (Hupe and Edwards, 2011) but also in servile forms of consciousness and social conduct. Democracy means a government accountable to its citizens. But the slave mentality and political status of civil society members implies that in reality, the government makes *us* accountable to *them*. We are inundated with prohibitions, legislation and public campaigns. For example, we are eating the wrong food or are lousy parents (Minogue, 2010: 4).

The new illiterates, in a grotesque inversion of the dream of the Age of Enlightenment about the emancipatory power of knowledge, are victims in the face of the symbiosis of power and knowledge (see Turner, 2001). Michael Polanyi and C.P. Snow were generally of one opinion that there is a dangerous gulf between science and the rest of the culture in modern societies. The renowned environmental theorist James Lovelock, inventor of the Gaia thesis, is more specific. Lovelock, extremely pessimistic and discouraged is convinced that contemporary humanity is just too stupid to avoid for example the dangers of climate change.[18] The Swedish media

---

[17] Paul Feyerabend (1978:234) employs a similar metaphor. However, he does so in exactly the opposite sense, when he demands of himself as a university teacher not to serve as a slave holder; that is, as a teacher merely promoting the ruling socio-philosophical curricula.

[18] James Lovelock quoted in interview published in the *Guardian* in March 2010 (also Chris Huntingford, "James Lovelock's climate change pessimism is unhelpful," *Guardian* 1. April 2010).

researcher Peter Dahlgren (2009) speaks of the "psychic havoc of the era of late modernity" in which citizens have lost all feeling for political participation because they just do not feel competent. The modern forces of globalization and the dominance of rational market behaviour supposedly reinforce the same trend towards alienation.

Is this gloomy diagnosis spot on? What therefore is the fate of democracy in modern societies? [19]

Is it rational to be ignorant?

In response to the primary question about the state of democratic governance in modern societies, equally difficult secondary questions arise. One may for example naively ask – aside from expressing doubt about the taken-for-granted assumption that the demand for evidence and science-based policy is on the upswing,[20] – isn't there a democratic right to ignorance? Isn't it rational to adopt a low profile (cf. Downs, 1967; Olson, 1965), especially in light of the fact that the transaction costs to be well informed politically are significant and become more costly with each passing year? While it may be common sense to readily defer to experts in many corners of the life-world, political expertise often prompts suspicion. Why is that? First, the suspicion political expertise generates is based on the

---

[19] The contemporary scientists I have cited can hardly be blamed for being contented with or even recommending and celebrating the "alienation" of the public from science. It is therefore worth noting that observations about an impoverished democracy resonate, in a peculiar sense, however, with early critics of what we now call and implicitly favour when concerned about the state of modern democracy, namely *deliberative democracy*. Just to name a few, Gustave Le Bon, Jacob Burkhardt, Karl Mannheim, Walter Lippmann and many other critics of the bourgeois society voiced their alarm about emergence of "mass society" that in the end sacrificed all that is sacred: "Position, property, religion, distinguished tradition, higher learning" (Burkhardt). Mass societies encourage the rule by the incompetent rather than what should be the case, namely the rule of experts. During the last World War and in the midst of the Nazi regime, Karl Mannheim (1940:86–87) observes that "the open character of democratic mass society, together with its growth in size and the tendency towards general public participation, not only produces far too many elites but also deprives these elites of the exclusiveness which they need to [perform their functions]."

[20] One of the less obvious accounts for the *rising demand* for evidence and science-based–policy from the political system is Steve Ryner's (2003:164) conjecture that the "displacement of moral judgement from the public sphere [has] something to do with the decline of electoral participation." After all, he argues, what difference does it make who is in charge if "the decision is to be based on purely 'technical' criteria?" The deference to judgements from science increases political indifference.

realistic observation that political expertise is extremely scarce and that "people who set themselves up as political experts often give off the whiff of snake oil" and, as Ian Shapiro (1994: 140–141) puts it, "experts always turn out to be on somebody's side, and not necessarily ours." That is, expertise is not immune to **motivated reasoning**.[21] But such fundamental skepticism towards the political role of experts may not be sufficient to assure that experts are expelled from the domain of politics. We also may ask, who is responsible for this dismal state of affairs of civil society?

Who is responsible for the deficit?

It is by no means the case, as one might expect that modern science or expertise is always blamed.[22] According to widely applauded views of Walter Lippmann or Joseph Schumpeter, ordinary citizens are simply incapable or disinclined to inform themselves. In political matters, the "typical citizen," the dispirited Schumpeter ([1942] 1950: 262–263) concludes, tends to yield to "extra-rational or irrational prejudice and impulse" and that ignorance will persist "in the face of masses of information however complete and correct."

But do higher volumes of knowledge and information among citizens lead to an increase in trust extended to political decisions and the political class or, more generally, democracy? What if the exact opposite is the case (see Termeer, Breeman, van Lieshout and Pot, 2010) and political trust declines with a more knowledgeable civil society? We suspect we know the answers to these questions but reliable knowledge skirts around the edges or is entirely missing.

One further answer to the question of co-responsibility for the enslavement of the public points the finger to professional journalism who mainly give voice to the views of experts – often without acknowledging the cultural contingency of scientific knowledge claims and thereby demoralizing and

---

[21] Steve Fuller (e.g. 1988 and 1994) has long maintained a highly sceptical attitude toward the special claims to expertise of experts and argued for a level playing field between expert and laypersons.

[22] One of the few scholars who put the blame on the shoulders of scientists and science is Philip Kitcher (2011:103): "Our investigations are not always directed towards the questions of most concern to most people, the results on which experts agree are not always based on reasons the broader public is prepared to endorse, and the dissemination of information is so distorted as to make supposedly free discussion and debate an unproductive shouting match." Also relevant is Frickel et al. (2010) reference to the phenomenon of "undone science"; that is, areas of research left unattended by the scientific community but of interest to civil society, for example, in the fields of AIDS and breast cancer activism.

immobilizing their readers, so that they are not able to take reflexive note of political decisions and are incapacitated to effectively take part in any discussion of the issues at hand (see Carey, 1993: 15; and much earlier Walter Lippmann in *Public Opinion* [1922]).

It is not just the individual scientists I quoted who identify the lack of knowledge of the public as a critical problem in modern societies. In fact, the entire scientific community is of the same opinion. For instance, 85 percent of American scientists acknowledge such a trend towards ignorance among the public in a survey in 2009 and cite it as the most critical problem.

Contrast this with what obviously contributes to the welfare of democratic society, namely its ability to mitigate or cope with an almost infinite number of man-made hazards and natural risks. These dangers and risks range from natural disasters – often exacerbated by the people themselves, to economic crises, to dangers of terrorism or epidemics. Since coping, in the form of risk regulation, for example, requires the best and often highly technical expertise available, how is one able to rationally deal with these risks and dangers without putting in question one of the fundamental prerequisites of democratic societies? Once again, the critical issue is how is it possible to uphold one of the key features of democracy, the culture of political participation, emphasized on many sides in contrast to traditional societies as the taken-for-granted feature of modern democratic politics? Is there a fundamental contradiction between system effectiveness and citizen participation in modern democracies? It seems whoever wants to govern efficiently and problem-driven, cannot afford to defer to citizen participation.

Democracy and Knowledge

I will continue my critical reflections with a rather broad set of questions and claims. As Max Horkheimer emphasized – in contrast to Karl Marx – justice or equity and freedom do not mutually support each other. Does this also apply to democracy and knowledge? Or is knowledge a democratizer? Is the progress of knowledge, especially rapid advances, a burden on democracy, civil society and the capacity of the individual to assert his or her will, if there is a contradiction between knowledge and democratic processes? Is it a new development, or is the advance of liberal democracies co-determined by the joint force of knowledge and democratic political conduct, that enable one to claim that civil society, if not democracy, is the daughter of knowledge? Is it perhaps a naive faith in knowledge that propels such a conviction?

Indeed, there are a couple of rarely contested but relevant assertions about our age; Scientific expertise is a salient political resource and most of the knowledge gained in the collective quest of knowledge is inaccessible to most living people. In the case of knowledge production and knowledge use, we are on an accelerating path away from what Otto Neurath ([1945] 1996:254; cf. also Siemsen, 2010) called for, namely a democratization of knowledge. However, as I will argue, the observations about the lack of democratic control of knowledge are not reason for premature despondency. Nor are these views necessarily unique to our age.

What can be done?

Among some of the immediate reactions to what can be described as moves toward a democratization of knowledge are prominent attempts to provide lay people or members of the public with more opportunities to participate in discussions on research activities, results and their implications, such as roundtables, hearings and consensus conferences. Here we see efforts to reanimate the hopes of the Age of Enlightenment for a knowledgeable public that also displaces some of the burdens of responsibility away from science itself. The practical problems of participation of laypersons cannot be neglected. It would be unrealistic to expect that one is able through improved communication about science, for example, in the tradition of the Public Understanding of Science for example, to abolish the boundaries between the science system and other social systems. [23] But the main drawback of PUS efforts is that the thesis of the profound gap between civil society's knowledge and expertise is uncritically taken on board and not questioned.

I will advance my own thesis expressing skepticism of the close alliance of power and knowledge in a series of steps. First, how does one best define knowledge? Secondly, I formulate my specific criticisms of the theory of the inevitable symbiosis of power and knowledge in the form of the **five** key assertions I listed at the beginning of the lecture.

---

[23] Taking the matter a radical step further than the notion of a public understanding of science, the idea of the co-production of knowledge between professional and layperson would come into view. Co-production of knowledge between scientists, non-scientists or interested constituencies is supposed to have a variety of benefits, not least opening up scientific knowledge production to more inclusive deliberations, local interests, accountability and a better fit with desired purposes (cf. Lövbrand, 2011).

The knowledge of the weak

With respect to the first key notion, there are a number of important, even dominant classic and contemporary sociological theories that assert a seemingly inevitable incapacitation of the consumer, the client, the public or the trade union member in modern society. I am thinking for example of Max Weber's theory of bureaucracy or the rule by virtue of knowledge or the so-called iron law of oligarchy by Robert Michels. In both cases it is the superior knowledge that leads to and nourishes positions of social power.

I would like to briefly refer, under the heading "the knowledge of the weak", to a specific example of such a perspective, namely Michel Foucault's theory of the microphysics of power. Foucault's work is an influential example of the prevailing social scientific representation of the societal role of knowledge – in which the power of knowledge is heavily oversubscribed and in which we therefore find the assertion of an iron law of an inescapable fusion of power and knowledge. As is well known, Foucault describes in his genealogical work the one-sided dressing of the individual by scientific disciplines such Penology (the prison research), psychoanalysis and the enormous, micro-managed power of regulation and measurement inherent in the major social institutions.

Knowledge/power are Siamese twins. Foucault's reflections on the "disappearance of the subject" are based on a view that ascribes to social institutions that use the knowledge to attain too much power. The critical issue for Foucault is therefore how the tight coupling of the "growth of skills" (knowledge) can be detached from an "intensification of power relations."

Despite this critical stance Foucault in his analysis of fields such as clinical medicine, psychiatry, the prison system or sexual relations as practiced, where he observes a symbiotic power and knowledge. He mainly shows how close the responsible scientific disciplines are implicated in organized practices and are concerned with what amounts to a "successful" controlling and shaping of society members.

In total, as I would like to emphasize, Foucault underestimates the malleability of knowledge and its profound contestability, as well as the assets of individuals and civil society organizations, to use knowledge to combat the oppression that may emanate from the most important social institutions in modern society and therefore resist und oppose the powers that may be. [24]

Are democracy and expert knowledge compatible?

Many observers are convinced that the gap between the powerful who command or have hijacked expert competence and civil society has widened in recent years and has done so apparently in an irreversible manner. Thus, there are loud voices who speak of an "inconvenient democracy". This is for example the conviction of a number of influential scientists. They argue that democratically governed societies are not in a position to respond in a timely fashion to warnings by science about impending disastrous consequences of human behaviour. I am thinking here primarily to climate change and swelling voices from academia and some in the media, who complain about an "inconvenient democracy."

However, such skepticism is not new: There are other, parallel justifications for the "power of knowing better" and the validity of decisions that may be based on superior knowledge. This will include for example a specific understanding of the role of the state. One of the founders of classical sociology, Emile Durkheim ([1957] 1992: 92), expresses these convictions about the proper role of the state as follows:

> The role of the State, in fact, is not to express and sum up the unreflective thought of the mass of the people, but to superimpose on this unreflective thought a more considered thought, which therefore cannot be other than different. It must be a centre of new and original representations which ought to put the society in a position to conduct itself with greater intelligence than when it is swayed merely by vague sentiments working on it.

A less encumbered statement would be to say you should not simply neglect the difference between expert and lay knowledge; there are indeed persons who are better informed or know more than others. Thus, if one is concerned about the effectiveness of political decision-making, it would be important to be able to distinguish between these groups of actors. We all

---

[24] Foucault (2008:1104) is able to recognize the capacity of human power that manifests itself in forms of discursive resistance: "Der Diskurs befördert und produziert Macht; er verstärkt sie, aber er unterminiert sie auch, er setzt sie aufs Spiel, macht sie zerbrechlich und aufhaltsam." [Source: Foucault, Michel (2008), *Sexualität und Wahrheit. Der Wille zum Wissen*, in ders. *Die Hauptwerke*, Frankfurt am Main: Suhrkamp Verlag]. But much more typical of Foucault's perspective is the indivisibility of the same capacity for action. His analysis of discursive resistance, its potential and productivity, is not convincing (also Giddens, 1984:157).

want to buy meat that is healthy, but not necessarily perform the function of food inspectors.

If one follows the *instrumental model* of social function of scientific knowledge, then the effect of scientific knowledge is direct, straightforward and useful. The flow of knowledge goes unilaterally from the expert to the layperson. Science speaks to power and to civil society. Scientific and technological phenomena are politically and morally innocuous.

An empirically much more accurate representation of the communication processes between science or experts and civil society, however, is far less impressed by the success or the automatic power of science to influence. As Dan Kahan and his colleagues discovered in experimental studies, the diametrically opposite reaction of the public in response consensual scientific knowledge (for example, to anthropogenic global warming), namely the strong expression of doubt, may be explained by the fact that the public assessment of scientific communication of this kind is strongly effected by already existing, culturally specific attitudes. These attitudes operate as an efficient kind of filter and confirm or refute the reputation of experts as experts. No matter how insistent reference is to the toxicity of a certain ingredient of food, provided that relevant cultural beliefs exist, such communication falls on deaf ears. The certification of science as a reliable or unreliable source of knowledge manifests itself not in a cognitive vacuum, it is dependent on pre-judgments. The answer to the question about differences in the decision calculus of knowledge and less knowledgeable citizens is that informed readers, voters, students reflect for example about a longer chain of consequences of political action, *but in the end* values or political ideology plays a crucial, or even decisive role in weighing the alternatives and assessment of the consequences.

It is therefore much more appropriate to speak of a precarious balance between autonomy and dependence, which describes the societal role of science in modern society. The loss of close intellectual contact between scientists and the public can very well be associated with both a diffuse support for science and with the consent of civil society to institute legal and political efforts to control the consequences of science and technology.

In another sense, however, the loss of cognitive contact is virtually irrelevant. That is, if one understands by "contact" the close cognitive proximity as a prerequisite for participation in decisions in which scientific and technological knowledge are at issue. Such a claim is virtually meaningless, because it requires public participation in the on-going work of the science itself.

In order to arrive at a realistic assessment of the role of expertise in civil society, one must take relevant contexts and issues that are at odds into consideration. It is also realistic that a small set of issues that need to be decided politically cannot be subject to *extensive* democratic deliberation, but that is not to say subject to the *abolition* of democratic process; at times, prompt decisions may be required, in case of some issues, only a small constituency needs to be consulted and in other instances, expertise does acquire special importance. The resolution of the question of the role of knowledge and democracy in modern society does not require a general "solution" but always only an answer from case to case. For every controversial political issue, new and differently composed publics tend to emerge.

If one formulates the question in this sense, it is apparent that the asymmetry between civil society and experts is not an insurmountable obstacle in order to challenge expertise. As empirical studies show, there is no need for symmetry in the volume of knowledge in order to question expert knowledge. The powerlessness of civil society is not cemented. We should not treat the relationship between expertise and public as a series of fixed events nor as a difference that can be fully abolished, but as occasions mediated by cultural identities and varying ideological views, for example with respect to beliefs about the societal benefits of science and technology.

I want to illustrate in my diagnosis that the relationship between knowledge and power must be analysed on a case by case basis with reference to the issue of climate change. If we are dealing with wicked problems in practice, and climate change is a wicked problem, it is impossible to directly derive instructions for action from scientific findings. This applies, for example, to earth science. Earth science is capable to work out scenarios of the potential of danger for regions with earthquake potential, but it is impossible to derive from such scenarios what kinds of risks society is willing to assume in the case of the construction of nuclear power plants.[25]

Rather than being a discrete problem to be solved, climate change is better understood as a persistent condition that must be coped with and can only be partially managed more – or less – well. It is just one part of a larger complex of such conditions encompassing population, technology, wealth disparities, resource use, etc. Hence it is not straightforwardly an 'environmental' problem either. It is axiomatically as much an energy problem, an economic development problem or a land-use problem, and may be better approached through these avenues than as a problem of

---

[25] I rely here on portions of our Hartwell Paper (2010) where the relevant issues are discussed in much more detail.

managing the behaviour of the Earth's climate by changing the way that humans use energy.

What makes a problem 'wicked' is the impossibility of giving it a definitive formulation. The information needed to understand the problem is dependent upon one's idea for solving it. Furthermore, wicked problems lack a stopping rule. We cannot know whether we have a sufficient understanding to stop searching for more understanding. There is no end to causal chains in interacting open systems of which the climate is the world's prime example. So, every wicked problem can be considered as a symptom of another problem. The practical, political consequence would be to argue that in order to achieve complex objective it is best to tackle them indirectly or obliquely (Kay, 2010).

This is of course frustrating for politicians. So policy makers frequently respond to wicked problems by declaring 'war' on them, to beat them into submission and then move on. Indeed, almost any 'declaration of war' that is metaphorical rather than literal is a reliable sign that the subject in question is 'wicked'. So, we have the war on cancer, the war on poverty, the war on drugs, the war on terror and now the war on climate change.

The public is often initially stirred by such declarations of war; but, as wicked problems demonstrate their intractability, the public soon grows weary of them. Recent polls suggest that public opinion in many developed nations is losing its previously intense preoccupation with climate issues as it becomes increasingly apparent that it is no more a problem to be 'solved' than is poverty, and as attention focuses on what people feel to be more pressing issues, like the economy.

In an era of knowledge politics (Stehr, 2003), there is the face of diverse and growing political efforts to regulate new knowledge and technical artefacts as well as the changing willingness among the public to support such efforts and welcome everything and anything because it is new. It does not make sense, to view the public in dealing with the new forms of action as naively resistant, but rather as cautious, uncertain and curious about the possible consequences of new scientific insights and technical possibilities. Science- and technology-based innovation will be judged by civil society against the background of their world views, values, preferences and beliefs, and despite the lack of detailed scientific and technical knowledge. Relevant examples are responses to stem cell research, medical genetics, or genetically modified maize. More generally, the rules of the political game are changing. In the context of knowledge politics and public discourse about the social authorization of innovative forms of action, this amounts to a change in the balance of power of science and civil society. Influence and power shifts in favour of civil society.

Without a measure of impersonal trust and confidence that members of civil society display toward experts, the expert would disappear, however. Trust if it is placed "reasonably" requires, as Onora O'Neill (2002) argues, "not only information about the proposals or undertakings that others put forward, but also information about those who put tem forward." Moreover, today's experts are constantly involved in all sorts of controversies. The growing policy field in which limits are set for certain ingredients in food, to safety regulations, risk management and the monitoring and control of hazards, have all as a side effect ruined the reputation of the experts. As long as a matter of public debate remains controversial, the influence of experts and counter-experts are limited. But as soon as a decision has been made and implemented, the experts regain much of their unchallenged authority.

To conclude:

Limited or lacking scientific and technical knowledge is constitutive of everyday life

> Der Wein schmeckt einem, der über seine Grundeigenschaften Bescheid weiß, deswegen doch nicht besser als den andern.
>
> (Michel de Montaigne 1998: 516)
>
> Wine is none the more pleasant to him who knows its first faculties.

The topic of my lecture was the allegedly unavoidable and dangerous convergence of knowledge and power in modern societies, especially in the world of politics. This diagnosis did not refer to the apparently growing disenchantment and skepticism of many groups in civil society toward certain existing or potential technical possibilities and consequences of implementing these potentials, for example, within the field of genetics, nanotechnology or the machine based medical treatment. Nor do I mean to refer to the alleged alienation of German civil society toward modern science as the result of the dominance of the English language in research and teaching in German speaking countries.[26]

---

[26] Compare the following articles by Heike Schmoll, „Wider den Englischzwang. Die meisten Fächer brauchen Mehrsprachigkeit aus historischen und methodischen

It would be quite interesting, as is often suspected – which I am unable to accomplish in this lecture – to explore whether we are not dealing with a deficit of knowledge among the public but with a *surplus* of readily available information and knowledge with the result as some suspect that we are incapable of reaching meaningful judgments (Hardin, 2006).

The philosopher of the French Enlightenment, Marquis de Condorcet, expressed the conviction the idea that "citizens could not participate fully in the entire discussion and that the opinion of each citizen could not be heard by everyone cannot claim to have any validity" (quoted in Urbinati, 2006:202). To Condorcet, participation was not a question of competence in relation to the particular problem, but of the existence the moral rules and appropriate contexts within which individuals could jointly deliberate. Thus, Condorcet had, as it were, a modern conception of the public in mind that relies on a dynamic, active conception of civil society. This conception is quite appropriate for the contemporary, knowledgeable public involving new forms of social and political interaction as well as social solidarities. Apart from the normative or even constitutionally enshrined right of citizens to be heard in political matters, even when these are coupled to highly specialized knowledge claims, Condorcet reminds us of the fact that collective thinking and collective commitment can only benefit from rules, contexts and opportunities that are conducive to reflection. As a matter of fact, Paul Lazarsfeld and colleagues (1974) in their electoral studies in the nineteen-seventies have shown that voters base their election decisions on a wide range of simple instructions as a substitute for complex information and a diversity of reference groups for support. That is one side of the question in the relationship between democracy and expertise.

The other side of the coin has to do with allegations that the public reflection about specialized knowledge claims is from the beginning doomed to fail because the average citizen is not able to participate in public discussions on such forms of knowledge. The deficit assumption, as I will call it, is mistaken. The assumption is already erroneous because it is incorrect to assume that the success or the persuasiveness of the communication of scientific findings is solely dependent on or determined by the attributes of the scientificity of such knowledge claims (e.g., their objectivity and impartiality). In fact, as I have already stressed, the reception and public response to scientific knowledge is strongly influenced by the worldviews, intellectual capacities

---

Gründen," *Frankfurter Allgemeine Zeitung*, 15. Januar 2011, Seite 10. Prompt and direct access to the findings of science by the public is limited also by the strict copyright laws benefitting mainly large publishing houses (cf. George Monbiot, Academic publishers make Murdoch look like a socialist," *The Guardian* August 29, 2011).

and epistemic cultures of the recipients of such communication. The common name for this kind of cognitive processes is motivated judgments (motivated reasoning).

The basic claim of my remarks is, however, that the development of modern societies into knowledge societies increasingly extends also to the democratization and negotiation of scientific knowledge claims. We are gradually moving away from what would be a case of an experts' society or the political rule of experts towards a much broader, shared governance of knowledge claims and their social consequences.

Finally, it is one of the strengths of liberal democracies, that citizens be involved in political decisions. Such involvement, in which formal basis does not whatsoever require that citizens have an extraordinary degree of factual or intellectual competence.

Also, I accept the assumption that scientific and technical knowledge is not only much more contested, flexible and accessible than the classical view – such as the "deficit model" let us expect and suggesting instead that – as the sociology of scientific knowledge has developed in recent years – the production of scientific knowledge is in many ways quite similar to other social practices, and that the wall between science and society, though it has not disappeared, is lower than is often assumed.

In addition and increasingly so in modern society, the problem we face must no longer be seen in that we do know enough but rather that we know too much. The social negotiation of new capacity of action (generated by science and technology) is less dependent on scientific and technical expertise rather on the enabling findings of the social sciences and humanities.

The general access of civil society to knowledge produced by the social sciences and the humanities is less strewn with obstacles as is the case of the knowledge generated in the natural sciences. Growing knowledgeability of many actors extends to the desire for a more participatory democracy and citizenship. All this creates special challenges not only in terms of access to social scientific knowledge, but also in the form of new forms of participation. At this point, the civil society organizations are increasingly required.

The social space for communication between science/social science and the public is already there. The possibility of democratic deliberation and scientific practice must be understood as part of a larger social enterprise and social context in which the professional scientists can take part as experts as well as the lay public in common forms of discourse. The scientific community can be an effective social force, because it involves itself in civil society organizations and relies on them. Activism on climate change and AIDS are already evident examples of social processes in which the boundaries between expert and lay public prove to be porous (Bohmann, 1999).

And last but not least, we should be content with the lack of our scientific basis in a good part of the knowledge we do with in everyday life. We need not to get too severely into task, because at least most of the time, we generally live with that knowledge quite well. As Ludwig Wittgenstein (1984: § 344) commented, in a soothing and restrained fashion, "My life consists in the fact that I am satisfied with many things."

References

Dahlgren, Peter (2009), *Media and Political Engagement*: Citizens, Communication, and Engagement. New York: Cambridge University Press.

Dow, Jay K. (2011), "Political knowledge and electoral choice in the 1992–2004 United States presidential elections: Are more and less informed citizens distinguishable?" *Journal of Elections, Public Opinion and Parties* 21:381–405.

Bourdieu, Pierre (1998), *Acts of Resistance*. Against the Tyranny of the Market. New York, New York: The New Press.

Carey, James W. (1993), "The mass media and democracy," *Journal of International Affairs* 47:1–21.

Downs, Anthony (1957), An Economic Theory of Democracy. New York: Harper.

Durkheim, Emile (1992), *Professional Ethics and Civic Morals*. With a New Preface by Bryan Turner. London: Routledge.

Feyerabend, Paul ([1978] 1980), Erkenntnis für freie Menschen. Veränderte Ausgabe. Frankfurt am Main: Suhrkamp.

Frickel, Scott et al. (2010), "Undone science: Charting social movement and civil society challenges to research agenda setting," *Science, Technology & Human Values* 35:444–473.

Fuller, Steve (1994), "The constitutively social character of expertise," *The International Journal of Expert Systems* 7:51–64.

Fuller, Steve (1988), *Social Epistemology*. Bloomington, Indiana: Indiana University Press.

Hardin, Russell (2006), "Ignorant democracy," *Critical Inquiry* 18:179–195.

Hupe, Peter and Arthur Edwards (2011), "The accountability of power: Democracy and governance in modern times," *European Political Science Review* (first online ...).

Kahan, Dan M. Hank Jenkins-Smith and Donald Braman (2010), "Cultural cognition of scientific consensus," *Journal of Risk Analysis* 14:147–174.

Kagan, Dan M., Paul Slovic, Donald Braman and John Gastil (2006), "Fear of democracy: A cultural evaluation of Sunstein on risk," *Harvard Law Review* 119:1071–1109.

Kay, John (2010), *Obliquity*. Why our Goals are best Achieved Indirectly. London: Profile Books.

Kitcher, Philip (2011), "Public knowledge and its discontents," *Theory and Research in Education* 9:103–124.

Lazarsfeld, Paul F. Lövbrand, Eva (2011), "Co-producing European climate science and policy: a cautionary note on the making of useful knowledge," *Science and Public Policy* 38:225–236

Mannheim, Karl (1940), *Man and Society in an Age of Reconstruction*. London: Kegan Paul.

Nelkin, Dorothy (1975), "The political impact of technical expertise," *Social Studies of Science* 5:35054.

Minogue, Kenneth (2010), "Morals & servile mind," *The New Criterion* 28:4–9.

Montaigne, Michel de (1998), *Essais*. Erste moderner Gesamtübersetzung von Hans Stilett. Frankfurt am Main: Eichborn Verlag.

Olson, Mancur (1982), *The Rise and Decline of Nations*. Economic Growth, Stagflation, and Social Relations. New Haven, Connecticut: Yale University Press.

O'Neill, Onora (2002), "Trust and transparency," 4. BBC Reith Lecture.

Popper, Karl ([1960] 1968), "On the sources of knowledge and of ignorance", in: Karl Popper, *Conjectures and Refutations*: The Growth of Scientific Knowledge. New York: Harper and Row, pp. 3–30.

Rayner, Steve (2003), "Democracy in an age of assessment: Reflections on the roles of expertise and democracy in public-sector decision making", *Science and Public Policy* 30: 163–170.

Schumpeter, Joseph A. ([1942] 1950), *Capitalism, Socialism and Democracy*. New York, New York: Harper Torchbooks.

Shapiro, Ian (1994), "Three ways to be a democrat", *Political Theory* 22:124–151.

Stehr, Nico (2003),

Termeer, Katrien, Gerard Breeman, Maartje van Lieshout and Wieke Pot (2010), "Why more knowledge could thwart democracy: configurations and fixations in the Dutch mega-stables debate, in: 't Veld (ed.), *Knowledge Democracy*. Heidelberg: Springer-Verlag, pp. 99–110.

Turner, Stephen (2001), "What is the problem with experts," *Social Studies of Science* 31:123–149.

Wallerstein, Immanuel (2004), *The Uncertainties of Knowledge*. Philadelphia, Pennsylvania: Temple University Press.

B. THEORY AND CONCEPTS FOR CIVIL SOCIETY

Civil Society as a System

André Reichel

Introduction

Civil society is prominent in political rhetoric and scientific discourse. The so-called "third sector" between the institutions of the state and the institutions of the economy is thereby often ascribed almost magical features. Civil society appears to be the crucial element of ensuring or reinstalling legitimacy and acceptance of political decisions and their institutions, providing a voice for the disenfranchised social and ecological environment in economic reasoning of businesses, and bridging the divide between the more abstract systems of modern society and the "lifeworld" of its citizens. Especially when it comes to the problem complex of sustainability, civil society's abilities are conjured by politics and business. Of course, the very same actors in politics and business often complain about civil society protesting and blocking or slowing down processes in voting, planning or building infrastructure.

The importance and benevolent contribution of civil society and its organisations is founded only partly on profane scientific enquiry or on empirical evidence. To a much larger degree this belief in civil society is founded on its explicit mentioning in chapter 27 of the Agenda 21, where it is stated that it plays "a vital role", possessing "well-established and diverse experience, expertise and capacity" for turning un-sustainable into sustainable development.

But what is civil society? And does it have something intrinsically benevolent to contribute to pressing problems of (un-)sustainability, of climate change or energy consumption? The notions of "credibility" or "diverse experience", even the scientific concept of "social capital", do not add to a deeper understanding of the empirical phenomenon we call civil society. Civil society is real. Our understanding of what it actually is, or as what we can observe it, is still very vague. In this contribution we develop a coherent notion of civil society using Niklas Luhmann's social system theory (Luhmann, 1984; Luhmann, 1995) as a theoretical lens and a heuristic tool for inquiry into its nature. We will also shed some light on civil society's role in the great societal challenges we are witnessing today and conclude with some implications for anyone active within civil society and its organisations.

Social system theory as conceptual tool

The strength of social system theory for addressing the questions we pose in this contribution lies within its conceptual focus on communication as basal operation in any social system, as well as in its "nature" as being a theory of modern society (Luhmann, 1992). The concept of communication in Luhmann's theory enables us to observe communication as the unity of a difference between content, intention and addressee. In Luhmann's words: between information, utterance and understanding (Luhmann, 1986; Foerster, 2003). Communication is realised when all these differences occur and form a unity. Empirically, communication then can never be observed when it happens but only in retrospect. Text, notes from conversations, media coverage and so on can be used to analyse what kind of communication occurred, what its themes were, how they changed and connected to other communication, or how they faded and ceased to exist. Communication in this view is an event, it happens in a moment and then it is already gone. In order to stabilise, there has to be an on-going stream of communication. Communication has to provoke other communication in order to continue and form stable social systems. Human individuals are observed as social addresses in communication and constructed as persons, but they are not "a part" of communication. When two human individuals talk to each other, they are not in the talk. Their bodies remain in their physical position, their thoughts remain in their conceptual position "in one's head"; they do not miraculously transform into a stream of words. This is the conceptual trick of social system theory, to exclude the human individual from social analysis because it cannot be conceptualised in a clear enough and precise manner. Who are we talking about when we use the term "human individual"? Do we mean the physical body? The psychological activities within the human mind? The conversation we are following? These questions point to the problem that we are not talking about an individual, but a dividual: the human individual is multifold and in order to make a scientific inquiry we always have to be clear what our system of reference is. For analysing social phenomena, the system of reference is society and there are some features observable in society that allows us to speak of them as systems (Luhmann, 1995).

The greater structure of modern society — the economy, politics, law, science, education, religion, art and so on — can be observed as systems in this view. To be more precise, these greater structures take the form of function systems, delivering one specific function for the rest of society that no other part can deliver. This structure is different from that in the past. Until the end of medieval Europe, the dominant structuring principle of society was hierarchy, dividing society in different social strata. On top were monarchs and gods, at the bottom peasants and slaves. The emergence of modernity from 1500 onwards broke up the stratified structure and different function systems developed with their own specific logic, modes of operation and organisations. In order to provide their function for the rest of society, they evolved into ever more independent parts with strict boundaries between them. The economy cannot operate politically, only politics can. If the economy tries to operate politically, we observe the social phenomenon of corruption; if politics tries to operate economically, we observe the social phenomenon of state capitalism. Civil society, if possible to be "systemised" as a function system of society, would then have to play a role that no other part of society can play.

Civil Society Systemised

In order to systemise civil society we have to observe the empirical phenomenon that is labelled as such. To observe in this respect implies the drawing of a distinction between civil society and the rest of society. The mark of distinction signifies civil society and in order to act as such a mark, we have to place everything else on its outside. Everything else is, according to textbook definitions and following Luhmann on his notion of functional differentiation, the totality of all observable function systems in society i.e. civil society is not: Politics, economy, science, education, religion, law and so on.

What we are left with on the one hand is *protest* (Luhmann, 1996). Protest in all its various forms does not reference any specific economic, political, scientific, judicial or other rationality. Protest operates in an "against" mode, often accompanied by fear, as in the case of anti-nuclear protests, and outrage, as can be observed with the current "Occupy" movement. Protest can give rise, on the other hand, to some more institutionalized forms like *citizens' initiatives* or full-blown *non-profit voluntary organizations*. Citizens' initiatives, however, have a more weak form of protest at their core, most often protesting against something "outrageous" in the spatial proximity e.g. building of a new road, closing of a local public service and the likes. The same can account for non-profit voluntary organizations addressing a social good e.g. protecting the natural environment or providing services the public or private sector is not. Both forms, citizens' initiatives and non-profit voluntary organizations, do not necessarily entail some form of protest, of fear and outrage. The local "Friends of the Earth" division or a local sports club can do just as well without. What these more institutionalized forms of civil society cannot do without, and what they have in common with protest, is the provision of stability for joint collective action for something greater than just individual benefits.

Whereas the textbook definitions allow for a certain vagueness, this "difference view" helps to draw sharp boundaries. These boundaries are drawn along at least five lines that will be detailed in this contribution:

- The *problem* that is solved by civil society, and only by civil society and no other functional part of society.
- The specific *medium* in which civil society operates that is different from other societal media e.g. money or power.
- Civil society's *code* that enables it to process and focus communication.
- Decision *programs* providing answers to the question what to do and how.
- The form of civil society *organisations* and how they operate and can evolve.

Problem, medium, code, programs and organizations are of course also distinctions we choose in order to operationalize and observe civil society. If all can be identified with civil society, we can speak of a function system that is not in the "in between" of everything, as so many definitions claim, but that has a clear locus in society with a clear and necessary function.

The Problem of Civil Society

In modern society no part of society can act for the other. Every function system solves one and exactly one problem. This is its purpose. The economy solves the problem of scarcity by producing goods and services, by providing employment and income. Politics solves the problem of how to arrive at legally binding decisions for all of society. This is a severe problem, as modern society does not have a centre or clear head; this has been decapitated along with the kings and emperors of pre-modern societies. Politics solves this problem by producing voting procedures, political parties, elections and the dichotomy of majority and minority. Neither politics nor the economy can act for another.

Civil society, following the line of reasoning behind the drawing of its distinction, tries to solve those problems that are not solved by any other part of society. These problems have to be of a specific class and their solution needs to be in the blind spot of all other parts: They cannot see it properly (Luhmann, 1997). From an economy perspective, such a problem's solution has to be of only minor liquidity gains compared to other investment options and probably too much risk of liquidity loss. For politics it has to be of uncertain power gains for winning or securing the majority and too much risk of losing power, e.g. by offending voters when introducing a "green tax" and thus becoming a target of the political opponent. Prime examples of such problems are climate change and the current financial crisis in Europe and North America. These problems are of course tackled by politics and the economy, but the results of international climate conferences in the past twenty years provide a sobering experience.

However, there has to be more to civil society and its specific problem than that. The already mentioned local sports club acts as a fruitful example. The problem it solves is not organizing personal fitness or physical health; a for-profit fitness club could also do this. The organisation of joint, collective action in a voluntary and "for the common good" environment appears to be the crucial factor here. It adheres to people's needs for social contact, for collaboration with and for doing something for others. This is done not as a side effect, as you could argue business is also doing something collaboratively (with a workforce) for others (their customers); it is the main purpose of these organised forms of civil society. In Stafford Beer's words: this is what they are doing and thus defines what they are (Beer, 1970).

None of the other function systems in society can deal with this problem of how to address their own blind spots by providing joint collaborative action for the common good and social coherence. Not only can they not see what they cannot see — however, they could hire political or economic consultants for that — but they cannot solve these "unseeable" problems in such a manner as civil society addresses them.

The Medium of Civil Society

Communication in society does not take place in thin air; it needs a medium through which it can take form. E.g. the English language is a medium and the sentences in front of the reader's eye are a form of the English language. Language is a very general medium for communication. Other media of communication include general distribution media, e.g. the printing press or the internet, and so-called generalised communication media. The latter are a specific kind of medium. Every function system in society has developed its own generalised medium for communication in order to make highly improbably communication probable. In the economy, money has evolved as such a generalised medium, making the unlikely event that a consumer chooses one product (buying it) more likely to happen. Without money, economic choice would be much harder to negotiate. For politics this role is played by power, for intimate relationships the generalised communication medium is love. All these media give their specific communication a backdrop against which they can take a stable form and thus providing connectivity to an on-going stream of communication. You can argue that the medium of communication is the key anchor point for stability in social systems (Luhmann, 2006).

What enables the various forms of civil society — protest, citizens' initiatives, voluntary non-profit organisations — to materialise stable communication? When regarding the protests against nuclear or the recent "Occupy" movement, outrage and also fear appear to be contenders for the medium of civil society communication. Fear of nuclear risks, fear of anonymous financial markets ruling personal lives, in combination with a moral outrage against the feeling of being deprived and disenfranchised make a powerful combination for realising all sorts of communication. But how can the local sports club, that is also taking part in civil society communication, utilise fear and outrage? What other, more general generalised media for civil society communication can be observed? Apart from all forms of revolutionary rhetoric as a form of outrage, the same what has been argued for the specific problem of civil society holds here as well. When asked what motivates them to occupy Wall Street or London or Frankfurt, protesters also argue that it is the joint action of many different people they would not have met otherwise, sharing certain common ideas and gut-feelings about what is going wrong in the world.

The only feasible medium to provide an anchor point for all of these forms of civil society communication appears to be values. With values we do not mean a specific form values can take e.g. freedom or equality, but their abstract backdrop, their function within society as providers of coherence and obfuscation of contingency (Luhmann, 2008). In the hierarchical society of medieval Europe, values in the form as we perceive them today were of little value themselves. In a hierarchy everything is already decided, the cohesion is provided by the structure of society itself. There is no point in questioning the role of the king or the emperor or God. However, when modernity evolved from the 15th century onwards, not only kings and gods were decapitated but also the ontological security they provided was lost. In modern society everything is questionable. There is no single truth but a multitude of truths of what is the best way to govern, what is the best product to sell or buy, who is the best partner to fall in love with, and of course what is truth anyway. The notion of contingency captures this feature of modern society where in every given moment no single individual and no single communication can refer to a "point of innocence" that everything is all right the way it is. The knowledge that it could be otherwise, and this would then be just as right, is always communicated, thought and felt along.

This is the situation in which values become of value. At first, the notion and idea of something having a value is quite profane. It evolved from measuring goods against each other, from measuring real-world instances and categorising them. The power to measure and categorise could then also be used to measure and categorise what is right and wrong: the notion of value was taken from goods to good — and evil. When we speak of values today, we are not speaking of some instrumental form of it, of what something is worth, probably in monetary terms. We use the term deliberately to refer to something bigger than that, something bigger than what we usually are dealing with. Why should any two human individuals agree on anything in modern society, apart from cases like clearly given one-upmanship, if it were not for the values they share – or at least: the belief that they are sharing identical values? Values today act as a form of social glue, a meta-medium of communication, binding together, if needed, all other media like money, power, love, truth and so forth, while at the same time obfuscating their fundamental assumptions. The question always is: what kind of freedom are we granting to whom, and not: why is freedom — or clearer, but never formulated that way: should freedom be — valuable? Somebody asking that question immediately has to bear the burden of proof why a value is not valuable. In brief, values from a social systems theory perspective are acting as a meta-medium that provides orientation for communication. Values allow communication to take for granted certain assumptions, "faking" a non-contingent communicative context, thus enabling the continuation of communication. In a way, values are filling the gaps modernity has created between the different function systems in society. They have intra-systemic relevance — the value of freedom as freedom of economic transaction or freedom to vote — as well as inter-systemic relevance, reassuring and thus faking unity in a functionally differentiated society.

The Code of Civil Society

In order to establish and continue communication, social systems need a mechanism to decide what to do with communication. If you ask a scientist "is this true or not?" and she answers "it costs about five Euro" then you would have to rethink the situation and if you are truly talking to a scientist or if there has been a change of reference from science to economy. This answer would irritate and maybe even destroy the continuation of communication. With the help of codes, social systems canalise contingency, they enable them to construct information out of communication. Without the existence of codes, the decision how communication can connect to other communication cannot be taken — without reference to a code you could not even decide whether or not there was anything communicated. In the economy the code is paying/non-paying, orienting all decisions taken in the economy towards securing liquidity in order to continue operation. In politics the code is majority/minority, orienting all decisions in politics towards securing power in order to continue operations. A code is giving orientation in decision situations to take those decisions in a way that secure the continuation of operations.

Given the medium of values, the code of civil society most likely will provide orientation how to continue value operations. The preferred side of the code is of course "value-laden" but we have to keep in mind that this means "value-laden for an observer". However what is of value to one observer need not be of value to another. Quite on the contrary, what is of value to one can be value-free or, more negatively, even value-less to another. The key feature of value as medium, its coherence provision through obfuscating contingency, is ensured through setting a value as a universal. There shall be no other values, that is the mantra of any value communication and this has deep impacts on the code and its operation. When civil society communicates along its own lines of values, it has to decide on which value to use as an anchor point and thus on what coin to flip. This explains why civil society communication is often so full of conflict with other kinds of communication. When you have values on your side, the other cannot have something similar on her side. There is always some form of dogmatism involved in civil society communication and this is not an aberration but constitutive for civil society as system. This holds for protest against nuclear or the financial markets just as much as it holds for the local sports club. At a local sports club, you are valuing doing sports together in a voluntary and local environment, with like-minded sports fans that enjoy doing their sport and organising it in such an environment with people like you. Everyone else who does not like to do that is excluded. Along values and its code, inclusion and exclusion are decided.

The Program(s) of Civil Society

Programs in social systems provide answers to the question how to reach the preferred side of the code. In the economy, the paradigm of Taylorism answered the question how to ensure liquidity and the ability to pay — instead of not paying — by means of algorithmisation of manual work, leading to large-scale automatisation of manufacturing industries and in fact the large-scale corporation that came do dominate the better half of the last century. In politics, social democracy used to be a program ensuring power and government by proposing mass welfare across all income groups, especially lower and medium ones. Programs can lose their ability to direct communication to the preferred side of the code in the system of reference; this then triggers evolution of other programs and in fact a battle of programs against each other. In science the clash of different paradigms in the Kuhnian sense (Kuhn, 1962) represents such a programmatic battle and depicts the general form of evolution of programs within society's function systems.

A good civil society program brings about more of it, more value communication through strengthening communication about values and getting "more value". Like Taylorism not only brought about an almost endless amount of literature and projects about itself, it also brought more liquidity for Taylorist organisations – at least in the short run. Values as medium are always giving form to more or less dogmatic communication, revolving about what has value and what is clearly atheist regarding values. Value communication thus resembles moral communication very closely, especially insofar as value communication is about having the right values. In everyday language the adjective "ethical" can be used to turn almost everything into a civil society program, you could even think of something like "ethical taylorism" that could be used by civil society activists to overcome traditional taylorism — which then would probably stop being an economic program. Similarly "green" or, even more notorious, "sustainable" are also playing such a role. The combination of an everyday activity in connection with a value-laden adjective can form the basis of a program for civil society.

However, there might be greater or deeper programs that encompass most of these rather new forms of programs, just like values lie deeper than outrage or fear. The recent protests in Germany against the railway project Stuttgart 21 can be used as a lens for focusing on such greater programs (Römmele, 2010). Protesters in this specific case wanted to protect their park, their city, their home — in brief, their identity against modernity risks. Ironically, the proponents of Stuttgart 21 also wanted to protect their identity against modernity risks, just against other modernity risks than the protesters. However, the dispute was decided by protest, as always, in such a way that the protesters had the "good" values, whereas the proponents had none at all. The proponents' arguments added to that as they adhered to established procedures, legitimate decisions already taken, expert knowledge on their side and so on. Clearly, they totally missed the value communication, which in turn fuelled the protest even more. Identity, protection, conservation are of great value to value communication. In fact, conservation and protection is likely one of the deepest civil society programs. Protection also accounts for the Anti-Nuclear or the traditional Environmentalist movement. For the local sports association, conservation and protection of community through joint organization and performance of sports and sports events, also appears to be a valid program. The protests against Stuttgart 21 show one more interesting feature as basis for civil society programs. It was predominantly a grassroots movement, routed in local activity, creating a counter public ("Gegenöffentlichkeit") and a form of counter expert knowledge with even a detailed concept of a railway alternative. Something similar can be seen in globalisation-oriented civil society movements, like the formation of Attac and also the latest Occupy protests. This is even more the case with grassroots democracy activists in developing countries, where there is only weak institutional power of governments, and most of it regarded as corrupt. The program at hand is a form of empowerment of people via building counter power (media attention, expert knowledge, organisations) against disempowering corporate and political interest. Subsidiary empowerment, to give that program a name, can just as much act for civil society in order to produce more value and more value communication as conservation and protection.

Interestingly, both programs can be combined: Empowering local communities in order to make them more autonomous against outside intervention and rule, thus sustaining their identity and culture. Needless to say that even in the local sports club, this greater and deeper program underlies value communication and directs that communication to the preferred side of the value code. Taken together, protection and empowerment is the classical program of emancipation, but with a conservative touch: to free us in order to become our true selves and maintain these selves.

The Organisations of Civil Society

Organisations have evolved as a special form of social systems in modern society. They are answering the question where in society decisions are formed and taken. In pre-modern societies decision power had a clear locus given through the structure of society itself e.g. in the form of the monarch or clan leader. As has been noted many times, in modern society its structure of functional differentiation evaporates decision power, thus needing a new locus for decisions. Organisations are that locus, in fact they can be observed as decision systems, with decisions as their specific form of communication (Luhmann, 1999; Seidl and Becker, 2006). The question what to produce is not decided on markets but in business organisations. The question what legislation to enact is not decided on the agora, but in parliaments and pre-formed in governments. The decisions are following the code of the system of reference, taking form against the generalised communication medium of the system of reference. For a business organisation the system of reference is the economy. However, it can be opportunistic i.e. ensuring continuation of operations to switch the system of reference and act politics or even values. Of course this change in reference cannot be followed for too long unless the organisation decided to change itself i.e. from a business organisation to a political party or a charity. It is interesting to note that this change in reference is a constant feature of social businesses, marking them as organisational chameleons.

In civil society organisations have to address the question how to take decisions with values as medium and code of reference and how to stabilise the continuation of value communication. In the past, protest movements have only sustained their influence and momentum when they evolved organisations to support them and carry on. The environmentalist movement invented the Sierra Club, Greenpeace, Robin Wood, the WWF, and even green political parties, thus transgressing the boundary between civil society, politics and the economy. The evolution of the green party in Germany is a prime example how civil society first evolved an organizational hybrid, which then became a full part of the political system — and stopped being a part of civil society, although the arousal mechanisms of the Greens still resonate strongly with the original value-laden communication of its origin. However it did not stop them from forming government coalitions with the Conservatives in several German states.

There are several methods how to form, discuss and take decisions in an organization with values as reference system. Preaching and converting is one method, gathering the already converted and preaching to them is even better. One sign of civil society organisations is that they demand the acceptance of their values before you enter the organisation. It was already argued that values are set dogmatic i.e. you cannot challenge them if you want to be included in the organisation and its decision process. To frame it more positively: civil society organisations propose values, they make some form of motivational offer to join their cause and it is up to their members-to-be to decide for themselves if they are buying into it. Values are the sole source and legitimation of any communication within a civil society organisation and beyond its boundaries towards its environment. In order to couple to that environment, to politics or the economy, methods are developed to "economise" or "politicise" its values and, in a kind of reverse engineering, economic and political programs are infused with value. We take the example of being green to illustrate this. Civil society organisations communicate to the economy that being green is good *and* paying off, therefore marking it as even "gooder" — thus all things green *must* be good economically, otherwise they are just carried out the wrong way. Or for politics, green is marked as good *and* winning you the elections. This is the game civil society organisations are playing and there is never a way out in system theory, but in value communication this is even "truer".

However, this view also points towards the permanent pitfall of civil society organisations. They are apt to betray themselves about their real impact on politics or the economy. When coupling to politics, to the economy, to science and so on, they have to carry out this "masquerading operation" and mark their value discourse as other, non-value discourse — being green is paying off — and vice versa — to do economically well is to be green. But which discourse is which? Is it necessary for being green to pay off? Or do you have to be green in order to make sound profits? What causes what and what needs to be proven first? The critique from protest groups against big civil society organisations like the World Wildlife Fund stems from this problem, which is a direct result of the coupling of a value-driven organisation with a non-value driven environment. Civil society organisations can also change their reference system, not only temporarily, but also completely and "fall out" of civil society like green parties or green consultancies.

Civil Society in the Next Society

From what has been developed so far, it appears sound to speak of civil society as a specific function system of modern society. However, when we follow the ideas taken from the more speculative parts of Niklas Luhmann's theory by Dirk Baecker and use a system-theoretical perspective to reason about a possible future of society, modernity might well come to its end (Baecker, 2007). Luhmann's system theory is not only a theory about the functional differentiated society we can observe today, but also an evolutionary theory of societal distribution media. Communication being the basal operation of any social system is shaped by the way it is distributed. The reader should beware that the notion of distribution is more a reference to everyday language and has no ontological implications for communication i.e. it does not imply that communication is a thing that can be distributed from one place to the other. Communication is created in the process of the threefold selection process described above. However, distribution media play a significant role in how communication is created. Three grand ages of societal evolution can be observed with the help of system theory: segmentation, stratification, and functional differentiation. The beginning of any of these ages is marked by a crisis in society, caused — not solely, but significantly — by the introduction of a new distribution media that enabled communication to increase its complexity. Complexity here means that communication gained more options to connect to other communication and to develop more communicative themes than before, including the disturbance of older communicative themes and their underlying societal structures. When the shift from oral language to scripture occurred, what has been handed down temporally by reciting stories, verses, rites and lore could now be solidified in text. The institution of landownership emerged, turning land into a property right with both economic and political significance. At the same time, these rights were made countable: if you had more of them you became more powerful. This accountability of property rights — in all the variety of meanings — is a necessary condition of a stratified society, with a king on top and peasants at the bottom. The advent of the mechanical printing press changed this society dramatically. Suddenly text was not in the domain of a sacred profession anymore — the stratum of the priests — but proliferated without control throughout society. For any text there was a counter-text criticising it and so forth. Old securities came under pressure, contingency loomed large and in the end, the hierarchical order of the stratified society itself dissolved in political and economic revolutions in the centuries to come. In fact, the cultural technique of critique had to be developed in order to cope with this new complexity introduced by the printing press. Had it not been developed, modernity would not have evolved the way it did.

In the last forty years a new distribution medium emerged. The computer in connection with electronic communication networks brings new possibilities and new problems. Communication via computer and networks not only evaporates authorship of texts — a key feature of the book society — it also destroys traditional ways of creating, storing, and selling texts, in other words: it destroys our book-keeping. Moreover, communication is now not only multi-sourced in a text — that was also the case with a book with many references — but multi-sourced instantaneously. The text being at the basis of a specific communication can be created simultaneously through the introduction of hypertext and automated search engines. What can be observed is loss: Loss of authorship and the legitimacy of the text by the author or by e.g. professional journalism, loss of control over text as regards its present state that can be constantly changing while reading and thus loss of the ability to provide a static reference. Of course this new medium also has great advantages that emerge from its downsides. The described losses enable communication to form more freely and unbound than ever before. Communication can connect to way more other communication in an instant, with virtually no temporal distance. For the first time, communication has a distribution medium at hand that matches its event-based character. To paraphrase Marshall McLuhan: the message has finally become the medium (McLuhan, 1962; McLuhan, 1964). But if communication is now almost omnipresent in our everyday lives, if we now can almost feel communication through touchscreen interfaces and gesture control, what implications does this have for society and its civil society? We will have to take an abductive inference from what has been said here or in other words: perform an informed speculation.

When communication becomes omnipresent and loses all the modern containers like authorship and references, the cultural technique of criticising text becomes obsolete. What can be criticised anymore? Selective attention, ironical curiosity and a certain kind of opportunistic playfulness all appear much more apt to cope with the newly proliferating complexity in society caused by computer communication. This of course disturbs codes and programs of function systems. How can you decide to pay or not to pay if you are either playing with many options at the same time or change your frame of reference permanently e.g. from economy to science and thus truth instead of payment? We have described civil society organisations as carrying out a masquerading operation, infusing values into other systemic references, thus in itself balancing on a multitude of references while trying to ensure their dogmatic stance on their chosen values. These organisations can become interesting empirical role models for economic and political organisations as to what extend a system reference can be kept and obfuscated at the same time. This of course calls for a certain form of accepted schizophrenia in organisations, the same schizophrenia civil society organisations exhibit when engaging with politics and business. Another possible role for civil society organisations can be that of an "airlock" for other organisations and the proliferating complexity of computer communication. Instead of becoming schizophrenic themselves, political organisations like governments or economic organisations like business enterprises can use civil society organisations as mechanisms to canalise this new complexity. This would then demand an even increasing schizophrenia from civil society organisations that can only be balanced by an even stricter adherence to values. Civil society as system, as the backdrop to which all civil society communication refer — be it protest, initiatives or formal organisations — can also merge into a new role. Up until today, civil society is either viewed as a nebulous third sector between or beyond anything else or as a troublemaker endangering the operations of the rest of society. The view on civil society as system makes it clear that it has its own function for the rest of society that no other part can take. In the "Next Society" that we can observe emerging after modernity today, civil society as system can perform a paradoxical operation for this society: it can blur the boundaries within society that functional differentiation created through schizophrenia — through being the truly postmodern jester with a license to de-differentiate and thus sustaining functional differentiation. The dangers of such a reliance on civil society are of course also significant. Schizophrenia in combination with a dogmatic adherence to values is a risky operation for both communication and its social systems as well as for thoughts and their psychic systems: the human mind. Without a certain amount of irony, of playfulness and an almost Buddhist-like cheerful serenity this operation appears to be impossible.

Conclusions

Civil society has been conceptualised as a function system with its own problem to solve, its own medium in which it can take form, a specific code to direct communication, decisions programs, and its own type of organisations. In this view it is clear that civil society is neither a textbook chameleon nor an aberration within society blocking its progress; quite on the contrary it is a clear differentiable part of society and plays a vital role no other parts can play. Furthermore it has been abductively guessed that, although being a child of late modernity, civil society can play an important role in the transition towards a next society with more diffused and less clear-cut forms of communication as we can see emerging today. The implications for the operations of civil society and moreover for its organisations are also clear: adherence to values and masquerading operations when connecting to other social systems beyond civil society. This also gives a clear warning to anyone working and taking responsibility in civil society. What is needed is an awareness of civil society's complete dependence on values and their inherent dogmatism while on the same time being able to translate and obfuscate their values to other systems of reference. Strict civil society activists would say: their sell-out, and thus they play a vital role for civil society itself as reminders of what it is about.

However, whether civil society can really stabilise itself fully as a function system of society remains unclear. It obviously is operating as you can tell by looking in the real world. But the problem of its organisations, their need to go looking elsewhere for resources, for recognition, for impact, constantly endangers civil society's decision core. Without such a decision core, no stable form of civil society. But this might not be necessary. Civil society could remain an unstable function system, a system in constant making and unrest, giving rise to protest which gives rise to initiatives which gives rise to organizations that, in the end, fall out of the realm of civil society from which they originated. Thus these organizations infuse other function systems with value communication and raise sensitivity for it. Maybe this restlessness is a necessary condition in itself or civil society in order to play the sketched role in the light of grand societal challenges like climate change and human well-being on a planet of nine billion people, the turn from modernity to the next society notwithstanding. Given the conflicting nature of value communication — there shall be no other values — it could well be the most dangerous role societal evolution can hold for any of its systems. "

References

BAECKER, D. 2007. *Studien zur nächsten Gesellschaft*, Frankfurt am Main, Suhrkamp.

BEER, S. 1970. *Decision and control: The meaning of operational research and management cybernetics*, London u.a, Wiley.

FOERSTER, H. 2003. For Niklas Luhmann: "How Recursive is Communication?". In: FOERSTER, H. (ed.) *Understanding understanding*. New York: Springer.

KUHN, T. S. 1962. *The structure of scientific revolutions*, Chicago, University of Chicago Press.

LUHMANN, N. 1984. *Soziale Systeme: Grundriß einer allgemeinen Theorie*, Frankfurt am Main, Suhrkamp.

LUHMANN, N. 1986. The autopoiesis of social systems. In: GEYER, R. F. & ZOUWEN, J. (eds.) *Sociocybernetic paradoxes: observation, control and evolution of self-steering systems*. London: Sage.

LUHMANN, N. 1992. The Concept of Society. *Thesis Eleven*, 31, 67–80.

LUHMANN, N. 1995. *Social systems*, Stanford, Calif, Stanford University Press.

LUHMANN, N. 1996. *Protest: Systemtheorie und soziale Bewegungen*, Frankfurt/Main, Suhrkamp.

LUHMANN, N. 1997. The Control of Intransparency. *Systems Research and Behavioral Science*, 14, 359–371.

LUHMANN, N. 1999. *Organisation und Entscheidung*, Wiesbaden, Westdeutscher Verlag.

LUHMANN, N. 2006. System as Difference. *Organization*, 13, 37–57.

LUHMANN, N. 2008. Die Moral der Gesellschaft. In: HORSTER, D. (ed.) Orig.-Ausg. ed. Frankfurt a.M: Suhrkamp.

MCLUHAN, M. 1962. *The Gutenberg galaxy; the making of typographic man*, Toronto, University of Toronto Press.

MCLUHAN, M. 1964. *Understanding media; the extensions of man*, New York,, McGraw-Hill.

RÖMMELE, A. 2010. Stuttgart 21 is a failure of deliberate democracy. *The Guardian*.

SEIDL, D. & BECKER, K. H. (eds.) 2006. *Niklas Luhmann and Organization Studies*, Copenhagen: Copenhagen Business School Press.

Bases of Power and Effective Participation of Civil Society Organisations in Development Partnerships – The Need for Governance?

Annekathrin Ellersiek

Introduction

Partnerships increasingly gained importance as a managerial imperative of international development cooperation (Brinkerhoff & Brinkerhoff, 2006; Robinson, Hewitt, & Harriss, 2000) in all parts of the world, where all kinds of organisations nowadays find themselves in the positions of managers and participants in such inter-organisational relations (Rochlin, Zadek, & Forstater, 2008). With their extremely diverse constituent bases, development partnerships in particular (Hastings, 1999), face grand challenges in governing inter-organisational power relations in order to enable effective partnering processes (Brown & Ashman, 1996; Fowler, 1998).

Yet, this course of events has gone rather unnoticed outside of the development domain (Brinkerhoff, 2002b). Despite the valuable insights that have been generated by inter-organisational relations and network research (Raab & Kenis, 2009) those almost solely derive from the study of partnerships operating in relatively uniform contexts, such as the service spheres of European and North-American countries (Hasnain-Wynia et al., 2003; Huang & Provan, 2007; O'Toole Jr & Meier, 2004; Provan, 1980; Zakus, 1998). Consequently, Raab and Kenis (2009) emphasise the need for their "external" validation in other domains of partnership operation.

Development scholars have pointed out the difficulties and needs for governing seemingly inherently unequal power relations and provided in-depth insights into their complex nature in international development cooperation (Lister, 2000; Morse & McNamara, 2006). Notwithstanding the valuable insights gained from this research, its majority to date has only been informed a little by theory (Brinkerhoff, 2002b) and is based on the study of only single or a small number of cases which hardly allow for any generalisation and cumulative knowledge building. Research on one of the rare existing comprehensive data sets[27] has found differences in the proportion to which certain groups, e.g. governments, businesses, and CSOs from the global South and North, (Andonova & Levy, 2003; Hale & Mauzerall, 2004), are represented in partnership initiatives. Yet, those groups are not powerful or powerless in all partnerships and politics of

---

[27] See: http://www.un.org/esa/sustdev/partnerships/partnerships.htm.

inclusion or exclusion represent only one mechanism of power through partnerships (Derkzen, Franklin & Bock, 2008). Lacking a level of specification applicable to the organisational level and comparable across cases, previous work cannot generalise and explain how these power proxies impact upon the development of power relations in partnerships.

The operations, the processes, relational dimensions and bases on which power enfolds once a partnership commences its operations, are core to the study of inter-organisational relations and the sociologically oriented management disciplines (Galaskiewicz, 1985). This study tests a conceptual framework that builds upon an understanding of the functioning of bases of organisational power within inter-organisational coordinative systems (Entwistle, Bristow, Hines, Donaldson, & Martin, 2007) and tests their applicability in the context of development partnerships. The question that guides this inquiry is formulated as follows: How do organisational bases of power relate to effective participation in development partnerships?

The contributions of this paper are twofold: First, it adds an inter-organisational perspective to the literature on CSOs' involvement and power in development partnerships, which so far has largely been neglected (Ashman, 2000; Brinkerhoff, 2002b). Secondly, by analysing the relationship between bases of power and effective participation across partnership cases, the study tests the systematic advantage or disadvantage of these groups and explores starting points for practical interventions and partnership governance that address inequities and make partnerships potentially effective for all partners.

Theoretical background

There is not one specific theoretical framework, which focuses on inter-organisational power in development partnerships but there are two bodies of literature relevant for such an inquiry. The first is on the study of inter-organisational power (Cook, 1977; Cook, 1978; Hardy, Phillips, & Lawrence, 1998; Huxham & Beech, 2003; Medcof, 2001; Provan, 1980) and the governance of collaborations, partnerships, and networks (Gray, 1989; Gray & Wood, 1991; Huang & Provan, 2007; Jones, Hesterly, & Borgatti, 1997; Kickert, Klijn, & Koppenjan, 1997a; Provan, Beyer, & Kruytbosch, 1980; Raab & Kenis, 2009). The second is on international development cooperation (Brinkerhoff & Brinkerhoff, 2006; Cooke, 2003; Cooke, 2004; Thomas, 2007) and the study of partnerships therein (Ashman, 2001a, b; Awortwi, 2004; Brinkerhoff & Brinkerhoff, 2006; Brinkerhoff, 1999; Brinkerhoff & Brinkerhoff, 2004; Brinkerhoff, 2002a; Dolan & Opondo, 2005; Johnson & Wilson, 2006; Morse & McNamara, 2006; Patel, 2001). To pave the way for a theoretical integration of these bodies of literature, first the main assumptions about bases of inter-organisational power and their functioning in development partnerships will be outlined.

The main rationale for partnership stated in the literature can be summarised as that of bringing together a diversity of organisations with a wide array of resources and capabilities (Blockson, 2003; Gray, 1989; Gray & Wood, 1991; Waddell, 2000, 2005). This "instrumental" perspective (Stewart & Gray, 2006) relates to an understanding of partnerships as "facilitating" interaction, collaboration as well as conflict (Gray & Putnam, 2005), in a way that "partners can best leverage their resources and capabilities so that goal-oriented processes can take place" (De Bruijn & Ten Heuvelhof, 1997; Kickert, Klijn, & Koppenjan, 1997b).

This understanding of partnership received critique because it seems to hypothesise a preliminary exchange, joint decision making and interactions between equals. This assumption is cast into doubt when considering that partners come to the table with all kinds of power inequalities (Stewart & Gray, 2006). Particular, concerns about this false egalitarian are raised by non-profit and development scholars, who argue that ignoring differences in power between partners as an essential part of the reality of partnership, is in contrast to the numerous accounts of the difficulties encountered by certain groups, in particular Southern partners and CSOs (Lister, 2000; Morse & McNamara, 2006) ineffective processes (Thomas, 2007), because it produces conflict, power struggle and partnership failure when partners end up "clashing" (Crane, 2000) and bargaining about basic rights instead of exploring mutual interests (Eweje, 2007: 21). By the same token, imposed partnership goals and processes risk resulting in a lack of ownership and ineffective processes (Fowler, 1998).

Acknowledging this reality of development partnerships, Thomas (1996) argues for partnerships to go beyond merely facilitating but "creating" the conditions that enable effective collaboration for all partners. At this point, however, one is left with the questions about how the inequalities in power that need to be addressed can be defined and how the conditions that enable effective collaboration can be created.

In the literature, the conditions for effective partnering build upon some tenets about the functioning of organisational bases of power, largely derived from two distinct perspectives (O'Toole, 1997):

Firstly, research on partnerships in the for-profit world, and a related exchange of theoretical understanding of inter-organisational power relations, (Emerson, 1972) posits that one organisation's power resides in another's dependence (Emerson, 1962). Dependency arises when organisations control or access resources which are needed by others (Pfeffer & Salancik, 1978). Knowledge of resource needs and dependencies are assumed to lead organisations towards partnering in the first place (Oliver, 1990) and to subsequently drive the development of functionally induced dependencies and relational control structures (Huang & Provan, 2006) that sustain effective collaboration (Jones et al., 1997).

Secondly, a public-administrative model emphasises the need for coordination and control to effectively utilise a diversity of potentially valuable organisational resources, services, products and capabilities for the achievement of the development task (Thomas, 1996). In administrative decision making, power derives from vertical dependencies and the extent to which a partner's services, resources, and capabilities benefit and are effectively coordinated and employed for the achievement of the development task (Pfeffer & Leong, 1977; Pfeffer & Moore, 1980; Provan et al., 1980).

The first model describes the development of individual goal driven horizontal – and the latter one the structuring of vertical inter-organisational power relations around the achievement of a joint task (Entwistle et al., 2007). Both models specify different functions of power but none of them seems to imply a need for "enabling" governance interventions as is proposed by development scholars (Thomas, 1996). The underlying mechanism on which both models build, however, require empirical validation in the context of development partnerships. The assumptions that common goals and joint decision-making are no prerequisites for effective exchange (Galaskiewicz, 1985) or that power is contingent on a partner's potential to create dependencies or benefit the achievement of the partnership task (Provan & Milward, 2001) are the theoretical linkages that will be explored in the first part of this study. If such links cannot be established this would define potential inequalities in power between partners and indicate the need to "create" the conditions for effective collaboration (Thomas, 1996), which will be explored in the second part.

Conceptual framework

Core to a definition of inter-organisational power in partnerships is the premise that the potential power of partners is not always enacted (Provan, 1980) and that agency is part and parcel of organisational life (Phillips, 1997). These ideas derive from the assumption of certain bases of power which can be accessed, utilised and enacted (Benson, 1975) or work indirectly (Provan, 1980). As summarised by Emerson (Emerson, 1962): "power will not be of necessity observable in every interactive episode between A and B, yet we suggest that it exists nonetheless as a potential to be explored, tested and occasionally employed by the participants". The bases of the potential power of organisations have been studied extensively (Clegg, 1989; Cobb, 1984; Cook, 1977; Cook, 1978; Dahl, 1961; Hardy, 1994) and can be summarised as resources and positions.

Resources as bases of power

The focus on resources as an essential component of an organisation's power emanates from a history of research on exchange relations (Cook, 1977). Resources can be regarded as anything that partners need for carrying out their activities, may create dependencies for others (Zeitz, 1980) and maybe utilised for the fulfilment of a partnership's task (Waddell, 2003, 2005). Resources can be more or less intangible (Huang & Provan, 2006; Rogers, 1974), and more or less institutionalised or discursive. That while some resources, such as financial means, may have implicit and universal value, others gain value as bases of power only through their enactment when partners "work to realise their goals and interests within the collaborative activity" (Lawrence, Phillips, & Hardy, 1999: 490). For all the many typologies and classifications of resources that exist (Alexander, 1996; Rogers, 1974), those are of a heuristic value only to the purpose of this research. The value of resources as bases of power is relational in nature, depends on the perception and assessment among partners, and may change over time and vary across the constituent bases and contexts of partnership cases (Gray, 1985).

Further, resources build only one component of the potential power of an organisation and cannot be set equal to power and influence. For example, Derkzen and colleagues (2008) describe how a governmental agency refrained from enacting its authority to decide unilaterally but left main decisions about the course of a partnership to its CSO partner. In contrast, resources may potentially be accessible to partners but cannot be enacted in partnerships. Brown and Ashman (1996) demonstrate how Southern CSOs exhibited potentially powerful resources, such as their social capital in the affected communities. Yet, these resources were only possible for them to enact in those partnerships in which the CSOs' involvement in decision-making processes was endorsed by the initiators. Hence, resources are important prerequisites for power in partnerships but no resource guarantees involvement and/or effective participation in all processes (Huang & Provan, 2006) or partnerships (Hardy, Phillips, & Lawrence, 2003).

Positions as bases of power

Despite the type and the extent to which partners access and control certain resources, partners need to be in a position to bring them their resources to bear. Positions define the "power infrastructure" (Huxham & Beech, 2003) of a partnership and indicate the level of involvement in partnership processes, interactions, negotiations, exchanges and decision-making processes. Hence, the same argument that applies to resources also holds for favourable positions in partnerships: both are analytically distinct from effective participation in partnerships. For example, Derkzen and Bock (2007) describe how limited the effects of CSOs' participation in partnership negotiations were when local knowledge and say in these processes was not considered an equally valuable resource to the technical and scientific expertise of the "professional" partners.

Bases of power and effective participation: Hypotheses

Together, the two bases of potential inter-organisational power: resources and positions; and their interplay in bringing about effective participation in partnerships, are analysed. The two analytical concepts and their theoretical relation to effective participation, in an exchange or public-administrative coordinative model, provide the bases for the hypotheses that guide this research. The first part of the study will answer the question to what extent resources, via the horizontal and vertical dependencies they create, lead to an advantageous position and/or effective participation in partnerships.

In internationally operating development partnerships we can hypothesise such dependencies to exist, e.g. between foreign and local partners. On the one hand, foreign partners depend on their local partners to identify and tailor partnership goals and processes to local needs (James, 2001), harness local private investment and ownership (Kolk, Van Tulder, & Kostwinder, 2008); (Sanyal, 2006), among other reasons. On the other hand, local organisations may depend on the technical expertise, management skills, and not least of all the financial means channelled through and provided by foreign partners (Lister, 2000). Based on this, one would assume that

H1: The extent to which an organisation can potentially contribute resources to a partnership that are valuable to others and/or are considered important for the achievement of the partnership task, positively relates to its position in a partnership.

H2: The extent to which an organisation can potentially contribute resources to a partnership that are valuable to others and/or are considered important for the achievement of the partnership task, positively relates to its effective participation in a partnership.

So far, the argument has been that resources, via the inter-organisational resource dependencies they create and via their utility for the performance of the partnership task, lead to an advantageous position and thus a greater potential power and chance for effective participation. By proposing an analytical distinction between the two bases of potential power and by distinguishing between potential, enacted power and effective participation, we have already suggested that potential power is not always enacted but in fact that both bases of power interact in defining a partner's chances for effective participation. Provan and colleagues (1980) highlight that it is as important to consider that neither one component of potential power, resources *or* an advantageous position alone is sufficient and that power cannot be enacted or perceived unless potential power is present. With regard to the two components, one can assume two ways of interactions. First, as demonstrated by Brown and Ashman's (Brown & Ashman, 1996) example of CSOs participation in partnerships, one could argue that resources alone are not sufficient for effective participation when a partner is not in the position to enact them. We hypothesise that:

H3: The extent to which a partner potentially can contribute resources to a partnership that are valuable to others and/or are considered important for the achievement of the partnership's task, only positively relates to effective participation when the partner is in the position to enact them.

On the contrary, as demonstrated by Derkzen and Bock's (2007) example, one would assume that an advantageous position in a partnership becomes useful only in the event that partners show the necessary resources to make use of their position and their claims and decisions "stick" (Phillips, 1997: 44). Related to the previous hypotheses, one can assume that:

H4: The extent to which a partner holds an advantageous position in a partnership only positively relates to effective participation when the partner has the potential to contribute resources to a partnership that are valuable to others and/or are considered important for the achievement of the partnership's task.

Effective participation: The dependent variable

Potential power, derived from alone or in combination with the resources and positions of an organisation in a partnership can result in effective participation. The literature on inter-organisational collaboration is fuelled with accounts of a variety of strategies and tactics that partners can employ to pursue their goals and gain a stake in partnerships. In the present framework, those are separately conceptualised as representing expressions of enacted power and are not further accounted for here.

Effective participation of partners is indicated by both the stake partners gain in the exchanges, negotiations and discursive struggles over partnership-related issues (Kim, Pinkley, & Fragale, 2005) and by the degree to which partners achieve, to attain their individual organisational goals (Hardy et al., 2003). On the one hand this is, because size, resource diversity and coordination may not always involve all organisations in all decision-making or exchange processes (Huang & Provan, 2006; Provan & Kenis, 2008). On the other hand, because partners may not always need to take influence (Provan et al., 1980) to pursue their goals.

Data collection, measurement, and methodology

In order to obtain information with regard to the concepts discussed above, survey data were collected from 175 organisations involved in 38 development partnerships. Equally in proportions, one half of the organisations was identified as foreign (47,4 %) and local (2,6 %) CSOs and the other half as International Organisations (IOs) and foreign national governments (13.2 %), national and regional local governments (21 %), foreign and local businesses (5.2 %), and research institutes (10.2 %). The partnerships, operating in and across 19 different African and Caribbean countries, derived from two financing instruments of the European Union: the European Union Water (EUWF) and Energy Facilities (EUEF).

The data collection has been conducted as follows: first, all 274 organisations which successfully applied for partnership funding were contacted and asked for participation explaining the purpose and procedure of the study. Forty-nine of the so-called intermediary organisations indicated their interest and asked to provide the contacts of all their partner organisations involved in the funded project partnership. This procedure resulted in a preliminary number of 249 participant organizations.

Second, all organizations of which the contacts were obtained were approached and asked for participation. If interested, the respondents could choose between three options: i) complete an online questionnaire which was provided in English and French; ii) receive a printed version of the questionnaire via post; or iii.) indicate a time and date and preferred language for a telephone interview. Questionnaire and interview guidelines were provided to each organisation and each partnership individually[28]. This was required due to the relational measures used in this study to be satisfied by both the personalization of all questions and the obtaining of the

---

[28] The full survey instrument and the description of its development are provided by the author upon request.

individual perspective of each responding organization about all its partners. Another consequence of this approach is that only those partnerships could be included which showed full participation, meaning, all partners completed the questionnaire or participated in the interviews. Eventually, full data was obtained for 38 partnerships, involving 175 organizations. After the first round of the data collection, the data was analyzed and complemented by follow-up telephone interviews, which were conducted in ten cases. Since only those participants were included of which the intermediary organisations provided the contacts, a non-response analysis was only conducted at the partnership and not the partner-level of analysis (see Appendix I).

Power has been conceptualized in the study of partnerships in a variety of ways. Different measures are not strictly comparable (Provan et al., 1980) and it is important to be explicit about the measures used (Provan et al., 1980), when trying to capture more than one dimension of the concept, in order to allow for systematic instead of generic interpretation.

Resources: The concept of resources was operationalised following an approach presented by Jacobson and Cohen (Jacobson & Cohen, 1986). Resources were measured presenting the same list of 18 resources at two points in the questionnaire/interviews. First, the respondents were asked to indicate on a five-point Likert scale (to "extremely important") the significance of each resource for their own organisation and/or the accomplishment of the partnership's task. Later the same list was presented again but this time the respondents were asked to indicate for their own organisation and their partners, to what extent they can potentially contribute each listed resource (again on a five-point Likert-scale, to "very high potential"). The average of the self- and others-perceived scores for each resource represented the objective resource measure.

Resource utility: From the first resource assessment, the total sum of the utility scores ascribed to a resource by all partners was divided by the total sum ascribed to all resources in a partnership. This partnership-specific percentage was taken as a weight representing the utility of a resource in a partnership. The objective resource scores of each resource were then weighted and the sum represented the individual *resource utility score* for each partner.

Position: The concept of position was measured in two ways: involvement in interactions with partners and in decision-making processes.

Interactions: Egocentric measures of the involvement of partners in the activities of the partnerships were used. Each respondent was asked to indicate for each partner, with whom the own organisation is most frequently involved with in four partnership-related activities. The activities were operationalised two-ways directed (giving/receiving, or both): reporting, resources, advice, and support. Because the focus was on the most eminent relations between partners, only confirmed linkages were counted (Marsden, 1990). The obtained in- and out-degree centralities for each activity were normalised, controlling for differences in the size of the partnerships. Despite the loss of data, this conservative approach was required, since no direct observations were obtained (Huang & Provan, 2006).

Decision-making: Involvement in the decision-making processes of a partnership was measured through involvement in the decisions about ten[29] partnership-related issues. For each issue it was asked to indicate own and other partners' involvement. Following these criteria, the data were aggregated and new variables were created. A percentage measure was derived from all issues for which involvement was indicated by the respondent organisation relative to the total number of issues.

Effective Participation: Effective participation was measured by two dependent variables i.e. goal attainment and influence.

Goal attainment: Goal attainment was measured by two items. The respondents were asked to indicate on a five-point Likert scale (to "far above expectations"). The averaged sum represented the overall measure for goal attainment.

Influence: The level of influence of an organisation was measured by using the same set of ten partnership-related decision-making issues as described for involvement. For each issue it was asked to indicate whether the own organisation and/or any of the other partners have been influential on the decision about this issue. This measure represents an issue-specific adaptation of Huang and Provan's (Huang & Provan, 2006) influence measure. Again, only those issues were counted as "influential" for which influence was confirmed by at least one partner. A percentage measure was created for confirmed influence relative to the total number of issues.

Before testing our hypotheses, three groups of variables were factor-analysed: the objective resource measures, the in and out-degree centralities in the four partnership-related interactions and the involvement in the decision-making. A principal component analysis (PCA) with subsequent orthogonal rotation and varimax solution was chosen for. When conceptually and statistically reasonable, sub-scales were created and the

---

[29] A description of the development of this list can be provided by the author upon request.

obtained regression scores were used in the following analysis[30]. The final list of variables measuring each concept is displayed in Table 1.

Variable		Definition
Resources:		Sum of the average, self- and others perceived potential to contribute the below mentioned resources:
	Relational resources	*Regression score* for factor one, representing the objective measure of seven resources: negotiation skills, relations to committees, reputation and reach, personal relations to partners, political support, relations to decision-makers, relations to the public and media
	Administrative resources	*Regression score* for factor two, representing the objective measure of four resources: technological and scientific knowledge, project management experience, administrative capacities, financial means
	Authority	*Regression score* for factor three, representing the objective measure of three resources: coercive authority, licensing authority, ownership of licenses/patents
	Production means	Average self- and others perceived potential
	Manpower	Average self- and others perceived potential
	Local knowledge	Average self- and others perceived potential
Representation of beneficiaries		Average self- and others perceived potential
Resource utility		Sum of self-and others-perceived *resource scores*, each weighted by the partnership-specific resource utility
Positions:		
Involvement in interactions		Normalised (for each partnership) confirmed in- and out degree centrality measures in the five partnership-related activities, described below:
Control		*Regression score* for factor three, representing four centrality measures: in-degree reporting, out-degree resources, out-degree support, out-degree advise
Resources		*Regression score* for factor four, representing four centrality measures: in-degree resources, out-degree reporting, in-degree support, in-degree advise
Involvement in the decision-making	Partnership design	Percentage of an organisation's confirmed involvement in the decision-making about the following five issues: partner selection, external monitoring, goal definition, resource contributions to the partnership, resource allocation to partners

---

[30] The results of the factor analyses are provided by the author upon request.

	Partnership implementation	Percentage of an organisation's confirmed involvement in the decision-making about the following five issues: tasks and responsibilities, outcomes, internal monitoring, ownership and maintenance, definition of beneficiaries
Effective participation:		
Influence	Partnership design	Percentage of an organisation's confirmed influence on the decisions made about the following five issues: partner selection, external monitoring, goal definition, resource contributions to the partnership, resource allocation to partners
	Partnership implementation	Percentage of an organisation's confirmed influence on the decisions made about the following five issues: tasks and responsibilities, outcomes, internal monitoring, ownership and maintenance, definition of beneficiaries
Goal attainment		Average perception of individual organisational productivity and goal attainment in the partnership.

Table 1: Variables and definitions

Empirical results

The descriptive statistics and mean comparisons for the whole sample are displayed for the partners and the intermediary organisations separately in Table 2. The results of the initial bivariate analysis testing the four hypotheses are presented in Tables 3. Each variable is listed in one of the groups representing the hypothesised concepts.

	Intermediaries				Partners						
	$N = 38$				$N = 137$						
Variable	Mean	Min	Max	S.D.	Mean	Min	Max	S.D.	s.e.	m.d.	Sig.[3]
Resources:											
Resources (unweighted)	2,86	2	4	0,505	2,59	1	4	0,577	0,103	-0,270	n.s.[1]
Relational	0,301	-3,984	2,001	1,193	-0,083	-4,118	2,230	0,926	0,181	-0,385	0,035[2]
Administrative	0,685	-0,910	1,996	0,816	-0,190	-2,887	1,692	0,964	0,171	-0,875	0,000[1]
Authority	0,233	-1,578	2,142	1,021	-0,064	-2,319	2,936	0,987	0,182	-0,297	n.s.[1]
Production means	2,27	0	4	0,867	2,51	0	5	1,107	0,194	0,236	n.s.[1]
Manpower	2,54	0	4	0,977	2,72	0	5	1,175	-0,235	0,208	n.s.[1]
Local knowledge	2,04	0	5	1,048	3,10	0	5	1,029	0,191	0,353	n.s.[2]
Beneficiaries	2,07	0	4	0,957	2,73	0	5	0,935	0,169	0,264	n.s.[2]
Resources utility	28,53	20	38	4,793	26,69	10	39	6,094	0,806	-1,84	n.s.[2]
Positions:											
Involvement in interactions:											
Control	1,129	-1,126	6,635	1,212	-0,315	-1,590	3,129	0,647	0,204	-1,444	0,000[2]
Resource	0,062	-2,106	3,797	1,282	-0,017	-2,166	3,143	0,910	0,222	-0,079	n.s.[2]
Involvement in decision-making:											
Design	0,836	0,25	1,00	0,198	0,562	0,20	1,00	0,275	0,046	-0,274	0,000[2]
Implementation	0,796	0,25	1,00	0,203	0,605	0,17	1,00	0,270	0,043	-0,192	0,000[2]
Effective Participation:											
Influence:											
Design	0,907	0,33	1	0,1607	0,389	0,00	1	0,359	0,040	-0,518	0,000[2]
Implementation	0,679	0,00	1	0,2743	0,573	0,00	1	0,346	0,053	-0,106	n.s.[2]
Goal attainment	3,39	0	5	0,377	2,26	0	5	0,219	0,486	-0,129	n.s.[1]

[1] T-test
[2] Welch
[3] two-tailed

Table 2: Descriptive statistics and mean comparisons between partner and intermediary organisations

	1	2	3	4	5	6	7	8
Resources:								
1. Resources (unweighted)	--							
2. Relational	,619**	--						
3. Administrative	,497**	,000	--					
4. Authority	,457**	,000	,000	--				
5. Production means	,532**	,095	,272**	,089	--			
6. Manpower	,566**	,223**	,141	,069	,578**	--		
7. Local knowledge	,427**	,163*	-,018	-,069	,137	,351**	--	
8. Beneficiaries	,325**	,004	-,013	,142	,093	,305**	,479**	--
9. Resource utility	,724**	,362**	,547**	,322**	,318**	,577**	,496**	,459**
Positions:								
Involvement in interactions:								
10. Control	,169*	,100	,297*	,098	,035	-,147	-,041	-,149*
11. Resources	,019	-,021	-,071	-,026	,134	,175*	,217*	,215
Involvement in decision making:								
12. Design[1]	,148	,139	,172*	-,021	,093	,038	,029	-,103
13. Implementation[1]	,197	,105	,180*	-,015	,129	,122	,125	-,015
Effective Participation:								
Influence:								
14. Design	,273**	,114	,298**	,089	,038	,032	,100	,059
15. Implementation	,215**	,047	,095	,009	,250*	,266**	,239**	,169
16. Goal attainment	,156	,212*	,134	-,035	,001	,134	,171*	,140

	9	10	11	12	13	14	15
Resources:							
1. Resources (unweighted)							
2. Relational							
3. Administrative							
4. Authority							
5. Production means							
6. Manpower							
7. Local knowledge							

	1	2	3	4	5	6	7	8
8. Beneficiaries								
9. Resource Utility	--							
Positions:								
Involvement in interactions:								
10. Control	,200**	--						
11. Resources	,233**	,597**	--					
Involvement in decision making:								
12. Design[1]	,168	,167	,260	--				
13. Implementation[1]	,285**	,323**	,266**	,365**	--			
Effective Participation:								
Influence:								
14. Design	,408**	,306**	,266**	,365**	,356**	--		
15. Implementation	,261**	,308**	,417**	,479**	,336**	,415**	--	
16. Goal attainment:	,174*	,122	,119	-,012	,116	,095	,090	

*: significant at the 10% level

**: significant at the 5% level

***: significant at the 1% level

Table 3: Correlation matrix: Whole sample

The descriptive statistics and mean comparisons between the intermediary and partner organisations show that the two groups significantly differ in the kinds of resources they potentially contribute and the activities they are involved in. No significant differences were found with respect to the *unweighted score* and the *resource utility score*, and the level of influence on decisions about the implementation of partnerships and the level of goal attainment. At least the decision on partnership design, seems to be to large extent in the hands of the intermediary organisatons. Since the design entails i.e. the selection of partners and resource allocations, the eminent role of intermediaries in these decisions seems to indicate that the translation of resources into favourable positions, is subject to administrative decision-making by primarily the intermediary organisations, rather than to horizontal, "functionally induced" dependencies (Huang & Provan, 2006).

The first two hypotheses posited that the resources a partner can potentially contribute to a partnership confer power through the dependencies created for other organisations and/or the fulfilment of the partnership task. The bivariate results show that the partnership specific measures of resource utility displays a stronger correlation with the positional measures and effective participation than the unweighted resource score. Those differences are significant for centrality in the control-related activities ($\alpha = 5\%$, $z = 2,643$) and influence on the design of partnerships ($\alpha = 5\%$, $z = -2,583$). These findings demonstrate the more accurate data obtained from the partnership-specific measures and suggest resources to relate to advantageous positions and effective participation.

Looking at the correlations between the resources and the utility score it appears that administrative resources, local knowledge, the representation of beneficiaries and manpower more strongly relate to the utility score than to the un-weighted resource score. These resources and the partners who can access or control them seem to benefit most from partnership-specific favourable perceptions. Yet, only administrative resources, manpower, and local knowledge at the same time show a direct significant positive relation to the positional measures and effective participation. In contrast, the representation of beneficiaries shows no such effect. Hence, this resource not only benefits the most from being perceived as valuable but also most strongly depends on such a perception. Relational resources, authority, and production means display stronger correlations with the un-weighted resource score than with the utility score and none of them directly relates to one of the positional measures but yet to effective participation. These resources, thus, seem to function as bases of power for partners, relatively invariant to partnership-specifc perceptions of their utility and to their actual enactment in partnership processes and decsion-making.

In summary, the utility ascribed to their resources seems to mediate the power of partners. The potential of partners to capitalise on the utility of their resources in predominantly administrative decision-making contexts of the partnerships under study will be analysed in the following. To test our first two hypotheses, the direct effects of the unweighted and the weighted resource utility scores on all other variables were tested for only the partner organisations, to control for the advantageous position of being an intermediary organisation. Because the sample consisted of only 38 intermediary compared to 137 partner organisations, it was not possible to test these assumptions on two equally sized groups. Table 4 displays the direct effects of the unweighted resource scores.

The results of the multivariate analysis for only the partner organisations give a different picture of the relationship between resources and the positional and effectiveness measures, compared to the bivariate results including the intermediary organisations. Most notably, the discriminating effect of resources on influence on partnership-level decisions seems to be indirect. None of the resources shows a direct significant effect on involvement in the decision-making processes but on favourable positions in the interactions among partners and on direct influence on decisions related to both, the design and the implementation of partnerships. While the effects of relational resources, authority, and production means appear relative invariant to utility perceptions, those seem to explain the direct effects of the other resources. Thus, it was chosen to more rigorously test the mechanisms that underlie these observed relationships via the inclusion of resource utility as the mediator variable[31]. Mediating models are tested for an effect of resource utility on each of the nine direct significant effects of the utility dependent resources (Table 5).

---

[31] For an overview of further testing strategies applied to latent constructs See Baron and Kenny's (1996) seminal work on the conceptual distinction between mediator and moderator effects.

		Independent variables: Resources								
		Relational	Administrative	Authority	Production means	Manpower	Local knowledge	Beneficiaries	R	Adjusted R^2
Resource utility:	Beta	,078	,496***	,105	,083	,357***	,242***	,214**	,816***	,648
	R	,214	,560***	,102	,389	,566***	,409***	,305		
Positions:										
Involvement in interactions:										
Control	beta	,061	,212***	,100	,171	-,138	,330***	-,270***	,386***	,102
	R	,046	,134	-,009	-,131	-,134	,129***	-,131***		
Resources	beta	-,105	-,119	-,056	-,162	,325***	,052	,197**	,415***	,127
	R	-,010	-,107	-,042	-,020	,246***	,240	,307**		
Involvement in decision-making:										
Design	beta	,061	,235	,226	,013	,013	,215	-,107	,342	,017
	R	,148	,242	,220	,096	,103	,216	,025		
Implementation	beta	,052	,125	-,092	,129	,015	,175	,036	,283	,009
	R	,132	,105	-,103	,165	,174	,195	,066		
Effective Participation:										
Influence:										
Design	beta	,002	,289*	,038	,071	-,028	,239*	,004	,306*	,042
	R	,038	,227*	,019	,118	,138	,270*	,196		
Implementation	beta	-,024	-,047	-,065	,116	,221*	,189*	,006	,408***	,119
	R	,098	,052	-,068	,243	,342*	,297*	-,002		
Goal attainment	beta	,106*	,204	-,053	,155	,108	,216	,027		
	R	,136*	,208	,027	,101	,090	,201	,102		

* Underlined betas are in the hypothesised direction
* significant at the 10% level
** significant at the 5% level
*** significant at the 1% level

Table 4: Multiple regression results and zero-order correlations of positional measures and effective participation on all resources (only partners)

Independent variable	Dependent variable	Effect	beta	s.e.	Sobel Z
Administrative resources	Control	XM	3,538	,450	0,288
		XMY	,185	,641	
Administrative resources	Influence: Design	XM	3,538	,450	0,876
		XMY	,304	,345	
Manpower	Resources	XM	2,935	,368	0,258
		XMY	,231	,892	
Manpower	Influence: Implementation	XM	2,935	,368	1,079
		XMY	,356	,326	
Local knowledge	Control	XY	2,425	,465	0,267
		XMY	,172	,642	
Local knowledge	Influence: Design	XM	2,989	0,235	2,077
		XMY	0,398	0,189	
Local knowledge	Influence: Implementation	XM	2,425	,465	1,964
		XMY	,448	,211	
Representation of beneficiaries	Resources	XM	2,395	,522	0,314
		XMY	,332	,329	
__ significant at the 5 % level (Sobel, 1982)					

Table 5: Mediating effect of resource-utility perception on the direct relationship between resources and positions and effective participation (only partners)

The findings show that their utility, only significantly mediates the direct effect of the resource of local knowledge on influence in the design and the implementation of partnerships. The other direct resource effects remain significant with only marginal mediating effects.

In summary, we can confirm our first two hypotheses. The extent to which partners are perceived to potentially have access to and control valuable resources has a positive effect on their power in partnerships. However, this effect holds only for some and not all resources and seems to follow different patterns. Furthermore, the attributed utility was found to mediate the power of only some resources not with regard to the involvement in but to the influence on decision-making processes.

While previous work found similar relations and discriminative effects of resources on, for example involvement in interactions and exchange (Huang & Provan, 2006), further inquiry is needed to explain why no significant effect was found on the involvement of partners in the decision-making processes. One explanation might be that utility perceptions are only one-sided. That is, partners who potentially access useful resources recognise them as such, whereas this perception is not shared by those who are in the position to involve them. Reversely, it could also mean that although the utility of the resources of partners is acknowledged by others, the partners themselves do not share this perception. Since data was obtained from both sides in a partnership, from the partners and the intermediary organisations, the average weights given to each resource by the two groups were compared.

	Partners	Intermediaries
Resource	Rank	Rank
Financial means	3	6
Production means	2	9
Manpower	1	8
Coercive power	18	16
Licensing power	13	17
Reputation/reach	17	14
Beneficiaries	15	2
Regional/local knowledge	4	7
Administrative capacities	8	5
Negotiation skills	6	12
Project management experience	11	3
Relation to decision-makers	12	10
Relation to committees	10	13
Relations to the public/media	14	15
Personal relations to partners	7	4
Political support	5	11
Regional knowledge	9	1
Ownership of licenses/patents	4	18
R	,187	
T	-17,118	
Significance	,000	

Table 6: Paired samples test of resource utility assessments by partners and intermediaries

The utility scores ascribed to the resources significantly differ across the two groups. Intermediary organisations and partners ascribe significantly higher utility to each other's resources than to their own. Partners however, assign equally high levels of utility to the resources potentially provided by the intermediary organisations, but not in particular to their own resources. This finding might explain why confirmation exists of a direct effect of resources on the level of influence of partners, but not on involvement. On the one hand, one could argue that resources can only confer power when they are perceived as such by those who can potentially enact them and demand to be involved in decision-making processes. On the other hand, one might apply a path-dependence argument and state that only when partners have experienced that their resources grant favourable positions, do they recognise them as such.

From the testing of the first hypotheses, it became clear that partners can be influential on the decisions about partnership design and implementation, although their resources show no discriminating effect on the involvement in these decisions. Intermediary organisations instead, display high levels of involvement in decision-making processes but not always equally high levels of influence, in particular, not on decisions related to the implementation of partnerships. These findings strongly support a distinction between the components of power (Provan, 1980) and directly refer to our last two hypotheses about the interaction between resources and positions in their potential to bring about effective participation of partners. To test these hypotheses the sample was divided into groups on two counts: Firstly, according to the resource-related potential power of partners, and secondly, with respect to their position, that is their involvement in the decision-making processes.

The third hypothesis states that resources can convey power only if the organisations that can enact them are in a position to do so. We already know, however, that some resources confer influence to partners without their involvement in the decision-making process. The question then becomes if such involvement can still increase the chances for effective participation of partners. Following our hypothesis, the four positional measures should have a strong impact on effective participation. To test this assumption, the weighted resource utility scores of all participants were normalised for each partnership and all partners were divided into two groups, with low and high potential resource power, respectively. The indicators for effective participation were regressed on the positional measures for each group. The unstandardised regression coefficients were compared across the two groups (Blalock, 1965).

The findings displayed in Table 7, show that the positional measures significantly increase the chances for effective participation for both groups. However, in particular for resource-wise less powerful groups. This is most likely because resource powerful partners already show high levels of influence and/or goal attainment, since their resources are acknowledged already and thus to a lesser extent depend on their enactment. Resource-wise, less powerful partners instead may increase the chances for their resources to be acknowledged by enactment through their involvement in partnering processes.

Positions:		Low potential power N=72			High potential power N=64		
		Influence: Design	Influence: Implementation	Goal attainment	Influence: Design	Influence: Implementation	Goal attainment
Control	ß	0,072	0,009	<u>0,813</u>	0,053	-0,051	<u>-0,340</u>
	b	0,110	0,014	0,159	0,118	-0,127	-0,076
	s.e.	0,077	0,075	0,401	0,061	0,050	0,443
Resources	ß	0,014	0,113	0,222	-0,069	0,104	0,126
	b	0,032	0,260**	0,060	-0,196	0,335**	0,034
	s.e.	0,055	0,054	0,479	0,055	0,041	0,537
Involvement: Design	ß	<u>0,269</u>	<u>0,167</u>	1,512	<u>0,146</u>	<u>-0,022</u>	1,218
	b	0,386***	0,240**	0,288**	0,187	-0,031	0,147
	s.e.	0,081	0,079	0,649	0,114	0,092	1,204
Involvement: Implementation	ß	0,147	0,179	1,246	0,198	0,229	1,354
	b	0,189	0,229*	0,189	0,192	0,251*	0,108
	s.e.	0,101	0,099	0,867	0,161	0,131	1,894
R		0,514***	0,536***	0,438**	0,336	0,500**	0,219
Adjusted R2		0,264	0,288	0,192	0,113	0,250	0,048
s.e.		0,308	0,308	2,459	0,353	0,287	3,707

* significant at the 10% level
** significant at the 5% level
*** significant at the 1% level
<u>___</u> Indicates significant differences (p < .05) between parallel coefficients in the two sub-samples (Blalock, 1965)

Table 7: Cross-sub-sample comparisons of regressions of effective participation on positions, between partners with high versus low resource power

The last hypothesis states that advantageous positions in partnerships result only in effective participation if partners access the decisive resources to substantiate their position (Jacobson & Cohen, 1986). To test this assumption, all partner organisations were again divided into two groups, this time according to their involvement in the decision-making processes of partnerships. All weighted resources were regressed on effective participation, for both groups, involved and not involved.

		Not involved N=59	Involved N=70	Not involved N=31	Involved N=89
		Influence: Design		Influence: Implementation	
Relational resources	β	,109*	-,024	,007	-,016
	B	,289*	-,076	,024	-,046
	s.e.	,040	,059	,067	,035
Administrative resources	β	,065	,072	,099	-,037
	B	,177	,221	,265	-,124
	s.e.	,071	,049	,122	,038
Authority	β	,052	,028	-,071	,015
	b	,139	,084	-,185	,049
	s.e.	,058	,042	,088	,032
Manpower	β	-,061	,110**	,178**	,009
	b	-,172	,428**	,451**	,038
	s.e.	,062	,052	,067	,039
Production means	β	-,106	,119**	-,057	,088**
	b	-,260	,477**	-,133	,353**
	s.e.	,080	,042	,111	,033
Local knowledge	β	,007	,121**	-,021	,114**
	b	,073	,408**	,080	,284**
	s.e.	,052	,012	-,068	,038
Beneficiaries	β	,010	,170*	-,013	-,014
	b	,027	,207*	-,035	-,046
	s.e.	,058	,052	,092	,038
R		,487*	,493**	,552	,491**
Adjusted R2		,104*	,243**	-,004	,173**
s.e.		,305	,296	,370	,251

* significant at the 10% level
** significant at the 5% level
*** significant at the 1% level
___ Indicates significant differences (p < .05) between parallel coefficients in the two sub-samples (Blalock, 1965)

Table 8: Cross-sub-sample comparisons of regressions of effective participation on potential resource power, between partners with and without positional power

The findings displayed in Table 8, indicate that indeed resources have a discriminating effect on the effective participation of those partners involved in the decision-making processes. However, not all resources have this effect. While local knowledge, the representation of beneficiaries and production means show such an effect, administrative resources, authority and relational resources display no or even slightly negative effects on effective participation in case of involvement. In addition, relational resources show a strong positive effect in the case of no involvement in the decisions about design, while manpower displays the same effect on the implementation of partnerships. This together with the finding of the bivariate analysis further supports the initial assumption that so-called "discursive resources" that depend on favourable utility perceptions also depend on their enactment, whereas already "institutionalised" resources remain effective bases of power, regardless of their enactment in partnering processes.

Conclusion and Discussion

This study set out to examine some of the basic tenets and underlying mechanisms of inter-organisational power in the empirical context of development partnerships. The findings confirm that the two main components of potential power, resources and positions, both represent bases for effective participation in partnerships. At the same time, the findings reveal several limitations to the present understanding of the functioning of bases of power of all partners in the context of development partnerships.

Following the structure of the paper, it will first discuss the two main findings presented in the first part of the analysis. The potential of partners to gauge power via their resources turned out to have discriminating effects on their positions in partnership-level interactions and on their effective participation. Yet, no comparable effects were found for their involvement in the decision-making processes; and this despite the acknowledgement as being valuable for other partners and/or for the achievement of the partnership task.

Similar to previous studies (Huang & Provan, 2006) the findings indicate that their resources partially define the level and kind of involvement of partners in partnerships. Seen in the context of the present study however, several implications of these findings become apparent. By being largely directed at co-financing and harnessing private capital for development[32], the partnership initiatives target and attract specific groups of financially strong partners, e.g. international CSOs. The resources of others, in particular the representation of beneficiaries by CSOs, showed comparably high utility scores, yet a significant negative effect on involvement in control-related activities and decision-making. These findings imply for these groups that an effective translation of their resources into positions and effective participation does not organically evolve. This is especially true for local CSOs, whose main resource was identified as the legitimate representation of beneficiaries. Since knowledge and capacity building of beneficiaries and recipient communities through their representation in partnerships by local CSOs is seen as decisive for development effectiveness (Brinkerhoff, 2002b; Brown & Ashman, 1996; Derkzen & Bock, 2007; Thomas, 1996), the findings lead to the question where governance interventions may best address the functioning of bases of power of such groups.

The second part of this study hypothesised the possible effects of governance interventions on the effective participation in development partnerships, through the interplay between the two components of potential power: resources and positions. Controlling for the resource-related potential power of partners, the findings showed that involvement in partnership processes indeed increases the chances for effective participation, in particular for resource-wise less powerful partners. This finding indicates that in the case of a lack of institutionalisation of their resources (Entwistle et al., 2007) amplified interactions and involvement in partnering processes, can increase the chances of effective participation of otherwise disadvantaged partners. In particular, this effect holds for the control-related activites and the descions about the design of partnerships. On the contrary, when controlling for actual involvement, it was demonstrated that those partners most strongly depend on and benefit from the enactment of their resources in decision-making processes.

The implications for governance interventions aiming at creating the conditions for the effective participation of all partners in development partnerships are twofold. First, contrary to what was expected based on the findings about broad but ineffective participation of, in particular, local CSOs, the present findings show that once these partners get involved in decision making processes, they can successfully enact their resources and participate. Secondly, since involvement in these processes does not

---

[32] See: EUEI. 2003. Proceedings of the EUEI Energy for Africa Event Nairobi 20–21 November 2003 19, EUWI, F. W. G. A. A. 2006. European Union Water Initiative: Key Sheet No. 1. In E. Union (Ed.), **Key Sheet Series**: 4. Brussels.

automatically evolve from valuable resources, addressing this issue by interventions can be seen as an adequate governance response.

More generally, such a response represents an important contribution to an institutionalisation of bases of power in diversely resourced partnerships and inter-organisational domains (Gray, Bougon, & Donnellon, 1985). Resources of groups such as local CSOs may be seen as valuable, what may be the reason for these organisations become invited and to engage in partnerships in the first place. Yet, such perceptions are of only limited use to these groups if their resources do not translate into favourable positions to effectively participate in partnerships. Such considerations, however, are rarely dealt with, e.g. by donor institutions such as the EU and foreign CSO partners. Mostly, funding requirements address the mere involvement of local partners in partnerships, without specifying how the issue of power inequalities among parties should be dealt with, once the partnership has commenced its operations. The findings of the present study indicate that direction is required not only with regard to who receives funding and gets involved in partnerships but to how the funds are used, administrated locally, and how partnerships are governed in order to enable the effective participation of all partners.

References

Andonova, L. B., & Levy, M. A. 2003. Franchising Governance: Making Sense of the Johannesburg Type II Parternships. In O. S. Stokke, & Ø. B. Thommessen (Eds.), *Yearbook of International Co-operation on Environment and Development 2003/2004*: 19–31. London: Earthscan Publications.

Ashman, D. 2001a. Civil Society Collaboration with Business: Bringing Empowerment Back in. *World Development*, 29(7): 1097.

Ashman, D. 2001b. Strengthening North-South Partnerships for Sustainable Development. *Nonprofit and Voluntary Sector Quarterly*, 30(1): 74–98.

Awortwi, N. 2004. Getting the fundamentals wrong: woes of public-private partnerships in solid waste collection in three Ghanaian cities. *Public Administration and Development*, 24(3): 213–224.

Benson, J. K. 1975. The Interorganizational Network as a Political Economy. *Administrative Science Quarterly*, 22: 229–249.

Blalock, H. M. J. 1965. Theory Building and the Statistical Concept of Interaction. *American Sociological Review*, 30(3): pp 374–380.

Blockson, L. C. 2003. Multisector Approaches to Societal Issues Management. *Business Society*, 42(3): 381–390.

Brinkerhoff, D., & Brinkerhoff, J. 2006. International Development Management: Definitions, Debates, and Dilemmas. In A. Farazmand, & J. Pinkowski (Eds.), *Handbook of Globalization, Governance, and Public Administration* 821–843. New York: US: Taylor & Francis.

Brinkerhoff, D. W. 1999. Exploring State – Civil Society Collaboration: Policy Partnerships in Developing Countries. *Nonprofit and Voluntary Sector Quarterly*, 28(suppl_1): 59–86.

Brinkerhoff, D. W., & Brinkerhoff, J. M. 2004. Partnerships between international donors and non-governmental development organisations: opportunities and constraints. *International Review of Administrative Sciences*, 70(2): 253–270.

Brinkerhoff, J. M. 2002a. Assessing and improving partnership relationships and outcomes: a proposed framework *Evaluation and Program Planning* 25(3): 53–74.

Brinkerhoff, J. M. 2002b. *Partnership for International Development: Rhetoric or Results?* Portland, OR: Lynne Rienner Publishers.

Brown, L. D., & Ashman, D. 1996. Participation, social capital, and intersectoral problem solving: African and Asian cases. *World Development*, 24(9): 1467.

Clegg, S. 1989. *Frameworks of power*. Newbury Park, CA: SAGE.

Cobb, A. T. 1984. An Episodic Model of Power: Toward an Integration of Theory and Research. *The Academy of Management Review*, 9(3): 482–493.

Cook, K. S. 1977. Exchange and power in networks of interorganisational relations. *Sociological Quarterly*, 18: 62–82.

Cook, K. S. E., R.M. 1978. Power, Equity and Commitment in Exchange Networks. *American Sociological Review*, 34(5): 721–739.

Cooke, B. 2003. A new continuity with colonial administration: Participation in development management. *Third World Quarterly*, 24(1): 47–61.

Cooke, B. 2004. The Managing of the (Third) World. *Organization*, 11(5): 603–629.

Crane, A. 2000. Culture Clash and Mediation: Exploring the Cultural Dynamics of Business/NGO Collaboration. In J. Bendell (Ed.), *Terms for Endearment: Business, NGOs and Sustainable Development*: 163–178. Sheffield, UK: Greenleaf Publishing Ltd.

Dahl, R. A. 1961. *Who governs?* New Haven: Yale University Press.

De Bruijn, J. A., & Ten Heuvelhof, E. F. 1997. Instruments for network management In W. J. N. Kickert, E.-H. Klijn, & J. F. M. Koppenjan (Eds.), *Managing Complex Networks: Strategies for the Public Sector*: 119–136. London: SAGE.

Derkzen, P. H. M., & Bock, B. B. 2007. The construction of professional identity: symbolic power in rural partnerships in The Netherlands. *Sociologia Ruralis* 47(3): 189–204.

Derkzen, P. H. M., Franklin, A., & Bock, B. 2008. Examining power struggles as a signifier of successful partnership working: A case study of partnership dynamics. *Journal of Rural Studies*, 24(3): 458–466.

Dolan, C. S., & Opondo, M. 2005. Seeking Common Ground: Multi-Stakeholder Processes in Kenya's Cut Flower Industry. *The Journal of Corporate Citizenship*, 18: 87–98.

Emerson, R. M. 1962. Power Dependence Relations *American Sociological Review*, 27: 31–41.

Emerson, R. M. 1972. Exchange theory, part II: Exchange relations, exchange networks, and groups as exchange systems. In J. Berger, M. Zelditch, & B. Anderson (Eds.), *Sociological theories in progress*, Vol. II: 58–87. Boston, MA: Houghton Mifflin Company.

Entwistle, T., Bristow, G., Hines, F., Donaldson, S., & Martin, S. 2007. The Dysfunctions of Markets, Hierarchies and Networks in the Meta-governance of Partnership. *Urban Studies*, 44(1): 63–79.

EUEI. 2003. Proceedings of the EUEI Energy for Africa Event Nairobi 20–21 November 2003 19.

EUWI, F. W. G. A. A. 2006. European Union Water Initiative: Key Sheet No. 1. In E. Union (Ed.), *Key Sheet Series*: 4. Brussels.

Eweje, G. 2007. Strategic partnerships between MNEs and civil society: the post-WSSD perspectives. *Sustainable Development*, 15(1): 15–27.

Fowler, A. 1998. Authentic NGDO partnerships in the new policy agenda for international aid: dead end or light ahead? *Development and Change*, 29: 137–159.

Galaskiewicz, J. 1985. Interorganisational Relations *Annual Review of Sociology*, 11: 281–304.

Gray, B. 1985. Conditions Facilitating Interorganizational Collaboration. *Human Relations*, 30(10): 911–936.

Gray, B. 1989. Collaboration Finding Common Ground for Multi-party Problems San Francisco: Josey Bass.

Gray, B., Bougon, M. G., & Donnellon, A. 1985. Organizations as Constructions and Destructions of Meaning. *Journal of Management* 11(2): 83–98.

Gray, B., & Putnam, L. L. 2005. Means to What End? Conflict Management Frames. *Environmental Practice*, 5(3): 239–246

Gray, B., & Wood, D. J. 1991. Collaborative Alliances: Moving from Practice to Theory. *Journal of Applied Behavioral Science*, 27(1): 3–22.

Hale, T. N., & Mauzerall, D. L. 2004. Thinking Globally and Acting Locally: Can the Johannesburg Partnerships Coordinate Action on Sustainable Development? *The Journal of Environment Development*, 13(3): 220–239.

Hardy, C. 1994. Power and politics in organization In C. Hardy (Ed.), *Managing Strategic Action*: 220–238 Thousand Oaks, CA, : Sage.

Hardy, C., Phillips, N., & Lawrence, T. 1998. Distinguishing trust and power in interorganizational relations: Forms and façades of trust. . In C. Lane, & R. Bachmann (Eds.), *Trust Within and Between Organizations.*: 64–87. Oxford: Oxford University Press.

Hardy, C., Phillips, N., & Lawrence, T. B. 2003. Resources, Knowledge and Influence: The Organizational Effects of Interorganizational Collaboration. *Journal of Management Studies*, 40(2): 321–347.

Hasnain-Wynia, R., Sofaer, S., Bazzoli, G. J., Alexander, J. A., Shortell, S. M., Conrad, D. A., Chan, B., Zukoski, A. P., & Sweney, J. 2003. Members' Perceptions of Community Care Network Partnerships' Effectiveness. *Med Care Res Rev*, 60(4_suppl): 40S–62.

Hastings, A. 1999. Discourse and Urban Change: Introduction to the Special Issue. *Urban Stud*, 36(1): 7–12.

Huang, K., & Provan, K. G. 2006. Resource tangibility and patterns of interaction in a publicly funded health and human services network. *Journal of Public Administration Research and Theory*, 17: 435–454.

Huang, K., & Provan, K. G. 2007. Structural embeddedness and organizational social outcomes in a centrally governed mental health services network. *Public Management Review*, 9(2): 169–189.

Huxham, C., & Beech, N. 2003. *Exploring the power infrastructure of interorganizational collaborations*. Glasgow: Scotland University of Strathclyde, Graduate School of Business.

Jacobson, C., & Cohen, A. 1986. The Power of Social Collectivities: Towards an Integrative Conceptualization and Operationalization *The British Journal of Sociology*, 37(1): 106–121

James, R. 2001. Southern NGO Capacity Building: Issues and Priorities In R. James (Ed.), *Power and partnership?*: 9–33. Oxford: INTRAC.

Johnson, H., & Wilson, G. 2006. North-South/South-North Partnerships: Closing the 'Mutuality Gap' *Public Administration and Development*, 26(1): 71–80.

Jones, C., Hesterly, W. S., & Borgatti, S. P. 1997. A general theory of network governance: Exchange conditions and social mechanisms. *Academy of Management Review*, 22(4): 911–945.

Kickert, W., Klijn, E. H., & Koppenjan, J. 1997a. *Managing complex networks: Strategies for the public sector*. London: Sage.

Kickert, W. J. N., Klijn, E.-H., & Koppenjan, J. F. M. 1997b. "Managing networks in the public-sector: Findings and reflections". In W. J. N. Kickert, E.-H. Klijn, & J. F. M. Koppenjan (Eds.), *Managing Complex Networks: Strategies for the Public Sector*: 1661–1191. London: SAGE.

Kim, P. H., Pinkley, R. L., & Fragale, A. R. 2005. Power Dynamics in Negotiations. *Academy of Management Review*, 30(4): 799–822.

Kolk, A., Van Tulder, R., & Kostwinder, E. 2008. Business and Partnerships for Development. *European Management Journal*, 26(4): 262–273.

Lawrence, T. B., Phillips, N., & Hardy, C. 1999. Watching Whale Watching: Exploring the Discursive Foundations of Collaborative Relationships. *Journal of Applied Behavioral Science*, 35(4): 479–502.

Lister, S. 2000. Power in partnership? An analysis of an NGO's relationships with its partners. *Journal of International Development*, 12(2): 227–239.

Marsden, P. V. 1990. Network data and measurement. *Annual REview of Sociology*, 16: 435–463.

Medcof, J. W. 2001. Resource-based strategy and managerial power in networks of internationally dispersed technology units. *Strategic Management Journal*, 22: 999–1012.

Morse, S., & McNamara, N. 2006. Analysing institutional partnerships in development: a contract between equals or a loaded process? *Progress in Development Studies*, 6(4): 321–336.

O'Toole, J., L.J. 1997. Treating Networks Seriously: Practical and Research-Based Agendas in Public Administration. *Public Administration Review*, 57(1): 45–52.

O'Toole Jr, L. J., & Meier, K. J. 2004. Parkinson's Law and the New Public Management? Contracting Determinants and Service-Quality Consequences in Public Education. *Public Administration Review*, 64(3): 342–352.

Oliver, C. 1990. Determinants of Interorganizational Relationships: Integration and Future Directions. *Academy of Management Review*, 15(2): 241-265.

Patel, R. 2001. "Stealing People's Decisions is Wrong!". In R. James (Ed.), *Power and Partnership*: 80–94. Oxford: INTRAC.

Pfeffer, J., & Leong, A. 1977. Resource allocations in United Funds: Examination of power and dependence. *Social Forces*, 55: 775–790

Pfeffer, J., & Moore, W. L. 1980. Power in university budgeting: A replication and extension. *Administrative Science Quarterly*, 25(4): 637–653.

Pfeffer, J., & Salancik, G. R. 1978. The external control of organisations: A resource dependence perspective. New York: Harper & Row.

Phillips, N. 1997. Bringing the organization back in: a comment on conceptualizations of power in upward influence research. *Journal of Organizational Behavior*, 18(1): 43–47.

Provan, K. G. 1980. Recognizing, Measuring, and Interpreting the Potential/Enacted Power Distinction in Organizational Research. *The Academy of Management Review*, 5(4): 549–559

Provan, K. G., Beyer, J. M., & Kruytbosch, C. 1980. Environmental Linkages and Power in Resource-Dependence Relations between Organisations *Administrative Science Quarterly*, 25(2): 200–225.

Provan, K. G., & Kenis, P. 2008. Modes of Network Governance: Structure, Management, and Effectiveness. *J Public Adm Res Theory*: mum015.

Provan, K. G., & Milward, H. B. 2001. Do networks really work? A framework for evaluating public-sector networks organisational networks. . *Public Administration Review*, 61: 414–423.

Raab, J., & Kenis, P. 2009. Heading towards a Society of Networks. Empirical Developments and Theoretical Challenges. *Journal of Management Inquiry*, 18(3): 198–210.

Robinson, D., Hewitt, T., & Harriss, J. 2000. *Managing Development. Understanding Inter-Organisational Relationships*. London, United Kingdom: SAGE Publications.

Rochlin, S., Zadek, S., & Forstater, M. 2008. Governing Collaboration: Making partnerships accountable for delivering development. In AccountAbility (Ed.), *Programme Paper*: www.accountability21.net.

Rogers, M. F. 1974. Instrumental and Infra-Resources: The Bases of Power. *The American Journal of Sociology*, 79(6): 1418–1433

Sanyal, P. 2006. Capacity Building Through Partnership: Intermediary Nongovernmental Organizations as Local and Global Actors. *Nonprofit and Voluntary Sector Quarterly*, 35(1): 66–82.

Stewart, A., & Gray, T. 2006. The Authenticity of 'type two' Multistakeholder partnerships for water and sanitation in Africa: When is a stakeholder a partner? . *Environmental Politics* 17(5): 362–377.

Thomas, A. 1996. What is Development Management? *Journal of International Development*, 8(1): 95–110.

Thomas, A. 2007. Development Management – Values and Partnerships. *Journal of International Development*, 19: 383–388.

Waddell, S. 2000. Complementary Resources: The Win-win Rationale for Partnership with NGOs. In J. Bendell (Ed.), *Terms of Endearment: Business, NGOs and Sustainable Development*: 193-207. Sheffield: UK: Greenleaf Publishing.

Waddell, S. 2005. Societal Learning and Change: How governments, business and civil society are creating solutions to complex multi-stakeholder problems. Sheffield, UK: Greenleaf Publishing.

Zakus, J. D. L. 1998. Resource dependency and community participation in primary health care. *Social Science & Medicine*, 46(4-5): 475.

Zeitz, G. 1980. Interorganizational Dialectics. *Administrative Science Quarterly*, 25: 72–88.

Appendix I: Non-response Analysis

	Respondents	Non-respondents		
	38 partnerships	212 partnerships	Difference	Significance
	Percentage	Percentage	Percentage	p-value
Variable				
Initiative:				
Energy	34,2	28,6	-5,60	0,454[1]
Water	65,8	71,4	5,60	
Region of operation:				
ACP	0	1,9	1,90	0,682[2]
Africa	94,7	89,0	-5,70	
Caribbeans	5,3	5,2	-0,10	
Pacifics	0	3,8	3,80	
Budget:				
5 5.0-77 Mill.	15,8	17,1	1,30	0,433[2]
4 2.5-5.0 Mill.	28,9	22,4	-6,50	
3 1.8-2.5 Mill.	7,9	22,9	15	
2 1.0-1.8 Mill.	15,8	20,5	4,70	
1 0.2-1.0 Mill.	31,6	17,1	-14,50	
Mean	2,82	3,02	0,20	
Percentage (%) of budget financed by partners:				
5 80-100%	2,6	1,0	-1,60	0,172[2]
4 60-80%	15,8	4,3	-11,50	
3 40-60%	21,1	17,6	-3,50	
2 20-40%	50,0	76,7	26,70	
1 0-20%	10,5	0,5	-5,50	
Mean	2,50	2,29	-0,21	
Intermediary organisation:				
IOs and Foreign National governments	13,2	18,6	5,40	0,823[2]
National local governments	18,4	13,3	-5,10	
Regional local government	2,6	5,7	3,10	
Foreign NGO	47,4	40,5	-6,90	
Foreign operator	2,6	2,9	0,30	
Local operator	2,6	8,1	5,50	
Local NGO	2,6	4,3	1,70	
Research Institute	10,6	6,7	-3,90	

[1] Binomial Test
[2] Mann-Whitney U-Test

Cooperatives and Climate Protection

Christine von Blanckenburg

The contribution of civil society in the development of climate protection measures and the complementary action potential of cooperatives

Climate change is an especially emphasized problem area for sustainable development, through which the dramatic extent of the effects of depletion of natural resources have upon social and economic development become apparent.

Organized civil society has participated in many aspects of the discourse surrounding climate change. The assessment of results of climate change research, the development of measures for mitigation and adaption, the setting of climate goals, especially for the reduction of CO_2, as well as the general handling of the topic in politics on global, national, regional and local levels results from the tireless effort of civic actors (Walk 2008).

On the normative level, NGOs are especially strong, reflecting their aim to influence climate policy. Both politics and citizens are the audiences of the campaigns of civic organizations. Policymakers are challenged to place sanctions on climate damaging behaviour, through legislation, or to increase the attractiveness of climate-friendly investments with tax incentives. A second strand of activity of civic organizations includes informational events and enlightenment campaigns, which are directed towards the wider public and aim at the implementation of climate protection measures (e.g. arguments in support of a sparing use of fossil fuels and, simultaneously, concrete suggestions for the reduction of daily energy use are disseminated). NGOs, therefore, operate opposite target groups of political decision-makers as well as opposite citizens as information mediators. They do not, however, take a neutral position. Rather, they advocate values intended to motivate changes in behaviour. They are not parties, but are party-like. In NGOs, however, the level of implementation of climate goals is poorly developed and limited to the observation of sustainability criteria within their own operations.

As part of the activity of "Local Agenda 21" groups, there are local projects directed by civic actors which contribute directly to climate protection. Such groups, which act on the local level in support of the achievement of sustainability goals, emerged globally after the *United Nationals Conference on Environment and Development* (UNCED), which presented the Agenda 21 in 1992. In Chapter 28 of this document on sustainable development, the global threat resulting from lacking sustainable development measures is presented in connection with options available in the immediate living sphere of individuals. An appeal is directed towards the governments of the signing nations to develop local action plans for increased sustainability through tri-sector (i.e. administration, civil society and business) cooperation (Earth Summit AGENDA 21 1996). This correlation is often transmitted by Local Agenda 21 groups with the challenge: *"Think globally – act locally!"* Upon analysis of the projects, however, one realizes that, at least on a local level of policymaking, the levels of influence on opinion shaping, decision making and implementation are so interconnected that distinguishing these stages is difficult. Local Agenda groups in communities and cities are not the actual implementers. Rather, these groups act as catalysers, mobilizing the support of local politics and other organizations, developing concepts (e.g. for energy saving) and rallying citizen support and participation. A genuine implementation function is not achievable by civic organizations on a local level. This gap can be bridged by cooperatives.

The implementation of sustainability goals on a local level is often impeded by the fact that economic aspects are notoriously neglected by civic organizations, their work being ethically motivated. In part, their latent anti-economic positioning crosses over into a fundamental critique of market economy. However, even where no ideological barriers seem to exist, economic aspects are not often incorporated enough into the local practice of climate protection. As a result, even in highly-praised, exemplary communities, which are oriented along the model of "Nachhaltigen Bürgerkommunen" (sustainable communities), businesses are only visible as partners in the process of modeling the quality of a location (Bürgerkommune Neumarkt i. Opf. n. d.), but not for climate protection. If one views climate protection as being a central action area of sustainable development, one must observe that the business sector is hardly being integrated into local activity on a global scale.

Civic organizations lack implementation potential, without which their normative claims and concepts remain weak. Additionally, the concepts for sustainable development lack an economic perspective and the integration of business in implementation processes.

Civic organizations engaged on behalf of climate protection focus on commonality and, thereby, on the individuals that must be convinced of the necessity to change their personal behaviour (e.g. in using less energy and in using less energy obtained from fossil fuels). Cooperatives are interesting actors in this respect, as they operate on a collective (i.e. not an individual) level, at which competencies and financial resources can be bundled and applied for mutual use.

Large cooperatives, with academically-qualified leadership, can incorporate, assess and adapt scientific results and corresponding options for action to their conditions much more easily than can individuals. When larger investments are required as a result of these assessment and adaption processes, cooperatives can apply vastly different amounts of financial resources for meeting their own climate protection goals.

A specific advantage of cooperatives is their democratic constitution. Acceptance of measures can be won through participatory processes, while their ratification can be made mandatory for all, regardless of personal opinion, by way of a majority vote. For example, the directorate of a cooperative may inform the members of ideas for climate protection after such measures have been developed and reviewed, in a manner that blends out the global implications and focuses on the specific conditions for implementation. By way of a more or less intensive opinion-shaping process, the members may develop their own opinions and exert influence. Even when measures are decided without prior approval of the general member assembly, such as those relating to the governance of the directorate, the directorate owes accountability to the members it represents. This form of democratic decision making and implementation of measures is based on a trust of the members in leading figures. This trust is fed with experiences demonstrating that the cooperative in turn supports its members. Naturally, even cooperative directorates cannot mandate individual behavioural change. However, they may launch discussion processes and shape framework conditions so that climate-friendly behaviour is recognized as being favourable.

The three mentioned deficits of the efforts of civic organizations for sustainability (e.g. implementation weakness, non-economical worldview and orientation at an individual level) can be covered by cooperatives. Cooperative action capabilities rest upon their collective foundation for the implementation of climate protection measures and upon their entrepreneurial logic, to which they are subject as organizations for economic self-help.

Excursion: The relationship between civil society and cooperatives

Cooperative capabilities for action complement the actions of NGOs. Cooperatives can, therefore, be seen as actors of the business sector, which can act together with local politics and administration and/or civic organizations. As cooperatives and not just businesses, and representing an association of persons, they can also be seen as civic actors. Both sides of the dual nature of cooperatives (Draheim 1955, p 16), association of individuals and economic entity, can be emphasized differently. This, of course, influences how cooperatives are perceived.

The assignment of cooperatives to organized civil society is unusual, especially in Germany, as the corporate status of cooperatives has had much influence on cooperative law and on the self-conception of cooperatives. Other nations have differing traditions which focus the functions of cooperatives more strongly to be on behalf of civil society. In France, Italy, Spain and Portugal, for example, cooperatives are part of économie sociale, the third sector next to the state and market economy (Göler von Ravensburg 2007b, p 40; Münkner).

The close connection between cooperatives and civil society becomes apparent on account of their shared values. The International Cooperative Association, an NGO which represents 233 cooperative organizations worldwide, states that cooperatives "are based on the values of self-help, self-responsibility, democracy, equality, equity and solidarity" while their "members believe in the ethical values of honesty, openness, social responsibility and caring for others" (International Cooperative Association 1995)[33].

The practice of cooperative organization is shaped in a participatory manner in accordance with these values. Cooperatives, like corporations, are led by a directorate making daily operational decisions and which is regulated by a supervisory board. However, the highest level of arbitration rests with the general member assembly in which, in contrast to corporations, all members have an equal voice, regardless of their percentage of shares. This culture of co-determination, which is constitutive for cooperatives, is one element which establishes the close connection between cooperatives and civic organizations. These civic organizations operate in a similar participatory manner and call for action on national and global levels.

> „Eine Genossenschaft lebt Demokratie in Reinkultur und zeichnet sich durch die hohe Transparenz und den Schutz der Mitglieder aus. Diese demokratische Verfassung prädestiniert Genossenschaften geradezu für Aufgaben mit sozialen und gesellschaftspolitischen Hintergrund." (Vogt 2011, p 8).

---

[33] The paper of the left wing of the parliamentary group of the Social Democratic Party in Germany draws from the shared value base when prompting unions to act cooperatively, stating that *"democratic values are a binding foundation, which can be built upon"*, Vogt (2011).

Although cooperatives are enterprises, belonging to the economic sphere and having an economic worldview, they are organizations which represent a link between economy and civil society, on account of their ethical values and democratic practice.

The here-described understanding of the relationship between civil society and cooperatives is based on the study of cooperatives in Germany. Two aspects are especially relevant for climate protection. First, cooperatives are, on account of shared values and participatory capabilities, economic partners for civil society and the state, especially on a local level. Second, the cooperative form of organization offers itself to actors of civil society who want to implement their own ideas.

Cooperatives as sustainable organizations

The mentioned action capabilities of cooperatives, which also pertain to the implementation of concepts for climate protection, such as their economic worldview and clout on account of their collective orientation, are not options exclusive to cooperatives. Rather, they are pertinent for other corporations and associations as well. If the thesis is presented here that cooperatives offer unique action capabilities on behalf of climate protection, it because cooperatives as such are sustainable organizations. This will be discussed in regard to the well-known triangular diagram of sustainability, which represents the balance of economic, social and ecological aspects.

Historically, cooperatives emerged as institutions for economic self-help. They served and continue to serve the economic security of their members. The guiding principle of economic conduct is not the shareholder value, as in a joint-stock company, but rather the support of the members. As cooperatives are able to limit themselves to this statutory purpose, they do not need to operate on a profit-driven basis. Whether or not dealings reflect this purpose is regulated by both the supervisory board and an audit by a cooperative regulatory association (genossenschaftlicher Prüfverband). Additionally, rules of cooperative law allow for legal and free provisions which protect creditors should insolvency occur, regulate the directorate's risk limit and protect the inventory of threatened cooperative assets. Furthermore, cooperative law places limits on the raising of capital. In the case of an exit out of the cooperative, only the nominal amount is paid by the cooperative (i.e. without the profit). Thus, the "internal value" is maintained. For investors, cooperatives are relatively unattractive. Due to the equal co-determination right of all members, they cannot attain decision-making power in accordance with their share. Profit expectancy remains vague, as dividend pay-outs are not required of cooperatives[34]. Cooperative law and statute protects cooperative organizations from risky dealings, speculative takeovers and divestitures. Especially during the current financial crisis, caused by highly speculative financial transactions, cooperatives are once again seen as an attractive alternative which make a sustainable economy possible. The left wing of the SPD parliamentary group in the German Bundestag presented the idea of a cooperative alternative to economic capitalism, apparent already in the title of their paper "Genossenschaften – eine andere Form des Wirtschaftens" (Cooperatives – another form of economy) (Vogt 2011).

Concepts of the social dimension of sustainability describe the sustainable society using the key terms *solidarity, justice* and *participation*. A certain standard of living in the areas of employment, housing, health and education are included in these social sustainability objectives (Bundesregierung 2002; Abgeordnetenhaus zu Berlin 2006). This pertains from the local to the global level. At each level, different standards are defined as being appropriate and just. At all levels, participation is a constitutive part of the social dimension of sustainability, especially on account of its linking of social goals with the demand for justice (Baranek, Fischer & Walk). The UN Division for Sustainable Development emphasizes the need for participatory and co-determination structures for sustainable development. The questions of how to do business and how wealth should be distributed and/or used must be addressed democratically, if they are to have a standing (World Commission on Environment and Development 1987; Hauff 1987).Justice and social cohesion only be generated through open processes involving civil society. The support of citizen engagement and the development of social capital, which also directly contributes to social cohesion, are seen as being additional results of participatory processes[35].

Cooperatives contribute to the achievement of social sustainability goals by creating housing and securing jobs. These are not the only areas, however, in which they prove to be socially sustainable organizations. Rather, it is because they represent the same principles and values upon which the social dimension of sustainability is based. The cooperative principle of solidarity provides that self-help and self-responsibility of its members are

---

[34] The revision of the German cooperative law in 2006 did, however, adjust the economic capabilities of large cooperatives to those of other corporations, by allowing investor-members and an expansion of multiple voting in primary cooperatives (Brockmeier 2007).

[35] The development of a solidary civic group as a complement to the social state and within the sustainability dialogue is assessed differently (Brand & Jochum).

complemented by mutual responsibility and caring for one another. Thereby, cooperatives offer not only the framework for the satisfaction of particular interests of their members. They also achieve balance and justice.

In addition to solidarity as a fundamental principle, the democratic nature of constitution must be emphasized, as it aims primarily for emancipation and equality. The participatory possibilities offered by cooperatives are recognized as means for the purpose of representing the different interests of members in the shaping of opinion and in decision making. Beyond this, they form a foundation for cooperatives as an *"emancipatory social system"* (Patera 1990), which provides the framework for the *"unfolding of individual livelihoods"* (Flieger 1996). This emancipation of cooperative members, which reaches far beyond its actual purpose and has a societal effect, is now hardly recognizable in the large Traditionsgenossenschaften (traditional cooperatives). However, it can be found in the beginnings of the cooperative movement, at a time when cooperatives began to assume educational responsibilities (Fehl 2007, p 100; Schädel 2000). Also, it can be found in the autonomous organizations of the new social movements (Atmaca 2007, p 572) and in the cooperatives of the developing world, which contribute to "empowerment" (Wade 1988).

The ecological dimension of the sustainability triangle served as the origin of the sustainability dialogue. Following the 1972 Club of Rome study "The Limits to Growth", the question of how limited natural resources can be used in the long-term came into focus (International Union for Conservation of Nature and Natural Resources, et al. 1980). The concept of sustainable development, which was developed in the Brundtland Commission report "Our Common Future" (World Commission on Environment and Development 1987), no longer focused on resource use, but rather on the threats to the natural foundation of societal development resulting from environmental degradation and excessive resource use. The depletion of the natural world is thereby declared as being a destructive evil. However, it is also placed in relation to development goals, which are composed of a social, economic and ecological dimension. One possible relativizing aspect of eco-political goal setting for the maintaining of the natural environment, which is possible in this concept through its link to development, was not accepted in the German dialogue. The environment is held as being the limiting factor. "The ecological dimension...plays a key role, as the natural basis of life limits the implementation potential of other goals. The natural preconditions for life on earth are non-negotiable" (Bundesministerium für Umwelt 1998; Deutschland / Umweltbundesamt 2002).

Especially here, in this non-negotiable sustainability dimension, ecology, cooperatives have not proven themselves to be sustainable organizations. They are not more ecological than other corporations and civic organizations. If a special role of cooperatives in climate protection is declared in the title of this essay, it is because hopes for solving pressing problems of the time have long been bound to the cooperative structure. This was true for the so-called "social question" of the 19th century, as well as for questions of internal democratization of economy and society in the second half of the 20th century. It remains this way today, when the need for protection of natural resources has come to be a question of survival and the global economic crises threatens sustainable development.

Principles of cooperatives and social utopias

Modern cooperatives emerged in the late 18th century and 19th century in order to overcome social injustice. Whether they were thought of by their "inventors" and proponents as being system-complementing or system-overcoming (Eschenburg 1988), they offered, on account of their organization principles, starting points for social utopias or the justified assurance that exemplary solutions to the pressing social injustice could be found within the cooperative framework. Even today, cooperatives are suitable, once again on account of their special organizational structure and value horizon, as projection surfaces for a diverse array of social modernization projects[36]. In practice, however, they are limited in the implementation of goals which stand outside of their defined purposes.

The various phases, through which the cooperative idea begins to carry these hopes, can each be attributed to one cooperative principle. Each of these principles offered the most solution potential in relation to the corresponding historical problem area. It must be emphasized, however, that the separation of principles only serves an increased understanding. The particularity of cooperatives continues to be that the principles relate to one another. As a result, a scope for design exists, which is otherwise unparalleled in both the economic sphere and civil society.

In the 18th and 19th centuries, the social question moved to the forefront due to the dissolution of corporative society. Liberalization and industrialization resulted not only in a wave of modernization, characterized by population

---

[36] The excess of idealistic goals becomes apparent in literature through the obvious phrasing in the subjunctive: „Cooperatives are predestined or would be an ideal form of organization for..." Karner (2010, pp 86 f.), Karner (2010, p 103), Göler von Ravensburg (2011), Becker (2011); Hanrath (2011, p 127), (Vogt 2011, p 8).

growth, technical advancement and urbanization, but also in the impoverishment and hardship in rural areas and in the most rapidly growing cities. Small farmers and craftsmen experienced a livelihood threatening decline. The situation was worse for the rural have-nots and labourers in the cities. The living, housing and working conditions were recognized, even by the bourgeois winners of modernization, as being catastrophic and inhumane, and often experienced as threatening. The cooperative movement emerged during this time period. It viewed the solidary union for self-help as a key to enabling market access for craftsmen and farmers and for securing livelihoods. By subscribing a cooperative share, they became members of an association of individuals and, at the same time, co-proprietors of a collective operation. The identity principle refers to the fact that all members of a cooperative are co-proprietors of the share capital (in an economic sense). The principle of identity means, that the member is in one person owner and customer or owner and supplier or owner and worker. The in socialist economic theory defined cause for the social question, the contradiction of capital and work, is, therefore, kept alive in producer cooperatives (Atmaca 2007, pp 521–525).

Those cooperatives most influenced by the labour movement are not, however, primarily concerned with this socioeconomic conflict between work and capital. Rather, they emerged in areas which were most effective in bringing about the improvement of the quality of life of their members. Housing cooperatives sought to provide an affordable and humane housing supply and consumer cooperatives enabled the supply of affordable, high quality goods. In both cooperative types, the members and customers are the same (Brendel 2011).

The next wave of enthusiasm for the idea of cooperatives was less dynamic as the movement of the founding period. Since the late 1960s, emerging from the student movement and non-parliamentary opposition, the topic of internal democratization of economy and society, which relates to the cooperative idea, has become established. Efforts to promote participation and democratization were strong in regard to diverse issues and came to be a staple, proving to be cohesive for the new social movement, which was soon to drift apart. Despite this, they did not touch equally upon the existential needs of the broader population, as did the social question during the 19th century. For activists of the time, however, the cooperative idea offered and ideal framework for experimenting with other forms of living and working. Most importantly, the central values of self- and co-determination could be implemented and tested in self-governing organizations.[37]

To the search for forms by which a direct democratic way of living and economy could be developed and lived, the cooperative model was very attractive. It was so attractive because the democracy principle reflected the enthusiasm by which the emancipatory power of participation was hailed by the new social movements (Hettlage 1987).

More specifically, the democracy principle states that every member, regardless of his or her capital share, has one vote in the general assembly.[38] This principle, which distinguishes cooperatives from corporations, is central to cooperatives, as they are first and foremost an association of individuals. These individuals, who each have one voice, collectively own capital which must be used for the main purpose of the cooperative. At the general assembly, the members decide on fundamental management questions, assess the annual report and decide on the appropriation of profits. The democracy principle does not only state that decisions must be made democratically (i.e. equally and transparently). It also states the management of the directorate and the regulatory functions of the supervisory board derive from the members. This is comparable to the principle of democratic nations, in which all power derives from the people. Accordingly, these office-holders must also be members of the cooperative.[39]

---

[37] To the connection of self-governing organizations, as part of the so-called "new social movements", with direct democratic, antiauthoritarian and emancipatory goals, Atmaca (2007, p 572)
The orientation to needs, engagement benefitting the socially disadvantaged, regional economy, the developing world, the reconciliation of family and career, and the preservation of livelihoods continue to be the ideals represented by self-governing organizations and cooperatives, whose members identify with the new social movements. The linking of these emancipatory ideals with the idea of cooperatives is viewed rather sceptically by cooperative associations and by the more conservative cooperatives, ibid. p 577.

[38] *Beuthien et al.* (1997, S. 31) suggest speaking more specifically of the "principle of individual (independent of the capital share of the individual member) vote equality." Beuthien, Brockmeier & Klose (1997, p 31).

[39] Members control the management activity of the directorate by selecting a supervisory board (§ 36 ff. GenG), which is made up of other members (§ 9 II GenG) and which is, alongside the general assembly, the highest-ranking decision-making body (§48 I GenG).

The solidarity principle and sustainability in the 21st century

The fact that the UN has declared 2012 as the International Year of Cooperatives is a sign of the hopes that rest on sustainable development through forms of cooperative organization. The resolution of the General Assembly honoured the contribution of cooperatives in the fight against poverty, to economic and social development and to the involvement of disadvantaged groups in development processes. Also, the General Assembly recognizes the role that cooperatives can potentially play for the "improvement of social and economic situation of indigenous peoples and rural communities" (United Nations General Assembly).

The United Nations recommend that their member states promote cooperatives, as this organizational form enables opportunities in combatting poverty, especially in developing and emerging nations. Market access resulting from solidary self-help is the key to emancipation from financial dependency, which is a reality that often confronts disadvantaged individuals and groups. Just how effective cooperative self-help can be in undeveloped regions, in enabling the establishment and securing the interests of small corporations through microcredits, has moved into the public consciousness. In 2006, the Nobel Peace Prize was awarded to Mohammed Yunus and the Grameen Bank, the microfinance organization and community development bank which he founded (Brendel 2011, pp 34 f.). Cooperatives secure not only livelihoods, but guarantee co-determination of fair living and working conditions as well. Not least, cooperatives have economic leeway in regard to the sustainable use of natural resources, as they are not driven by profits.

The success of this and other lending cooperatives, especially in developing and emerging nations, is reminiscent of the beginnings of the cooperative movement in Germany and its rural loan societies and Raiffeisen credit unions. Actors of development policy are less euphoric than the United Nations about the contribution of cooperatives to social development. Decades of experience with cooperative organizations as vehicles for rural development cannot be ignored. The contribution which cooperatives can provide in combatting poverty, hunger and underdevelopment depends largely on the underlying conditions (Göler von Ravensburg 2007a).

While the "contribution of cooperatives to socio-economic development" is highlighted through the International Year of Cooperatives, the cooperative idea is simultaneously experiencing a renaissance in times of financial and economic crisis. The cooperative orientation towards long-term existence and member support, which seemed antiquated in boom times, is being valued highly once more, as cooperative enterprises have proven to be less vulnerable in the face of the crisis (Birchhall & Ketilson 2009).

The comprehensive hopes which rest upon cooperatives, in regard to sustainable social and economic development in the 21st century, fall in line with deliberations on specific possibilities for handling climate protection. We can observe that the environmental dimension is gaining importance within the current cooperative movement and appearing more often in statutes as a main or side purpose. While the number of cooperatives has been declining continuously over the past decades, a counteracting movement of cooperative establishment has been developing since the amendment to the cooperative law. Although this counteracting movement cannot offset the overall decline, it is a clear indicator that the idea of cooperatives is being filled with new life (Stappel 2010, p. 72; pp. 76 ff.; Volz 2010). Not infrequently, these new cooperatives are focused explicitly on environmental goals[40].

Even tradition cooperatives and cooperatives which do not explicitly associate themselves with environmental protection have an approach to the issue of climate protection. Solidarity, a fundamental organizational principle of cooperatives, is the key issue which can be addressed here. Solidarity is an ethical value advocated by members of cooperatives. Values have an action-directing function which is not limited to one specific area. In other words, solidarity, as the organizational principle which first and foremost justifies the solidary, internal responsibility of the members, transcends the boundaries of the cooperative as a value held by their members.

This type of ethically orientated behavior, especially, which is understood as being not only the ensuring of one's own interests through a balancing of interests, is crucial for active climate protection. This is so because the principal cause of the development of environmental consciousness and motivation of active climate protection is missing in regard to the topic of climate protection. In reality, it is the experience of having one's own health threatened or of having the belief that severe harm may be inflicted, if relief is not provided for (Hinding 2002). In regard to climate change resulting from harmful greenhouse gases, negative effects can hardly be expected in developed nations, which are responsible for the largest percentage of CO_2

---

[40] In the project „Solidarische Stadt – Genossenschaftliche Handlungsmöglichkeiten in Zeiten des Klimawandels" (City of Solidarity – Possibilities for cooperative action in the era of climate change) 7 new cooperatives and 2 tradition cooperatives from different interest areas are assessed. www.solidarischestadt.de.

emissions. Their citizens do not need to feel acutely threatened. Therefore, they do not, as becomes apparent when one interprets the often-heard, flippant appreciations of warmer temperatures as being a reflection of the widespread mind-set of the population. Different surveys on the perception of climate change produce varying results. One trend, however, remains consistent. In developed nations, negative effects on the immediate environment, resulting from climate change, are expected only on the distant horizon. Government and industry are viewed as being primarily responsible for development, as their potential for action is much greater, while the individual contribution to climate protection is viewed as being insignificant (Walk 2008, pp. 171 ff.).

The main greenhouse gas emitting nations will suffer less severely from drought, floods, famines and desertification than will developing nations, which hardly contribute to CO_2 emissions on account of their lack of wealth. Without a fundamental insight into the global interconnectedness of the developed and developing world and the consequent acceptance of responsibility in form of solidary behavioural changes in developed nations, an important pillar for reaching ambitious climate goals is missing.

As solidarity, as described, is such a fundamental aspect of active participation in climate protection, cooperatives and their members, for whom solidarity is a central value, have a special starting position regarding the minimization of the use of energy produced by fossil fuels. The assumption that cooperatives will open themselves to the issue of climate protection and more strongly incorporate the environmental dimension rests on the hope that a historical tradition can be propagated. This tradition is one through which cooperatives have delivered solutions for the most pressing problems of their time. The hope that cooperatives will play a role in the survival issue of the 21st century, sustainable development, rests once more on solidarity. Solidarity, as an orientating ethical value, must transcend the narrow boundaries of cooperatives and provide the impulse for behavioural change, which would otherwise be too weakly pronounced on account of the lack of experience with the direct threats of climate change.

We do not want to deny that cooperatives per se do not demonstrate ecological orientation. The theoretical connection to solidary values offers only a weak bridge between the cooperative movement and climate protection. There is evidence, however, that the affinity for climate protection, deduced here on a theoretical basis, will gain importance in the practice of cooperatives. We can observe that an explicit link to climate change is increasingly developing within the new cooperative movement. Many of the new cooperatives set sustainability goals. Hereby, they propagate a tradition of the cooperative movement, to promote ideological goals alongside the main goals. For the cementation of the issue of climate protection, therefore, there are proven examples throughout the history of cooperatives.

It cannot yet be determined whether or not the principle of solidarity and a therefrom resulting consciousness of global responsibility were the reasons for the incorporation of climate protection into the goals and orientation of new cooperatives. This explanatory approach would gain strength if a stronger consideration of climate change would present itself in the actions of tradition cooperatives as well.[41] If the implementation of climate protection measures continues be an issue exclusive to new cooperatives, however, a second explanatory approach would be more plausible. This explanatory approach explains the connection between cooperatives and climate protection as resulting from the ecological orientation of the founders and members of these cooperatives. For individuals living a "green" lifestyle, who share the ideals of the new social movement and value its pronounced participatory culture, cooperatives offer an attractive form of organization.

Conclusion

Cooperatives have a unique approach to the issue of climate protection on account of the value of solidarity. If a cooperative has defined climate protection as one of its goals, whether as a result of an orientation towards solidarity or because the environment is important to the members, the cooperative form of organization offers unique potential for action. This potential differs from that of civic organizations and/or that of other corporate forms. Cooperatives can be especially effective in contributing to the achievement of climate protection goals on a local level. This is because, as economic self-help organizations, they stand between civil society and the economy and must not operate on a profit-oriented basis. Therefore, they have leeway in implementing even costly ecological solutions, as long as these do not threaten their own economic survival. As a result, they distinguish themselves from other corporations, which view the sustainability issue in light of the conflict between economy and ecology.

Cooperatives operate on a collective basis, rather than on an individual one, upon which competencies and financial resources can be combined and

---

[41] With the Spar- und Bauverein Hannover eG and Konsum Dresden eG, the project "City of Solidarity" assesses two tradition cooperatives having an orientation towards climate protection.

applied for mutually beneficial uses. Therefore, they can develop a specific potential when it comes to climate protection. They have unique chances, as they can invest large sums, absorb scientific findings more quickly and adapt these to their own terms and conditions. An additional advantage of the collective approach lies therein that decisions regarding climate protection are made on the basis of majority decision. A certain degree of directional decision making is thereby secured and even the unconvinced members included.

Cooperatives will become increasingly important for sustainable and cooperative solutions on a local level, as they have the potential to lead new behavioural and social patterns of action, which are oriented towards more sustainable paths. In addition, cooperatives, in principle, allow for the highest possible level of civic involvement in decision-making processes. Value creation remains citizen-centric and communally available. Thus, the cooperative movement, and especially the formation of new cooperatives, has the potential to inject new life into the mobilization of individuals, civil society, policymakers and economic actors by actively supporting a transition to sustainable practice in Europe.

References

Abgeordnetenhaus zu Berlin 2006, Berlin zukunftsfähig gestalten. Lokale Agenda 21.

Allgeier, M (ed.) 2011, *Solidarität, Flexibilität, Selbsthilfe,* VS Verlag für Sozialwissenschaften, Wiesbaden.

Atmaca, D 2007, 'Produktivgenossenschaften – zwischen Utopie und Realismus' in *Volkswirtschaftliche Theorie der Kooperation in Genossenschaften,* eds T Brockmeier & U Fehl, Vandenhoeck & Ruprecht, Göttingen, pp. 509–590.

Baranek, E, Fischer, C & Walk, H, *Partizipation und Nachhaltigkeit. Reflektionen über Zusammenhänge und Vereinbarkeiten.* Available from: http://www.tu-berlin.de/uploads/media/Nr_15_Bara-Fisc-Walk_01.pdf.

Becker, P 2011, 'Bioenergieprojekte brauchen Bürgerbeteiligung', *LandInForm – Magazin für Ländliche Räume,* no. 3.

Beuthien, V, Brockmeier, T & Klose, H 1997, Materialien zum Genossenschaftsgesetz Band V. Genossenschaftsrecht der SBZ und DDR (1945–1990), Vandenhoeck & Ruprecht, Göttingen.

Birchhall, J & Ketilson, LH 2009, *Resilience of the cooperative business model in times of crisis. Responses to the global economic crisis,*, Sustainable Enterprise Programme. Available from: http://www.ilo.org/wcmsp5/groups/public/---ed_emp/---emp_ent/documents/publication/wcms_108416.pdf.

Brand, K & Jochum, G, *Der deutsche Diskurs zu nachhaltiger Entwicklung.* Abschlussbericht eines DFG-Projekts zum Thema „Sustainable Development/Nachhaltige Entwicklung – Zur sozialen Konstruktion globaler Handlungskonzepte im Umweltdiskurs", Münchner Projektgruppe für Sozialforschung e.V.

Brendel, M 2011, 'Genossenschaftsbewegung in Deutschland – Geschichte und Aktualität' in *Solidarität, Flexibilität, Selbsthilfe,* ed M Allgeier, VS Verlag für Sozialwissenschaften, Wiesbaden, pp. 15–36.

Brockmeier, T & Fehl, U (eds.) 2007, *Volkswirtschaftliche Theorie der Kooperation in Genossenschaften,* Vandenhoeck & Ruprecht, Göttingen.

Brockmeier, T 2007, Zur Reform des deutschen Genossenschaftsgesetzes – Frischer Wind durch das Statut der Europäischen Genossenschaft (SCE)' in *Volkswirtschaftliche Theorie der Kooperation in Genossenschaften,* eds T Brockmeier & U Fehl, Vandenhoeck & Ruprecht, Göttingen.

Bundesministerium für Umwelt 1998, *Nachhaltige Entwicklung in Deutschland : Entwurf eines umweltpolitischen Schwerpunktprogramms,* Bundesministerium für Umwelt, Naturschutz und Reaktorsicherheit, Bonn.

Bundesregierung 2002, *Perspektiven für Deutschland. Unsere Strategie für eine nachhaltige Entwicklung.* Available from:
http://www.bundesregierung.de(nsc_true/Content/DE/_Anlagen/2006-2007/perspektiven-fuer-deutschland-langfassung,templateId=raw,property=publicationFile.pdf/perspektiven-fuer-deutschland-langfassung.

Bürgerkommune Neumarkt i. Opf. Available from: http://www.buergerhaus-neumarkt.de/buergerhaus-projekte.html.

Deutschland / Umweltbundesamt 2002, Sustainability in Germany. Creating a lasting environmentally compatible future, Erich Schmidt, Berlin.

Doluschitz, R (ed.) 2010, *Aktuelle theoretische und empirische Beiträge zur Genossenschafts- und Kooperationsforschung*. Veröffentlichungen der Forschungsstelle für Genossenschaftswesen an der Universität Hohenheim 29, Stuttgart

Draheim, G 1955, *Die Genossenschaft als Unternehmungstyp*, Vandenhoeck & Ruprecht, Göttingen.

Earth summit AGENDA 21 1996, *The United Nations Program of Action from Rio*. Available from: http://www.un.org/esa/dsd/agenda21.

Eschenburg, R 1988, Systemüberwindung oder Systemergänzung durch Genossenschaften gegensätzliche Positionen in der frühen wirtschaftswissenschaftlichen Diskussion um Genossenschaften, Westfälische Wilhelms-Universität Münster, Institut für Genossenschaftswesen, Abteilung Lateinamerika, Münster

Fehl, U 2007, 'H. Schultze-Delitzsch und F.W. Raiffeisen: Die Gründerväter und ihr Vermächtnis – die 'klassische' Genossenschaft' in *Volkswirtschaftliche Theorie der Kooperation in Genossenschaften*, eds T Brockmeier & U Fehl, Vandenhoeck & Ruprecht, Göttingen, pp. 87–117.

Felber, C 2011, *Die Gemeinwohl-Ökonomie. Das Wirtschaftsmodell der Zukunft*, Deuticke, Wien

Flieger, B 1996, *Produktivgenossenschaft als fortschrittsfähige Organisation. Theorie, Fallstudie, Handlungshilfen*, Metropolis, Marburg.

Göler von Ravensburg, N 2007a, 'Genossenschaftliche Selbsthilfe in der Entwicklungspolitik' in *Volkswirtschaftliche Theorie der Kooperation in Genossenschaften*, eds T Brockmeier & U Fehl, Vandenhoeck & Ruprecht, Göttingen, pp. 741–807.

Göler von Ravensburg, N 2007b, 'Ideen und Traditionen im neuzeitlichen Europa' in *Volkswirtschaftliche Theorie der Kooperation in Genossenschaften*, eds T Brockmeier & U Fehl, Vandenhoeck & Ruprecht, Göttingen, pp. 39–83.

Göler von Ravensburg, N 2011, 'Sozialer Betrieb Sulzbach eG: Ein Experiment der lokalen Ökonomie' in *Solidarität, Flexibilität, Selbsthilfe*, ed Allgeier, M, VS Verlag für Sozialwissenschaften, Wiesbaden, pp. 123–139.

Hanrath, S 2011, 'Selbstbestimmung in Gemeinschaft – Wohnungs- und Sozialgenossenschaften als Zukunftsoption' in *Solidarität, Flexibilität, Selbsthilfe*, ed M Allgeier, VS Verlag für Sozialwissenschaften, Wiesbaden, pp. 121–136.

Hauff, V 1987, *Unsere gemeinsame Zukunft Der Bericht der Weltkommission für Umwelt und Entwicklung. Der Bericht der Weltkommission für Umwelt und Entwicklung*. Brundtland Bericht, Eggenkamp, Greven.

Hettlage, R 1987, *Genossenschaftstheorie und Partizipationsdiskussion*, Vandenhoeck & Ruprecht, Göttingen.

Hinding, B 2002, *Wahrnehmung der globalen Erwärmung und Energiekonsum ,. Eine empirische Untersuchung zur psychischen Verarbeitung von Klimaänderung und ihrer Beziehung zu Mustern des Energiekonsums.* Diss. TU Berlin.

International Cooperative Association 1995, *Values of Cooperatives.* Available from: http://www.ica.coop/coop/principles.html#values.

International Union for Conservation of Nature and Natural Resources., United Nations Environment Programme., World Wildlife Fund., Food and Agriculture Organization of the United Nations. & Unesco. 1980, *World conservation strategy. Living resource conservation for sustainable development,* IUCN, Gland Switzerland.

Jackson, T 2009, *Prosperity without growth? The transition to a sustainable economy*, Economics Commissioner Sustainable Development Commission. Available from: http://www.sd-commission.org.uk/data/files/publications/prosperity_without_growth_report.pdf.

Jeantet, T 2010, *Economie Sociale – eine Alternative zum Kapitalismus.* Aus dem Französischen übersetzt von Hans-H. Münkner, AG-SPAK-Bücher, Neu-Ulm.

Karner, A, Rößl, D & Weismeier-Sammer, D 2010, 'Genossenschaftliche Erfüllung kommunaler Aufgaben in PCP-Modellen: Typen und Determinanten einer erfolgreichen Entwicklung' in *Neue Genossenschaften und innovative Aktionsfelder. Grundlagen und Fallstudien,* eds HH Münkner & G Ringle, Nomos, Baden-Baden, pp. 85–105

Laurinkari, J (ed.) 1990, *Genossenschaftswesen: Lehr- und Handbuch,* Oldenbourg, München.

Münkner, H, *Economie Sociale – eine Alternative zum Kapitalismus.* Beitrag zur Ringvorlesung „Konflikte in Gegenwart und Zukunft" Wintersemester 2010/2011. Available from: http://www.online.uni-marburg.de/isem/WS10_11/docs/es.pdf [13 September 2011].

Münkner, H 2010, 'Gründungsimpulse aus der Novelle zum Genossenschaftsgesetz 2006 und weiterer Reformbedarf – Zwischenbilanz und Perspektiven' in *Neue Genossenschaften und innovative Aktionsfelder. Grundlagen und Fallstudien,* eds Münkner H. & Ringle G, Nomos, Baden-Baden, pp. 37–53.

Münkner, HH & Ringle, G (eds.) 2010, Neue Genossenschaften und innovative Aktionsfelder. Grundlagen und Fallstudien, Nomos, Baden-Baden

Patera, M 1990, 'Genossenschaftliche Förderbilanz Laurinkari, Juhani (Hrsg.): Genossenschaftswesen: Lehr- und Handbuch, München 1990, S. 285–301.' in *Genossenschaftswesen: Lehr- und Handbuch,* ed Laurinkari, J Oldenbourg, München.

Pleister, C (ed.) 2001, *Genossenschaften zwischen Idee und Markt. Ein Unternehmenskonzept für die Zukunft?*, Campus-Verl., Frankfurt

Schädel, C 2000, *Humanvermögensbildung durch Genossenschaften. Einzel- und gesamtwirtschaftliche Betrachtung,* Vandenhoeck & Ruprecht, Göttingen.

Schauer, T, Weiler, R & Schaubacher, D (eds.) 2006, *Civil Society Monitoring the EU-Strategy for Sustainable Development: From Commenting to Shared Ownership,* protext, Bonn.

Stappel, M 2010, 'Neugründungen von Genossenschaften in den Jahren 2000–2008' in *Neue Genossenschaften und innovative Aktionsfelder. Grundlagen und Fallstudien*, ed HHuRG Münkner, Nomos, Baden-Baden, pp. 67–81.

Stern, P & Dietz, T 1993, 'Value orientations, gender and environmental concern', *environment a behaviour*, no. 43, pp. 269–302

United Nations General Assembly, *Die Rolle der Genossenschaften in der sozialen Entwicklung. Resolution der Generalversammlung der Vereinten Nationen.* A/RES/64/136. Available from: http://www.unesco.ch/fileadmin/documents/pdf/resolutions/ares64136de.pdf.

Vogt, W 2011, *Genossenschaften – eine andere Form des Wirtschaftens. ein Reader der Parlamentarischen Linken in der SPD Bundestagsfraktion.* Available from: http://www.parlamentarische-linke.de/fileadmin/Texte/2011/Reader_Genossenschaften_final.pdf.

Volz, R 2010, 'Stand und Entwicklungsmöglichkeiten von Bürgerenergiegenossenschaften in Deutschland' in *Aktuelle theoretische und empirische Beiträge zur Genossenschafts- und Kooperationsforschung*. Veröffentlichungen der Forschungsstelle für Genossenschaftswesen an der Universität Hohenheim 29, ed R Doluschitz, Stuttgart, pp. 37–65

Wade, R 1988, Village republics – Economics Conditions for Collective Action in south India, University Press, Cambridge.

Walk, H 2008, *Partizipative Governance. Beteiligungsformen und Beteiligungsrechte im Mehrebenensystem der Klimapolitik*, VS Verlag für Sozialwissenschaften, Wiesbaden.

World Commission on Environment and Development 1987, *Our Common Future. Report of the World Commission on Environment and Development.* Transmitted to the General Assembly as an Annex to document A/42/427, UN. Available from: http://www.un-documents.net/wced-ocf.htm.

C. CASES IN COLLABORATION BETWEEN CIVIL SOCIETY AND SCIENCE

Democratic culture for sustainable development in Slovenia: Outcome of a European action research project involving CSOs and researchers for sustainability

Milena Marega, Andrej Klemenc, Mateja Sepec, Gilles Heriard Dubreuil, Stephane Baudé, Matthieu Ollagnon

The European research project Civil Society for Sustainability (CSS) has been developed from 2009 to 2011 with the aim of linking civil society with research activities on sustainable development issues. The project relied on three partnerships (or "tandems") between one civil society organisation (CSO) and one research organisation. The present paper focuses on one of the three tandems, formed by the Slovenian office of the Regional Environmental Centre for Central and Eastern Europe (REC) and Mutadis, a French research group specialised in governance of sustainable development and hazardous activities.

From the initial phase of joint review of REC history, context and methods of work, the concept of *democratic culture* has been identified by Mutadis and REC as a subject of interest for both a research and an operational point of view in the framework of the CSS project. This concept proceeds from the idea that democracy is grounding on both democratic institutions and rules in order to produce legitimate decisions on the one hand and, in the other hand, on citizen's capacity and experience to address and influence "public affairs" and to build relations and networks in this perspective. Whereas "participatory processes" have more to do with reinforcing legitimacy and quality of decisions, democratic culture refers to the capacity of people to investigate autonomously "public affairs" and to develop their influence as a result of their own will. In this perspective, democratic culture focuses on the activity of persons and on quality of societal bonds rather than on procedures and institutions. The development of a White Paper on "Democratic Culture and Sustainable Development in Slovenia" has been chosen by the tandem as a pilot project to test cooperation mechanisms.

A participatory process has been developed by the Regional Environmental Centre (CSO) with the support of Mutadis within the CSS European action research project in order to investigate the need for democratic culture in the Slovenian context as an intrinsic dimension of sustainable development, in the perspective opened by the Aarhus convention. This process gathered various Slovenian actors (public and private actors, national and local, CSOs, lay citizens, economic operators, etc). It aimed to investigate strategies and means in order to create favourable conditions for its development in Slovenia and addresses each target group's contribution to democratic culture (CSOs and citizens engaged in civil initiatives, public authorities at local, regional and national level, experts and enterprises). This process has produced a White Paper on "Democratic Culture and Sustainable Development in Slovenia" in order to catalyse concrete project and initiatives which will contribute to develop democratic culture in Slovenia.

In the first part, we will describe the cooperation developed between REC and Mutadis as a tandem in the framework of the CSS project. The cooperation has been built in two phases: an exploratory phase, in which the two organisations have sought objects and modalities of cooperation which could be relevant and meaningful from the perspective of both a research organisation and the one of a CSO with strategic objectives. The second phase has been the development of a joint project i.e. the White Paper on Democratic Culture and Sustainable Development. In the second part, we will present the content of the White Paper, which has a two sided value for the REC/Mutadis tandem: an operational tool for developing future projects from the CSO point of view and a conceptual work on the notion of democratic culture from the research point of view.

The tandem of a CSO and a research organisation: building new hybrid objects of cooperation

The Regional Environmental Center for Central and Eastern Europe (REC) is an international organisation established in 1990 by the United States, the European Commission and Hungary with a mission to assist in solving environmental problems. It fulfils this mission by promoting cooperation among governments, non-governmental organisations, businesses and other environmental stakeholders, and by supporting the free exchange of information and public participation in environmental decision-making. The REC has its head office in Hungary and has offices in 17 central and eastern European countries, including Slovenia. The REC actively participates in global, regional and local processes and contributes to environmental and sustainability solutions within and beyond its country office network, transferring knowledge and experience to countries and regions. In the framework of the CSS project, REC Slovenia, which main direction of work is to encourage public participation in environmental decision making, has formed a tandem with Mutadis.

Mutadis is an independent French research group focussed on governance of activities involving risks and impact for health and the environment (e.g. nuclear energy, nuclear waste management, nanotechnologies but also more traditional activities like agriculture or forest management). It gathers specialists from various fields (social and political sciences, administration and science) and has a significant expertise in the fields of cooperative research. Its values are oriented towards a greater engagement of citizens into public affairs. In this perspective, Mutadis has developed various partnerships and projects with French and European NGOs and with national or European public institutions. At the beginning of the CSS project, Mutadis and REC Slovenia had previous experience of cooperation in the framework of European projects. Contrarily to the two other tandems of the CSS project, the Mutadis/REC tandem in the CSS project involves institutions from two different member states.

Cooperation between the two organisations developed through three different steps. The first one was a review of the REC's history, strategies, and activities and the identification of subjects of common interest to be investigated by the tandem. The second and third step involved cooperation on two concrete pilot projects: a participatory process of spatial planning developed by REC and the development of a White Paper on "Democratic Culture and Sustainable Development in Slovenia".

Identifying common objects of cooperation

The cooperation between REC Slovenia and Mutadis started with a historical review of the REC's activities since its foundation in order to assessing its contribution to sustainable development and its institutional sustainability. This included revisiting its main goals and stakes and structures and reviewing its main evolutions since its creation. This also included an extensive review of the REC's projects, back falls, successes and capitalised knowledge and skills since its creation. In addition, Mutadis performed interviews of key partners of REC Slovenia from CSOs and from the public sector, in order to identify the key stakes regarding public participation to environmental decisions in the Slovenian context. The two organisations then analysed this material in order to identify research areas and problems met by REC Slovenia to be investigated by the tandem. This analysis focused on the specific context of each partner CSO with special emphasis on their views on their role and on the problems they meet in contributing to the sustainability of development in Slovenia. As a result, REC Slovenia and Mutadis identified three issues or "research gaps" to investigate.

First "research gap": development of public participation policies in Slovenia

The first "research gap" was linked to the development of public participation policies in Slovenia. A pilot project was identified by the tandem in relation with this first topic: the design of a participatory procedure for a regional road infrastructure planning in the Mežica Valley, for which a mandate has been given to the REC by the Slovenian Ministries of Environment and Spatial Planning. Related to this process, the research topic identified by the REC and Mutadis was: how to ensure actual co-construction of decision framing by institutional decision makers and civil society organisations engaged in the participatory process? In effect, public participation processes are often initiated in relation to the action of a specific actor (government, industry ...), which frames the issue at stake in the process. This issue may then appear as specifically sized according to the preferences of the institutional decision maker. A key stake here is to include into the participation process itself time and opportunities to reframe the issue at stake in order to keep and enhance the common dimension of the process. This is in particular true for the delimitation of the territorial entities to be considered in a specific participatory process.

Second "research gap": sustainability of the REC as a CSO

The second "research gap" was linked with the sustainability of REC Slovenia itself and with the economic model attached to its goals and activities. In effect, the REC is a specific kind of organization: born as a branch of an international intergovernmental organization, it has built its identity in Slovenia in the context of the integration of former communist countries in the European Union and benefited from large funding and network from REC headquarters. The achievement of the process of integration of Slovenia into the European Union changed this context for the REC with a decreasing international funding since 2004. In this context, REC Slovenia faces three challenges: addressing issues of concern for the Slovenian society in order to be considered as a relevant partner, keeping its reputation and credibility as a reliable actor environmental field and preserving its integrity regarding its values and history.

Third "research gap": conditions and means for the development of democratic culture in Slovenia

Eventually, interviews conducted in Slovenia by Mutadis led the REC and Mutadis to identify that a major issue regarding the contribution of the CSO to sustainable development is related to the building of a democratic culture, which was identified as a third "research gap". The concept of *democratic culture* is based on the idea that citizens can contribute to sustainable development not only by adapting their behaviour, habits and practices, but also by engaging into participatory processes in order to influence institutional public or private decision-making processes. In this perspective, citizens are also expected to bring an autonomous and steady contribution to the framing of public affairs through vigilance, information building and spreading, and engagement into new patterns of governance of complex sustainable development issues. This picture relies on an active role of civil society as well as on cooperation between citizens and CSOs and institutional actors (e.g. public authorities, local governments, public technical and scientific organisations ...). It involves the existence of means of counter-power (Fung & Wright 2005) of which civil society can take advantage in order to force more powerful actors to take their views into due account in the perspective of the second pillar of the Aarhus Convention. The development of democratic culture is a co-evolution process involving the various categories of concerned actors (and not only citizens). This model has been developed in the TRUSTNET IN ACTION European research project (Hériard Dubreuil, Bandle & Renn 2007, Hériard Dubreuil & Baudé 2008). It includes both the openness of decision-framing and decision-making processes to stakeholders and the development of autonomous self-organisation capacities of civil society. These self-organisation capacities are not limited to traditional advocacy of a determined cause or defence of private or sectorial interests but include the capacity to interact with different public and private actors and contribute to the definition and implementation of the common good. In this perspective, democracy is a dynamic equilibrium that results from continuous interactions of society with institutions.

Democratic culture fits into a perspective of *constructive democracy* (Lavelle et al. 2011), in which inclusive governance of public affairs supposes continuous forms of interactions, be they cooperative or conflicting (Simmel 1995), between civil society and institutionalised actors. Public affairs in the perspective introduced by John Dewey (Dewey 1927), does not refer to issues that are dealt with by public authorities. As opposed to private activities, public activities are the activities that impact other categories of people (namely the public) than the ones that undertake the activity for their own benefit. Whereas an activity of stamp collecting for instance would be regarded as a private, a nuclear power plant would typically be regarded as a public activity. As underlined by Joëlle Zask (Zask 2000), the social inquiry in the perspective of Dewey is the result of the public (the affected or potentially affected people) investigations in order to identify their stakes and interests regarding the public activity while developing strategies and actions in order to recover some kind of control or influence on the activity and to make their views and concerns taken into account.

The Mežica Valley participatory spatial planning project

The REC, together with two other organisations, had received mandate from the Slovenian Ministries of Environment and of Spatial Planning to design a participatory procedure for spatial planning and to test it in a regional road infrastructure planning process in the Mežica Valley. Mutadis and REC developed a self-evaluation tool (questionnaire) for the participants to assess the quality of the process all along its duration. The questionnaire focused on themes linked with the first two research gaps: capacity of the process to address actual relevant stakes from the stakeholders' perspective; capacity of the participants to influence the framing and sizing of the process (notably the sizing of the territorial entities concerned by the planning process) and integrate new dimensions and stakes into the process; access to technical expertise; consequences of the process beyond the spatial planning decisions; impact of the project on the REC's reputation and credibility. It was decided to implement this self-evaluation tool all along the duration of the process. At the same time, REC designed and started the implementation of the participatory procedure (from September 2010 to January 2011). However, it appeared very soon that this process raised some scepticism among the population. Moreover, after the kick-off, the institutional side seemed to try to delay the process to an indeterminate horizon.

In this context, confronted with a complex and blocked situation, REC expressed the need to explore new strategies in order to contribute to more global changes of its social and strategic environment in the perspective of sustainable development.

Drawing lessons from the Mežica Valley project and rethinking the cooperation within the tande

Discussions between REC Slovenia and Mutadis showed that addressing this very issue required to re-evaluate the content of the cooperation within the tandem. The partners considered a possible option that would be to investigate the question of democratic culture as a part of sustainable development in the framework of a REC promotion campaign in Slovenia, and to involve some CSOs in its elaboration. This was the purpose of a second pilot project, which included the organisation of a conference on "Sustainable development and democratic culture" and the participatory development of a Slovenian White Paper on this issue.

Cooperation within the tandem was developed on a different ground than in the Mežica Valley project, with a concern of deepening the common dimension of the project. In effect, the Mežica Valley process was the subject of a contract between REC Slovenia and the Ministry of Environment and Spatial Planning, which did not involve Mutadis. REC and Mutadis were therefore contributing to the project on an unequal standing, as REC was responsible for the implementation of the project while Mutadis' role was to support REC Slovenia in the evaluation of its experience in the project along its development. Moreover, the Mežica Valley process mainly relied on the REC's core competences as facilitator of participatory decision-making processes. Mutadis was therefore sometimes in the position of providing external elements of evaluation, which could be perceived as some interference with the main process.

Consequently, a key stake in latter stages of cooperation has been to avoid a relational situation where each of the tandem members was in position to give assessment on matters belonging to the core identity of the other partner. Concretely, this entailed for researchers contributing in another way than evaluation or "top-down" expertise and, for CSO member to invest in an object that had some distance with operational constraints. This type of common epistemological space, where the partners were provisionally freed from their identity pressures was called a "third room". This could constitute a ground for further thoughts on cooperation modalities between research and civil society actors.

Participatory development of a White Paper on "Democratic Culture and Sustainable Development in Slovenia"

Common analysis of the experience of cooperation on the Mežica Valley process has led the tandem to the conclusion that a new pilot project should be co-developed from the start by the two organisations. This allowed identifying a new object of cooperation, relevant both from the REC's operational perspective and from Mutadis' research perspective. This object (the conference and the White Paper) differed from the mainstream activity of both organisations, which facilitated a common ownership of the new object of cooperation and a good articulation of the competences of both organisations. In this process, Mutadis provided conceptual background and case studies while REC Slovenia provided its analysis of the Slovenian context of CSOs while involving various Slovenian stakeholders and feeding the process with various practical experiences of CSO engagement in sustainable development in Slovenia. The architecture of the conference and of the White paper was co-developed by both organisations.

From February to September 2011, REC Slovenia and Mutadis developed together a participatory process within the framework of the CSS project in order to investigate the need for democratic culture in the Slovenian context as an intrinsic dimension of sustainable development. This process gathered various Slovenian actors (public and private actors at the national and local level, CSOs, Citizens, economic operators, etc). It aimed to investigate strategies and means in order to create favourable conditions for its development in Slovenia and addressed each target group's contribution to democratic culture (CSOs and citizens engaged in civil initiatives, public authorities at local, regional and national level, experts and enterprises). The final outcome of this process is a White Paper on "Democratic Culture and Sustainable Development in Slovenia"[42], which will be presented in the following section of the present article. This White Paper was developed not only as a diagnosis of the Slovenian situation but also as a practical tool to catalyse concrete projects and initiatives which will contribute to develop democratic culture in Slovenia.

The White Paper was developed using a collaborative drafting process involving various stakeholders. The first step of this process was the conference "Strengthening Participatory Culture in Slovenia" organised on 3rd February 2011 in Ljubljana. This conference gathered representatives of CSO and civil initiatives, governmental bodies, local authorities and enterprises to discuss the state of the art and experience with public engagement, the conditions and means for public engagement to become permanent and the conditions for effective participatory development of society. The conference addressed three main topics: the state of the art of Slovenian experience in public participation, the conditions and means for public participation to become permanent, and the ways to ensure conditions for effective participatory development of society and the conditions for its continued existence. The conference involved conceptual presentations on democratic culture and various case studies on Slovenian and European processes of civil society engagement in sustainable development issues.

On the basis of the outcomes of this conference, a first draft of the White paper has been produced, under the form of questions to be debated during two workshops organised in June and July with experts in the field of public participation in sustainable development in Slovenia and representatives of

---

[42] At the time of redaction of the current article, the White Paper is under finalisation. It will be presented in November during a meeting organised by REC Slovenia with the support of the National Council of Slovenia (second chamber of the Slovenian Parliament).

CSO, business organisations as well as national and local authorities active in the field of sustainable development.

The White Paper on Democratic Culture and Sustainable Development

The issues addressed in the White Paper are organised into three distinct parts. As democratic culture is the result of a history and experience of democracy in each country, the first part addresses the specific historical background of Slovenia regarding civil society engagement in public affairs. The second part identifies key democratic challenges for sustainable development in Slovenia and proposes a diagnosis of the needs for meeting these challenges. The third part of the White Paper refers to the conditions and means for creating a favourable systemic environment for the development of democratic culture in Slovenia: what is required and who can contribute to this development. It addresses four particular dimensions of democratic culture development: access of civil society and CSOs to expertise, strategies, organisations and economic models of CSOs, contribution of public authorities to the development of democratic culture, enterprises and business contribution to the development of democratic culture as a contribution to their global performance and corporate social responsibility.

The Slovenian historical background as regards civil society engagement in public affairs

In order to understand present situation regarding civil society engagement in public affairs one needs to take into consideration specificities of transition from the Yugoslavian communist regime to the current form of liberal parliamentary democracy and European Union member state. Historians and political scientist characterise this evolution as "soft transition" both from "self-managing market economy" to "liberalised opened market economy" and from "self-management form of communist rule" to "parliamentary form of political rule".

Development of "new social movements" in Yugoslavian post-Tito communist regime

In the 1980's post-Tito era, Slovenia entered in a specific political dynamic of engagement of citizens in public affairs with the development of semi-autonomous and semi-formal civil political associations known as "new social movements", which were tolerated and sponsored by State institutions. About 20,000 associations in all fields of social life (sports, culture, health and social care etc.) were registered and integrated within the

"Socialist Alliance of Working People" – a "transmission socio-political organisation" for participatory communist rule in the country. This provided a vivid dynamics of emancipation of public society and of civil society engagement in policy making.

Some of those associations started to organise and defend stakes, in particular in the environmental field, opposing the goals and strategies of authorities regarding development. Opposition of associations within the Yugoslavian framework of "self-management pluralism of interests" entailed the development of "wild" forms of participation, mainly from students who were inspired by contemporary green movements in Western Europe. These "wild" forms of participation started public actions against environmental polluters and projects related to expansion of large power plants and intensive energy industries as well as against the "military-industrial lobby". In this context, activities with environmental impact (notably energy), as well as military affairs, were marked by uncertain and open ended decision making processes. Parallel to these developments, claims of dissidents for basic human rights arose, including the right to freely assemble and speak in public (Knep & Fink-Hafner 2011).

Transition to parliamentary democracy and adhesion to the European Union

At the end of the 1980's, the League of Communists of Slovenia (Slovenian communist party) entered dialogue and negotiations with dissidents for transition to parliamentary democracy. New proto-political parties were established from leaders of different environmental movements and civil initiatives. A coalition of newly established parties, Demos, won the first legislative election[43] against political parties formed on the basis of the

---

[43] The election was hold for three-chamber Assembly of The Socialist Republic of Slovenia constituted from the Socio-political Chamber, the Chamber of Municipalities and the Chamber of Labour. Only for the first Chamber the election was hold based on proportional electorate principle and with clearly recognisable party candidates. In other two Chambers, the election was based on the majority principle and with not fully recognisable partisanship to political parties. Therefore it was not directly transparent which of the political parties won since the alliances within Socio Political Chamber were not identical to those in other two chambers. Although reformed communists and socialist youth placed 1st and 2nd within Socio-Political Chamber they did not achieve relative majority and Demos as a coalition managed to achieve the dominant influence within the Assembly. After the election the competition between the "new" and "old" parties was significantly reduced due to challenges that were demanding overall national political consensus: establishment of parliamentary

socio-political organisations of the former regime[44]. However, because of this dynamics of "soft transition" and their left-winded ideology, neither the new political party Greens of Slovenia nor environmental civil society movements and civil initiatives supported attempts to transform Demos into a strong "anti-communist" political party[45]. In this context the reformed League of Communist of Slovenia maintained its legitimacy, as well as its relations with the majority of CSOs established prior to change of political regime. Reformist former leader of League of Communist of Slovenia Milan Kučan was elected for the President of Slovenia by the Parliament (Ferfila & Philip 2010, Fink-Hafner 1992).

Despite the important role played by civil society in this "soft transition" and in the emergence of establishment of non-governmental organisations independent from political parties, participatory democracy has been denounced as "communist nostalgia" by the dominant political discourse in the country in the beginning of the 1990s. Regardless to their ideology or origin, political parties successfully established a monopoly of the form of the political party in the political field and the dominance of political parties in policy making. At the same time, in order to reinforce their political influence, most of the new political parties started either to design pragmatic alliances with traditional corporative organisations of civil society[46] (Fink-Hafner 1996) or to create new civil society organisations supporting their political orientations. As a consequence, CSOs that rejected these forms of "neo-corporative" relationship with political parties (Tomšič 2008, Lukšič, I 1992) lacked public support, in particular in terms of funding (Lukšič, A 1998). In this context, much of the support to CSOs in the 1990s came from the USA or foreign foundations. From 1998, with the opening of

---

institutional order and assurance of independence and international recognition of the country.

[44] The League of Communists of Slovenia reformed into The Party of Social-democratic Renewal that merged in 1993 with some small non-parliamentary parties into The United List of Social Democrats (renamed as Social Democrats in 2005). Socialist Alliance of Working People reformed in Socialist Party that merged in 1993 into the United List of Social Democrats. Socialist Youth reformed into Liberal Democracy of Slovenia.

[45] After achieving independence and international recognition of Republic of Slovenia in 1992, Demos dissolved into number of small parties. From Socialist Youth of Slovenia originated Liberal Democracy of Slovenia under the chairmanship of Mr. Janez Drnovšek, which ruled the country in coalition with reformed communists and one or the other ex Demos party till 2004 – interrupted only by short intermediate governance of ex Demos parties during the political crisis in 2002.

[46] e.g. Roman-Catholic Church, trade unions, Chamber of industry, Chamber of farmers …

adhesion negotiations between Slovenia and the European Union – especially from 2002, when Slovenia was proclaimed as a developed country by the OECD – these sources of funding decreased and European Union integration process provided new sources of funding for CSOs, in particular in the environmental field.

CSOs in the field of environment followed the general above-described trends. In the beginning of 1990s, many "new social movements" based environmental initiative turned into NGOs, with the support of western European and American organisations. In the first decade of the new millennium, most of environmental NGOs, lacking public support to serve as vehicles for public participation, turned into promotion of the EU, its principles and environmental, climate and energy policies. They played the role of public participation vehicles and "watchdogs" in regard to transposition of EU policies into national legislation. However, in the specific Slovenian context as regards public participation and development of CSOs, environmental NGOs are recognised as partners and contributors to the quality of public decisions only nominally since the national funds for public participation are very limited[47]. In this context, some NGOs managed to access to European funds as partners in EU projects.

After Slovenian accession to the EU in 2004, environmental NGOs lost to a great extent their role to represent civil society in environmental conflicts, at very first on local level. Number of new civil initiatives and some new NGOs emerged, predominately focused on challenging polluting industrial practices and larger infrastructural projects (roads, wind farms, high voltage electric grids, low quality coal power plants etc.). Consensus oriented local partnership arrangements have been replaced to a great extent by media campaigning in combination with the use of legal tools of environmental protection and of innovative forms of civil disobedience. To get expert legitimisation of their claims, they rely on ad hoc solutions, primarily based on identification and exposition of contradictions of official expertise and on reputation of single experts that support their cause (Lukšič, A 2005).

---

[47] Parallel to and after the process of Aarhus Convention ratification environmental NGOs and Ministry of Environment engaged in process of "Environmental Partnership" that resulted with agreement aiming to provide support to NGOs in public participation in environmental matters. However the process did not result in significant improvement of funding and treatment of NGOs in environmental decision making. Nevertheless compared to cooperation with other relevant ministries (economy, transport, regional development) the cooperation with Ministry of Environment improved at very first at consultancy level on legislation and policy.

This historical background is characterised by some degree of distrust regarding the issue of public participation, by limited access of CSOs to the funds and expertise that would allow effective public participation and by the lack of articulation between public policy making and civil society. The reflection on democratic culture initiated through the White Paper is of particular relevance in this context. In effect, this concept grasps both the institutional issue of structuring public participation and the socio-political issue of the emergence of an autonomous, sustainable and influential civil society sector. This sector notably contributes to sustainable development by supporting citizens' capacity to address and investigate public affairs in an autonomous way and develop influence on public policies and institutions.

The state of experience of civil society engagement in public affairs

After situating the historical background, the White Paper establishes a diagnosis on the current context regarding civil society engagement in public affairs in Slovenia in the field of sustainable development. This diagnosis has been developed by a working group composed of CSO representatives and social scientists on the basis of a set of questions developed in common by REC Slovenia and Mutadis. The outcomes of the discussions of the working group are presented hereunder, organised following the different themes addressed by the questionnaire.

Civil society and CSOs influence on public decision-making processes?

In the fields of environmental and nature protection the civil society and environmental NGOs in general have an influence in Slovenia. However, this influence is mostly limited to blocking or impeding decisions they oppose, while the capacity of environment-related CSOs to propose and promote self-affirmative actions is weak.

This oppositional standing stems both from the radical character of CSO's alternative proposal, but also from a situation of "media trap". In effect, Slovenian media tend to report CSO actions only if they oppose the decision of public authorities or of private or public investors. However, CSOs depend on the media to expose either procedural mistakes or to raise awareness on negative consequences of the considered project or option: environmental or health risks and/or possible taxpayer money losses.

In the Slovenian context, formal participatory procedures do not appear as actual opportunities to influence decisions. One the one hand, CSOs and civil initiatives lack skills and resources to effectively engage equitably in highly complex and timely formal decision making procedures. On the other hand, most public authorities in the Slovenian context consider that formal processes of societal participation are to achieve legitimacy of decisions which have been in most cases already made within a non-formal decision making arena of key stakeholders who have a privileged access to information and expertise. The participatory procedures are in many cases used as a tool for providing advantage to those groups.

This context does not therefore favour a constructive inclusion of new actors (CSOs) in the decision-making processes. CSOs and civil society have therefore limited opportunities for contributing to the reframing of the rationales and values on which ground the decision-making processes.

Respective roles of citizens and CSOs in sustainable development

Within a dominant political and media discourse, citizens are seen as people pursuing their individual interests and are recognised as contributors to the common good essentially in charity contexts. In practice, their degree of engagement in public issues depends on their degree of proximity to the issue. On issues of more abstract level (or upper levels of decision) which have no direct immediate (visible) impact on the citizen's everyday life, there is usually little citizen engagement even in cases in which views and statements of CSO are backed by prominent experts and get media coverage. However, when people are directly affected they form in most cases a civil initiative.

Whereas environmental NGOs are usually recognised as actors following and promoting common good, this does however not fit to the reality of the civil initiatives, which most often have difficulties to develop the stakes they defend beyond their narrow interest (or difficulties to make explicit their disagreement regarding the way general interest is framed by more powerful stakeholders). Moreover, civil initiatives generally have difficulties to back their demands by either providing strong evidence on violation of legal and/or administrative procedures or by providing strong evidence then an alternative solutions might better fit public interest. They therefore try in most cases to create alliance with CSOs that will support their claims but they very scarcely seek to establish links with CSOs that could broaden their perspective or independently mediate between them and the investor and/or public authorities. Conversely, CSOs and self-affirmative actions that provide mediation and capacity building are still rather the exception than the rule.

Economic models of CSOs

Economic models of Slovenian CSOs usually combine membership fees, national and international grants, donations and sponsorships. In most cases, membership fees provide very marginal source of revenues given the small number of members and supporters. National grants are scarce and in most cases of very limited amount. Fund raising as a result of media campaign is only recently started in Slovenia as core funding for some NGOs or as the main source of funding for a certain action. Expertise is a relevant source of revenues for NGOs essentially in the field of nature protection, whereas information and media services are usually offered for free based on grants which have been obtained for those purposes. Because of the small size of the Slovenian market for any kind of services, no CSO can manage to survive on the exclusive basis of its expertise and services in relation to sustainable development. CSOs either need to develop, more commercial services or to assure other forms of revenues, at very first sponsorship or international grant. However, this presents a risk of dependence on sponsors, of diversion from the CSOs core missions or of degradation of their image (in the case of the development of commercial services). Strong engagement in EU co-funded projects demanding heavy administrative duties might also result in loosing focus of the mission of organisations and/or weakening of the capacities for being engaged in public participation processes within the country.

Access of civil society to expertise

An important resource for CSOs is the access to expertise. Since mid-1990s, environmental CSO have had considerable opportunities to raise their skills and knowledge through capacity building programmes of regional (e.g. the European Commission or the REC) or foreign organisations supporting the development of civil society and CSO. It also took the form of grants given to some CSOs for their project of raising skills and knowledge of NGOs in different fields relevant for public participation. A considerable number of NGO activists attended trainings on campaigning, fund raising, use of information and communication technologies ... Since 2004, CNVOS (Centre for Information Service, Co-operation and Development of NGOs) and PIC (Legal Information Centre) regularly offer trainings on basic technical, legal and communication skills for CSOs.

However, due to their unstable financial situation and/or weak institutionalisations a lot of the skills are lost or cannot be adequately used.

Access of CSOs to scientific expertise is also very restricted for financial reasons (notably the nearly absence of public funding for counter-expertise) or because of the lack of diversification of expertise sources due to the size of the country.

Relationship between business and civil society in the field of sustainable development

As private decisions from business obviously impact sustainable development, interactions between firms and civil society have been addressed. In context in which "green consumerism" have also made roots in the recent decade, some Slovenian companies showed interest for forms of cooperation with CSOs. However, this trend faces two types of difficulties. The first one is the reluctance of most CSOs either because of incompatibility of these forms of cooperation with radical positions or because of a lack of capacities to assess the proposed cooperation and to distinguish between "greenwashing" and actual improvement of companies and/or consumer behaviour. The understanding of the nature of a "partnership" also differs among companies. Some companies consider it as a way to avoid critical standings from the partner CSOs on their overall business activities while other companies are much more in favour of an open relation of exchange on specific common activities, which does not mean that the partner CSOs should keep silent about all other aspects of their activities. Active participation of CSO in reframing the goals and activities of industrial and trade companies in spite of some attempts has not make ground yet.

Systemic nature of the democratic culture development

This diagnosis shows that the development of democratic culture in Slovenia is not only a matter of evolution of the legal and institutional context, but also requires co-evolution of different types of actors – notably public authorities, business, expert institutions, together with lay citizens and CSOs – towards more inclusive modes of governance and more cooperative relationships. It also entails shift from a focus on public authorities towards more self-affirmative strategies of civil society and CSOs regarding sustainable development. Change towards more sustainable patterns of development as a result of the spreading of democratic culture is therefore of a systemic nature.

The creation of a favourable environment for developing democratic culture

Building on the above-exposed diagnosis, the White Paper identifies four fields of action to create a favourable environment for democratic culture, each one linked to one of the four types of actors concerned by the diagnosis: technical and scientific expertise institutions, CSOs, public authorities and enterprises.

Development of societal capacities & competences, access to expertise and openness of public and private expertise to society

In the perspective developed in the White Paper, expertise is seen as a procedure preparing public decisions. This procedure is often delegated to individual experts but also to groups of experts usually connected or linked with some categories of stakeholders, albeit in various manners. In some very conflicting environmental contexts (such as post-uranium mining in the south of France) public authorities have created "Pluralist Expertise Groups" (gathering experts with a scientific background representing the various stakeholder values involved and notably scientific from CSOs) in order to prepare public decisions. A key stake regarding expertise is the extent to which the result is (or not) entrusted by the various stakeholders.

Expertise is involving three complementary aspects. The first one is the gathering of the existing reliable scientific knowledge and the identification of uncertainties and gaps of knowledge – some of them may be irreducible such as in the case of very long term decisions of radioactive waste management for instance. The second aspect is to incorporate key values that would lead choices and the selection of proposed options. The last key aspect is to incorporate not only scientific knowledge but also the one of directly concerned people living for instance in the concerned area, which is of particular importance for environmental or public health decisions. In other words, expertise is never a scientific exercise although it should ground on robust scientific knowledge and methods.

Regarding social trust vis-à-vis the expertise, it is observed that most of the time, individual experts are not entrusted for they do not take on board the values of the various stakeholders – or even worse the expertise is presented as "scientific", denying therefore its political and ethical dimension. This is why the access of civil society to expertise is an important issue, which is not limited to accessing the result of expertise processes but also includes rethinking the role of civil society actors in the whole expertise process, from the early framing of the question posed to experts to the final dissemination of results, through the design of the process and contribution to modelling and data collection. This could encompass the development of autonomous societal expertise with appropriate resources altogether with societal access to public sources of expertise. These public sources of expertise are expected to have a certain level of independence vis-à-vis the economic operators although it is noted that it is scarcely observed that lay citizens have an actual and detailed access to the expertise developed by public authorities to support their decisions.

Opposition, evaluation, partnerships, mediation ... what strategies and organisation for CSOs to contribute to sustainable development?

At international level as well as in many national, regional and local contexts, CSOs are recognized as a key player in sustainable development and play a wide variety of roles such as raising public awareness on emerging environmental or social issues (e.g. nanotechnologies, shale gas), campaigning to promote sustainable behaviours or to denounce unsustainable behaviours, evaluating organisations or States, developing their own expertise in their core field of competence, and contributing to the definition of both hard law (laws, decrees, regulations) and soft law (standards, statements, principles, codes of conduct etc.).

Opening governance of issues affecting the three pillars of sustainable development is often seen as a condition and means to improve sustainability. In this regards, one can observe a movement towards inclusion of NGOs into institutional decision making processes, alongside with public authorities, enterprises, workers organisations, researchers and experts, and international or regional organisations. This is often seen by decision makers either as a way to reinforce the quality of decisions or as a means to facilitate their acceptation by society. It can also be considered as a way of reducing the "democratic gap" between public authorities and society in representative democracy. However, some CSOs express frustration regarding the limited influence on final decisions of institutional participatory processes. Moreover, questions can be raised regarding institutionalization of the role of CSOs: does it actually reduces the democratic gap, or does it simply result in incorporating CSOs as another class of representatives? Is this beneficial for CSOs or does it weaken their positions (notably regarding their relations with their constituencies) and, ultimately, their capacity to trigger change towards more sustainable ways of development? Should CSOs contribute to the empowerment and direct engagement of citizens into the public affairs that affect their everyday life rather than becoming themselves a kind of representatives of those affected people (in connection with the above consideration on the interaction of CSOs and civil initiatives)?

A key issue in the contribution of CSOs to sustainable development is their capacity to trigger or facilitate systemic change: a permanent evolution in the way people, organisations and society as a whole act and interact, with positive effects on sustainability. In this perspective, strategies, roles, organisation and economic models of CSOs can be considered regarding their capacity to catalyse this systemic change. In which extent and how do CSOs engage in the system they try to change? How do actions developed by CSOs as well as processes they take part in articulate in a longer-term process of change? Do they try to defend a model through communication, campaigning and lobbying or do they favour co-evolution of different actors, thus assuming a role of mediation and facilitation?

The possible contribution of public authorities to the development of democratic culture

The concept of democratic culture refers both to the openness of decision-framing and decision-making processes to stakeholders and to the development of autonomous self-organisation capacities of civil society. These self-organisation capacities are not limited to traditional advocacy of a determined cause or defence of private or sectoral interests but include the capacity to interact with different public and private actors and contribute to the definition and implementation of common good (notably as regards integration of long-term and intergenerational perspective). In this perspective, self-organisation capacities of civil society can be identified by public decision-makers as a resource for tackling emerging complex issues (e.g. reduction of pesticides, nanotechnologies, climate change).

In effect, democratic culture is therefore the other face of a coin whose first face is the opening of public decision-making process to participation. It determines the quality of civil society contribution to public affairs involving sustainability of development. This contribution is not limited to improving the quality of public decisions and actions (in a weak understanding of improving "acceptability" of decisions or in the stronger sense of reframing issues in a meaningful way for citizens and effectively modifying the outcomes of the decision making process). Civil society is not only an object of public policies; it can also be a subject and an active partner of public authorities, with complementary resources and levers of action.

As a key resource for tackling public affairs, public authorities may wish to catalyse the development of democratic culture – notably for emerging issues for which civil society awareness, competence and engagement may be limited. Facilitating the development of democratic culture however necessitates other tools than the traditional levers used by public authorities to mobilise society: communication, incentives (e.g. tax reductions) and regulations. This drives public authorities to develop (or resort to) new skills of professional facilitation and mediation. This also poses the question of the legitimate and efficient conditions and means for public authorities to catalyse and support self-structuring of civil society without weakening its autonomy.

Business and CSOs: adversaries or partners?

As a result of globalisation and extension of the fields of action of private enterprises (e.g. to sectors initially under State monopoly in Slovenia), private sector and enterprises become actors of public activities for those activities entail consequences for other actors (workers, local communities, professional sectors, etc.) not only in the economic and social field (relations with workers) but also in the societal (e.g. issues of human rights, privacy, access to services, …) and environmental fields.

This situation can in return impact the activities of the enterprises, including its economic performance. For instance, reputation of the enterprise can be affected by campaigns, trials can entail financial penalties, lack of credible ethical values of the enterprise can affect motivation of the employees, trust in the management and therefore can increase the turnover, … Conversely, responsible behaviour can represent a competitive advantage in terms of reputation, attractiveness for both customers and workers, capacity to develop sustainable local projects, etc. Interpenetration between business and non-business spheres therefore tends to intensify.

This understanding of enterprises as societal actors and potential contributors to sustainable development have been increasingly formalised under the concepts of global performance or corporate social responsibility (CSR) which led to the creation of new regulations (legal obligations of firms to report on their social and environmental impacts), normative standards (e.g. ISO 26000 on social responsibility of organisations), codes of conduct (socially responsible investment), societal control activities (e.g. CSR rating agencies, audit agencies, consultancies …), which impact directly the activities of enterprises.

In this context, developing constructive engagement with stakeholders (both at the local and national or international level) should contribute to the global performance of the enterprise. In particular, some enterprises and CSOs have developed new types of cooperation relationships based on the identification of common stakes and interests. For enterprises, CSOs expertise and know-how can constitute a valuable resource for developing their performance regarding their social responsibility and their contribution to sustainable development. For CSOs, favouring evolutions of the conceptual framework of enterprises as well as of their practices can be identified as an efficient way to promote sustainable development, while some (but not all) partnerships also entail contribution of the enterprise to the resources of their organisation.

Conclusion

The form of cooperation developed by the REC office Slovenia and Mutadis has allowed developing a hybrid object that is situated at the frontier of concept exploration and CSO activism. In effect the White Paper on democratic culture stems both from previous research development of Mutadis in the fields of inclusive governance and from the REC's practical experience and knowledge of the Slovenian context as regards sustainable development.

From the point of view of REC, cooperating with a research institution gave the opportunity to take a step back from day to day management and exert some reflexivity both on the organisation's work and strategy and on the national context as regards CSO action in the field of sustainable development. This reflexive thinking has been fuelled by conceptual analysis and foreign experiences from other political and cultural contexts (case studies) brought by Mutadis and allowed to identify the concept of democratic culture as a key object of reflection in the current national context. Besides providing resources in terms of concepts and analysis, cooperation with a research organisation in the particular context of the CSS project provided an arena to address strategies of the REC in the long term, which is usually difficult to address in the normal context of a CSO, which is marked by constant changes and turnover of members and staff.

From the point of view of Mutadis, cooperation with the REC was an opportunity to refine and develop further its conceptual reflection while ensuring practical applicability and effectiveness of the developed tools by linking it closely to the reality of the particular Slovenian situation. It also represented an occasion of testing the validity of the concepts in a social and political context of a new member State of the European Union. Eventually, direct cooperation with a CSO helped grasping the reality of CSO work and constraints in the political and social context of Slovenia.

This cooperation necessitated a process of mutual adaptation of both organisations in the framework of the CSS project to bring the different perspectives, logics and point of views together and finally identify and build a common object. Mutadis had to understand the practical political and social context in which the REC developed its activities while REC had to assimilate the concepts brought in by Mutadis while dealing with its own constraints. This process was not achieved overnight, as underlined by the difficulties encountered by the tandem in a first attempt to cooperate on a project belonging to the usual field of competence of the REC. In effect, in this first attempt, the two organisations had to identify mutually relevant and practically effective roles within the research action format. This has shown that one of the conditions for successful cooperation in a hybrid CSO/Researcher tandem is to step aside from their usual positions and practices to define a hybrid cooperation object that will both serve the purposes of knowledge building of the research organisation and the political objectives of the CSO.

References

Dewey J 1927, 'The Public and Its Problems', New York: Holt, 1927; London: Allen & Unwin, 1927, republished as The Public and Its Problems: An Essay in Political Inquiry, Chicago: Gateway, 1940.

Ferfila, B & Philip, PA 2010, *Slovenia's transition: from medieval roots to the European Union*, Lexington Books

Fink-Hafner, D 1992, 'Political modernization in Slovenia in the 1980s and the early 1990s', *Journal of communist studies*, year 8, no. 4, pp. 210–226.

Fink-Hafner, D 1996, 'Organized interests as policy actors in Slovenia', *Parliaments and organized interest: the second steps*, eds Agh, A & Ilonszki, G, Hungarian Centre for Democracy Studies, Budapest, pp. 222–240.

Fung, A & Wright, EO 2005, 'Le contre-pouvoir dans la démocratie participative et délibérative', *Gestion de proximité et démocratie participative*, eds MH Bacqué, H Rey & Y Sintomer, La découverte, Paris

Hériard Dubreuil, G, Bandle, T & Renn, O (Dir) 2007, *Trustnet In Action (TIA), Final Scientific report*, http://www.trustnetinaction.com/IMG/pdf/TIA-Final_Report.pdf

Hériard Dubreuil, G & Baudé, S 2008, 'Innovative Approaches to Stakeholder Involvement in Risk Governance. Lessons from TRUSTNET IN ACTION European Research Project', *European Risk Governance: Its Science, its Inclusiveness and its Effectiveness*, E. Vos (Ed.), Connex Report Serie, vol. 6, chapter 4

Knep, M & Fink-Hafner, D 2011, 'Key Periods in the Development of Slovenia's Environmental Policy', *The Open Method of Coordination*, Fink-Hafner (ed), Faculty of Social Sciences, pp. 112 – 118

Lavelle S et al. 2011, 'Démocratie constructive et gouvernance de la technique. Les conditions de la gouvernance démocratique dans un processus technique et social complexe : l'exemple du projet européen Cowam-in-Practice dans la gestion des déchets radioactifs', *Gouvernance*, vol. 7, n°2, February 2011, p. 2

Lukišič, A 1998, 'Okoljske nevladne organizacije v Sloveniji : prve portretne poteze' (Environmental NGOs in Slovenia – first sketch), *Teorija in praksa*, year 35, no. 5, pp. 877–894

Lukišič, A 2005, 'Modificiranje in odpiranje okoljskih političnih aren' (Modification and Opening of Environmental Policies Arenas). *Časopis za kritiko znanosti*, year. 33, no. 219, pp. 91–107

Lukišič, I 1992, 'Preoblečeni korporativizem na Slovenskem', *Časopis za kritiko znanosti, domišljijo in novo antropologijo*, year 20; no.148–149, pp. 47–55

Simmel, G 1995, *Le conflit*, trans. S Muller, Ed. Circé, Paris

Tomišič, M 2008, *Elite v tranziciji* (Elites in Transition), Nova Gorica : Fakulteta za uporabne družbene študije, Ljubljana

Zask, J 2000 *L'opinion publique et son double (2 vol.) : Livre II : John Dewey, philosophe du public*. L'Harmattan, Paris

Participatory Action Research for Local Human Rights – The Case of Roma Minority in Szeged, South-Hungary

György Málovics, Barbara Mihók, István Szentistványi, Bálint Balázs, György Pataki

Acknowledgment: The authors would like to acknowledge the contributions to the projects by Györgyi Bela, László Jakab, Elizabeth Lakatos and the two volunteers: Dániel Takács, Szilárd Ledán. Györgyi who provided essential administrative support, while Eliz and Laci were involved in field work and conducting desk research on local human rights issues related to the Roma people in Szeged. We are particularly grateful to our local informants and cooperating partners in Szeged. The work leading to these results has received funding from the European Community's Seventh Framework Programme (FP7/2007–2013) under grant agreement n° 244264 (the PERARES project).

Introduction

There is a growing concern among academics that the vast amount of knowledge accumulated at universities and research institutes is hardly utilized by local communities, particularly the marginalized ones. Consequently, academic institutions hardly fulfill the positive social functions of sharing knowledge with and empowering marginalized social groups in society made possible by their available resources (Bodorkós & Pataki, 2009).

Within the framework of a science-society European project, a research group (Environmental Social Science Research Group, ESSRG) and a civil society organization from Szeged, Hungary (Szeged Group of Protect the Future) joined forces to design and conduct a participatory action research with special focus on local human rights of marginalized groups. The objective of the project is to significantly increase the efficiency in utilizing the research potentials and the accumulated knowledge and other resources of universities and research groups on a local level for the benefit of local communities, particularly marginalized ones. The present paper intends to give account of the on-going research and its preliminary conclusions.

The Problem/Context

Human Rights and Sustainability

Sustainability is primarily a future oriented concept which refers to negative environmental consequences of todays' socioeconomic processes endangering future human well-being over time, i. e. intergenerational equity (see e.g. Bruntland 1987, Hanley 2000). However, it seems similarly important to emphasize that "in our anxiety to protect the future generations, we must not overlook the pressing claims of the less privileged today. A universalist approach cannot ignore the deprived people today in trying to prevent deprivation in the future" (Anand & Sen 2000, p.2030). Consequently, concentrating exclusively on future well-being is clearly an elitist approach in the sense that wide social groups have extremely pressing well-being claims already in our times (see e.g. UNDP 2010).

Securing certain human rights (HRs) of marginalized social groups may have both intrinsic and instrumental value related to sustainability. Intrinsic value appears if present human rights in themselves are related to the notion of sustainability. One can argue that the social pillar of sustainability may be related to human freedoms as Amartya Sen has defined (see Sen 1999). Human rights constitute an important part of human liberties and freedoms, therefore HRs are clearly connected intrinsically to social sustainability. On the other hand, sustainability is also about future well-being. If securing HRs serves as an instrument of future well-being then the concept has an instrumental value regarding sustainability. HRs in the present promote future well-being by contributing either to (1) the capital stock enabling future well-being or (2) to the preservation of environmental resources (protecting natural capital). Sachs (2003) shows how concentrating on basic human rights (subsistence rights) of marginalized resource users globally may contribute to the preservation of environmental resources (capital).

Thus it is reasonable to define sustainability as a notion connected to both present and future human well-being, i. e. both intra- and intergenerational equity and justice. Applying such a definition means that HRs associated with present well-being (intra-generational equity) of marginalized groups are implicitly connected to sustainability (e.g. Hawkins 2010).

The Social Context: the Roma in Szeged

In 1997, the Roma community consisted of 2500–3000 people in Szeged (Rátkai 1997), while based on the interviews conducted the current number is more likely to be 4500–5000. There are two larger segregated areas in the town but the majority of the Roma in Szeged live scattered all around the town (Rátkai 1997). Based on their descent and social situation the Roma population in Szeged shows a rather diverse picture. Because of the high level fluctuation (i. e. people migrating from the countryside and also leaving the city) it is difficult to estimate their number. By the 1980es the majority of the Roma population had legal income from employment while the level of schooling did not increase. After the regime change in 1989–1990 – that brought about a swift decrease in the demand for unskilled labour – members of the Roma population could not find their place in the new job market (Rátkai 1997). Recent research points out that the problems have become significantly greater – for instance, the housing situation of the Roma, a generation after the regime change, returned to its level in 1971 (Dupcsik 2009). The lack of education and professional training is the primary obstacle to employment. In addition, increasing social prejudices also contributed to this employment situation, thus the social welfare system has become the major source of income for Roma as early as in 1997.

Rátkai (1997) also points out the low level of self-organization and political representation of the Roma in Szeged (as elsewhere in the country), and our interviewees confirm the same about the current situation. These problems have only deepened in the upcoming years. The functioning of the Roma Self-Government (RSG) is continuously hindered by the lack of human and financial resources. *"The financial sources available to support the community disappear on various levels of the administration and these initiatives cannot reach our main objective. We need a well thought out education program that would enable us to create a layer of intellectuals in 20–25 years that is a prerequisite for the emergence of a middle class."* – the president of the RSG in Szeged stated in our interview. An effective political representation of Roma would require that all of the representatives in the Szeged Local Assembly considered this as a crucial issue and the RSG had its influence on the decisions – this is however not the case currently.

The Context of the Research Project

The research is conducted within the framework of an EU 7 Research Program under the title, "Public Engagement with Research and Research Engagement with Society" (PERARES). The program is intended to increase the social engagement of scientific research conducted by supporting the long-term cooperation between various research groups and civil society organizations (CSOs). The researchers cooperate with civil organizations in creating research plans and conducting research. By generating and facilitating public debate about issues at the science-society interface, the program helps articulating the research demands of civil society and contributes to the establishment of a science-society dialogue.

Our research is a part of a work package of the PERARES project that intends to provide a common research topic for academic research groups and civil organizations by defining the research agenda about Roma and Traveller communities. Within an international cooperation in the work package we attempt to define new research agendas, trends and problems related to Roma and Traveller communities. There are three research institutions involved in this part of the project (ESSRG, Hungary; Cork University, Ireland; and the University of Tarragona of Catalonia) that join forces with civil organizations (the Szeged Group of Protect the Future; Traveller groups around Cork; and the Federation of Roma Associations in Catalonia) to carry out a joint research about local human rights related to Roma and Traveller communities. Finally, the participants offer their research results about the social segregation of Traveller and Roma communities for a European debate from January 2012, under the title *Forgotten Citizens of Europe*, that provides an online forum for the open debate of esteemed researchers and experts and allows for the effective communication of local human rights issues as well as the active involvement of those concerned in policy making processes (Balázs 2011).

Means and Methods

The Thematic Focus of the Research

The focus of our research is **on one (or more) Roma communities** and the related **human rights in their local context**. We hope that our research allows us to examine the local appearance of certain human rights problems associated with the Roma communities.

Participants of the Research

The research project is basically a cooperative enterprise between an academic group having special expertise on the social aspects of environmental problems and a local group of a national eco-political civil organization involved in environmental justice issues in Hungary. Since the local activists of the civil organization do not consider themselves as legitimate representatives of the interests of the Roma in Szeged, the cooperation is extended from two to three parties. Members of the Roma community are involved as a third party as well as experts familiar with the conditions and the problems of the local Roma population. Thus, one aspect of the cooperation is realized between ESSRG and the Szeged Group of Protect the Future (further referred to as SGPF) in which the research group supports the work of the civil organization by its formerly accumulated knowledge and expertise. The other aspect of the cooperation connects the Szeged group of Védegylet with the members of the community and a group of experts, more or less familiar with the problems of the community. The research and actions described in the following sections were conducted by the SGPF members with the continuous support from ESSRG in terms of project planning, conceptual framework and finances.

Currently there are 6 persons continuously and actively participating in SGPF, three of them are volunteers and three participants work for a modest compensation. The group consists of two college students, one person with a newly obtained master degree, a member of the local government, and two scholars holding a PhD. Five out of the six participants have former experiences in volunteer work and civil activities. By profession, there is a social worker, a politologist, an economist, an ecologist, an IT specialist and a literature teacher among the members of the group. Two members of the group are of Roma descent.

The Research Process

<u>First phase: problem identification and choice of methods</u>

The research started in February 2011 with the forming of the research group and by **studying the professional literature on participatory research**. Those scientific studies that contrasted participatory research with traditional (conventional) forms of research proved to be the most helpful (Cornwall & Jewkes 1995, Chung & Lounsbury 2006). We have observed these characteristics in order to comply with the criteria of participatory research during the entire research process (*Table 1*).

In addition to literature discussing participatory research in a dichotomy of participatory/traditional research, we also studied writings on research methodology, especially in the contexts of **critical communicative methodology** (Gómez et al. 2011, Munté et al. 2011), **means of community engagement** (Egészséges Városok Magyarországi Szövetsége 2004, Tanaka é.n.), and **photovoice** (Zenkov & Harmon 2009, Strack 2004, Streng et al. 2004, Dennis et al. 2009, Castelden et al. 2008, Catani & Minkler 2010). We also devoted attention to **power related problems** emerging in participatory research (Chung & Lounsbury 2006), as well as **ethical challenges** (Minkler 2004).

	Participatory research	Traditional research
What is the objective of the research?	Action	Understanding, possible subsequent actions
For whom is the research conducted?	For the local people	To satisfy institutional, personal and professional interest
Whose knowledge counts?	The local people	Scientists
What influences the choice of topics?	Local priorities	Funding priorities, institutional agendas, professional interests,
What is the main factor in selecting the methodology?	Empowerment, collaborative learning	Disciplinary traditions, "objectivity" and "truth"
Who is involved in research?		
Problem Identification	Local people, researchers	Researchers
Data collection	Local people, researchers	Researchers,
Interpretation	Local concepts and frameworks	Disciplinary concepts and frameworks
Analysis	Local people, researchers	Researchers
Presentation of the results	Locally available and useful	In the researchers community or to the funding agents
The results-based action	Is an essential element	May or may not be taken
Who acts?	Local people, with or without external assistance	External agencies
Who owns the results?	Shared	Researchers
What is the focus of the process?	Process and Outputs	Outputs

Table 1   Participatory and traditional research: a comparison of processes (Cornwall & Jewkes 1995)

Along with literature on participatory research we also started to overview the **Hungarian literature focusing on the Roma population**. We conducted a literature review both offering a national overview (Bodorkós & Szombati 2009, Kóczé 2011, FRA 2010, Rostás & Farkas 2001, Szuhay 1999, Dupcsik 2009, Ladányi & Szelényi 2004) and focusing on local issues (Rátkai 1997, Rátkai & Sümeghy 2001, Boros et al. 2007, Boros 2007).

We started the **field work** simultaneously with our library research. As a first step we created contact with the local Roma community, and started to obtain relatively significant information about their conditions and internal network of relations (to understand their situation in the context of their possibilities). For this reason, we decided to conduct a **semi-structured interview research** (Kvale 2005). The structure of the interview drafted by the SGPF was discussed and commented by the ESSRG members. Before the interviews, those group members without experience were trained. We interviewed about two dozens of people in March and April of 2011. The interviews were made in pairs (sometimes in threes, including at least one experience interviewer) with notes taken that were later recorded in interview summaries of a formerly defined format.

We applied the method of snowball sampling when selecting our data providers and we tried to find people working for or being in an active relationship with the Roma population of Szeged, people with a general understanding about their past and present problems. The range of interviewees includes local Roma leaders, social workers, experts responsible for the field in government institutions, representatives of civil organizations, the leaders of a school integration program, as well as other experts related to the field. Our interviewees also included a few Roma families living in and around one of the segregated areas, but at this phase of the research we made only limited contacts with the Roma families and their community.

We raised and discussed the following topics in the interviews:

Topic 1 The general situation of the Roma population of Szeged (the most crucial problems affecting the lives of Roma families in Szeged, their living conditions and possibilities, etc.).

Topic 2 The situation of those living in the segregated Roma areas of Szeged.

Topic 3 The organizations and the self-organization of the Roma community in Szeged (which organizations have the greatest influence on the lives of the people in the Roma community, is there self-organization within the Roma population).

Topic 4 Anything else that may help us understand more about the situation of the local Roma community.

Second phase: feedback and joint action-planning

In the second phase we processed the available information broken down into thematic groups based on the interviews, and evaluated the data we received in the context of civil rights. We gave account of the findings of the analysis in a short summary (see Results).

We used this summary as an invitation for all of our data providers to a **group discussion (forum)** as the next step suggested by the ESSRG in the discussions regarding the appropriate methods for further action research. As we indicated in the invitation, our intention with the forum was to receive feedback from our interviewees, to find out *"whether we managed to gain an accurate insight into the situation of the Roma population in Szeged"* and to provide space within a discussion for *drawing up plans for our future* *cooperation.* We also indicated that we were expecting suggestions *"about the topic(s) we should focus our scientific resources on for the interest of the Roma population of Szeged."*

Seven out of the two dozen interviewees participated in the forum. The participants were deeply interested and very active, and we reached our primary objective: we gathered research/project ideas for the upcoming phase of the work. The forum also contributed to further enhancing a mutual attitude of trust among the participants.

Third phase: joint selection of the action/project

The aim of the **second forum** was to select one or two projects that we would realize together. Our team presented five ideas for discussion that had come up in the interviews or during the first forum (see Results), and the participants of the second forum chose two out of them, both (or one) of which we planned to realize together.

Before the second forum the potential participants were sent a summary of the project ideas as an invitation for forum. When planning the second meeting we paid special attention to **1) prepare a realistic schedule (as a consequence of the very limited time available for the participants); 2) create a process in which the final decision is not made on the basis of the preferences of a few dominating participants but by engaging a wider circle of people; 3) apply a decision making process that prefers cooperation over competition.** For this reason – and for other reasons – we may describe our research as a "pragmatic approach" (Bodorkós 2010). This approach aims at the production of practical knowledge by creating consensus, developing feasible action plans, engaging a wide range of participants, relying on close cooperation, and forming a mutual platform for the participants. Thereby we tried to limit the possibilities of conflicts or disagreement that are in the center of the criticisms of participatory research. A consensus seeking process would have best served this purpose, but it seemed difficult to control in light of our former problems of keeping the schedule – a potential problem of deliberation mentioned by the relevant literature (Csanádi et al. 2010). Therefore, we tried to create a decision making process in which a "moderate" debate, characterized by balanced power relations, ends with a non-competitive majority decision.

Based on the above considerations, we followed the steps below during the decision making process:

1. **Selection of the three most attractive projects and providing reasons for the choices.** The participants were asked to choose three ideas that they liked the most and to give reasons for the choices. After this point, however, there was no space for further debate or reflecting on each other's positions and arguments
2. **Decision on which ideas to realize.** After the first step participants were asked to select the two most attractive projects and to put them in order of preference giving them a score each. The two projects with the highest sum of scores were selected for further work and detailed planning.

Where are we at the moment?

By July 2011, the present state of the research, we have managed to select two project ideas as a result of a thinking process together with those concerned (considering all of the conflicts within the circle of those concerned – see below) that they also regard as relevant for the future of the local Roma population. Our research is currently before the phase *"action based on results"* in the process presented in Table 1. At the present phase of the research we cannot venture to evaluate the entire project but we can reflect on the processes that are visible so far. This is the goal of the following section.

Results

The Results of the First Phase

According to the information we received, the problems of the marginalized Roma population of Szeged are centered on the major problems detailed below, similarly to the results of more comprehensive international studies (Rorke 2011). Despite this focus on the problems, we should not consider the Roma population as a social group that is characterized by problems, but rather, as a socially marginalized ethnic group that plays the role of an outside "mirror" in which the majority of the society can see itself in a more favourable light (Dupcsik 2009). The human rights context in itself was not articulated explicitly by our interviewees as an operative concept. They mentioned the violation of rights (e.g. discrimination at workplaces) in certain cases, but not as an overall perspective when discussing the situation.

Housing, housing conditions and related issues on medical conditions: During our interviews we gathered disillusioning experiences about the housing conditions of the segregated areas in Szeged. These conditions clearly violate the right for appropriate housing (set up in the Universal Declaration of Human Rights (UDHR, the International Covenant on Economic, Social and Cultural Rights (ICESCR)) in terms of conditions, legal status and affordability. The living area is generally very small; 8–15 people live in 20–30–50m^2 apartments. At least 20% (some say more) of the inhabitants in one segregate live there without a legal title. Many families are behind with payments for the utilities, and the rent for the houses is relatively expensive. The general health conditions of the inhabitants of the segregated areas are very poor, the average age is relatively low, and many people suffer from asthma and pulmonary diseases.

Job opportunities and Employment: According to the interviews 90% of the marginalized Roma population is affected by unemployment. Low level of schooling, social prejudices and the lack of opportunities nearly make employment impossible – creating a situation of constant violation of the right to work (see UDHR, ICESCR). Changes in the community work program negatively affected the Roma population, several interviewees pointed out that their situation is that of a "poverty trap".

Education: Views on education are diverse: our interviewees claim that education cannot provide opportunities for the marginalized families before their basic needs are met – they may only aspire to learn a trade. Families need to find income as early as possible and a part of this is making the child learn a trade. While attitudes towards desegregation processes are rather contradictory, everybody agrees that segregated schools are not the way to go but they are also critical about "integrated" education. The right for appropriate education is a fundamental human right also declared. Many Roma children apparently do not get the appropriate education due to the lack of appropriate professional programs, capacity and experts (e.g. Roma teachers). They (and their non-Roma peers) also do not receive any particular knowledge of Roma culture, literature etc. which would be a necessary implication of this HR concept.

Security, access to information, perspectives for the future: A majority of the Roma population in Szeged is facing an insecure future when it comes to long-term housing – many of them do not know whether they will have anywhere to live in the future. This insecurity also characterizes their general outlooks (work, future perspectives), and it is made worse by never being sure what new regulations come out and how they actually affect the people in the community. This is due to the fact that these people are never asked to offer their opinion about the decisions and they are not even informed about them. As an important component of the feeling of security, many of them mentioned the need for a confidential relationship with the representatives of authorities and social organizations.

Equal treatment, self-management: Negative discrimination as a direct link to the human rights violation appears in every aspect of life, especially in employment and education, as well as in the relationship with the public service providers. The negative discrimination of the Roma population (in Szeged) is probably closely related to poor self-management skills in the Roma population, and the lack of representation of their interests both locally and in the national context. The HR perspective was the most recognizable issue here mentioned in the interviews.

Action/Project Ideas and the Selected Action/Project

1. **Public debate or public hearing in the Local Government**: The interviews and the first forum made it clear that the members of the community think that the Roma population does not have proper representation in Szeged, and they feel that this should be changed. The objective of this project idea was to organize a public debate or a public hearing in the Local Government that focuses on the situation of the local Roma population (or more generally: the disadvantaged local groups), and discusses the plans, measures and the activities of the Local Government and the local community in this context.

2. **The situation in kindergartens, an experimental program for kindergartens**: According to the interviews and the first forum the members of the community believe that kindergartens have an outstanding role in improving the later performance of their children in school and in the process of catching up with the majority children. The objective of this project is the realization of an experimental program for the education of Roma children in a particular kindergarten.

3. **A series of forum discussions/lectures:** The members of the community practically all confirmed that prejudices against the Roma population have increased in the past period. Along with the growing social prejudices only a few people are familiar with the Roma culture, customs, traditions, their history and position in society. The goal of the project is to launch a series of forum discussions/lectures that helps eliminate the various misbeliefs and to raise awareness in the general public about the Roma population.

4. **"The place where we live and where we wish to live"** – **Photovoice survey**: Nearly all of the interviewees mentioned housing, i.e., the lack of proper housing and poor housing conditions, among the most severe problems. The objective of this project is to find out how people living in

segregated areas in Szeged see their environment and their home, and what they mean by an ideal home/residential area.

5. **Chances/possibilities to establish a special school**: Several people mentioned in the interviews the need for a well-functioning public space – a special school/community center. It also turned out that the current official educational system alone – despite the effects of the former and ongoing desegregation experiments in Szeged (Fejes & Szűcs 2009) – is not capable of solving/decreasing the disadvantages of Roma school children. The objective of the project is to identify the characteristics of "special school" needed for Szeged and to reveal its professional and practical requirements – thus enabling the realization of the right for appropriate education as a fundamental HR.

During the second forum two projects were selected out (see Methods and means) of the projects listed above: the **special school project** (13 points) and the **kindergarten project** (7 points).

Evaluation of Results and Reflections

Theoretical Dilemmas and the Preliminary Results of the Collaborative Learning Process

Before we contacted the members of the community we expected to face certain dilemmas that we could not or did not want to solve right at the start. Below is a list of the dilemmas that have emerged so far and the answers given to them by the members of the community, at this phase of the mutual learning process:

1) We needed to clarify the use of certain terms, when (how) and why do we use expressions like Roma, Roma and the Roma community. We wanted to find out about the views and the suggestions of those concerned (and educated in the history of the Hungarian Roma community). Our experiences show that the members of the local Roma population (as well as the experts working with them) do not entirely agree on the proper terminology. Some of the participants found the wide-spreading of the term, Roma as controversial (because they felt it is more of a private expression that entails a rather intimate relationship) They repeatedly emphasized that the term, Roma community is ambiguous and it is important to clarify who we mean by it. (For instance, whether they are Carpathian, Boyash or Olah Gypsies.)

2) Another basic dilemma was to clarify what we mean by the term, Roma population of Szeged (at least during the project) that we defined as our

target group. Originally we intended to contact marginalized people living in segregated areas (Cserepes sor, the Roma settlement in Dorozsma). Our first contacts, mostly from the elite of the local Roma population, expressed their opinion that we should not limit our approach to those living in the segregated neighbourhoods because the Roma community also includes integrated Gypsies who do not really differ in their life style/living standard from the majority of the society.

3) Another dilemma was to find out whether we can talk about disadvantaged (or marginalized) group(s) "en bloc" within the context of the Roma population of Szeged, and if we can, what are the well-defined criteria to do so. This problem did actually emerge in the interviews and during the discussions afterwards: several participants emphasized that we should not identify the disadvantaged social groups (living in poverty or deep poverty) with the Roma community as such, even on the level of terminology. They also questioned the existence of a clear-cut and close correlation between these categories.

4) In close relationship with the previous dilemma we needed to decide whether we want to define and characterize the Roma population as a social category (group) and/or an ethnic (cultural) community. The members of the community themselves are likely to have diverse views about this question as well, in the sense that it is difficult to weed out whether the problems we intend to solve/treat are social questions or those of the Roma population in general.

5) Regarding the focal issue of integration, or the need for such efforts, we were primarily interested, again, in the views of those concerned: what integration means from the perspective of their own culture and identity. The discussions showed a diverse picture concerning this issue as well: sometimes integration is so successful that people trying to break out of their original environment do regard full assimilation as the key to their upliftment. Others emphasize the preservation (or even strengthening) of cultural and ethnic identity: they claim that the integrated (intellectual etc.) layers have a special responsibility to serve as catalysts for the less successful members of the community by strengthening their cultural and ethnic identity.

6) The question of segregation is a closely related issue. People tend to view segregation in a negative light if it refers to forcing people into a segregated area/ghetto/camp despite their volition (prison, labour camp, refugee camp, etc.). But when the members of a community choose to segregate themselves (e.g. ecovillages), the term may have positive connotations, too. The fact that the EU does not deny the right of Travellers to lead an unusual

life style may be considered as another example for the positive interpretation of segregation in which it takes place in the interest of the community from a human rights perspective. Some of the participants voiced their opinion that a simplistic approach to the problem of segregation often leads to a (more or less inevitable) resegregation process in education: in the higher grades of primary school most of the Roma students end up in special schools despite all efforts for their integration.

7) We also expected the need to thematize the way some of the classic dichotomies operate. For instance, how can we properly use the majority society/minorities distinction and what are the practical consequences of an adequate interpretation. How does this ethnic divide relate to such broad(er) distinctions as privileged/marginalized social groups, or the relationship between the prevailing elite and the majority society in which the ethnic category is replaced by a social/economic category. The prominent, respected figures of the local Roma population (that we were mostly able to contact) have nearly all become members of the social elite (in a broader sense). When we (primarily) focus on the problems of the (mostly) disadvantaged groups of the segregated areas, to what extent can we consider them as a concerned party.

Dilemmas and Challenges Faced

We may summarize the problems and challenges we had to face during the actual working process in the following way.

1) **Who did we reach?** The approaching of marginalized (and mostly vulnerable/defenceless) social groups, and earning their trust as strangers coming from outside, is an extremely hard task. However, the two university students of Roma descent in our team made things easier for us, and we also planned to rely on help from experts familiar with the "field" in locating and contacting the members of the community. In the second round (during the planning process of the special school) we will make attempts to perform a more effective channelling of the opinions and views of the most directly affected groups.

2) **The influence of power structures and power relations within the community on the research.** Internal relations of the local Roma population fundamentally influence people's willingness to cooperate. It became clear for us that our interviewees have a long past together that is not free from conflicts (and might inhibit further collaboration between them), as we found ourselves among solid structures of hierarchy and power relations.

3) **Conclusions of organizing and conducting focus group discussions.** One of the greatest challenges in the forums was the task of moderating the discussion. Some of the participants were not willing to keep the time limits we suggested and the moderator (a member of our team and not an outsider) could not "discipline" them in this respect. One of the reasons was that (1) these "undisciplined" participants were on the top of the hierarchy of the community with unquestionable authority (or at least position), and therefore, the moderator's efforts to control them would have negatively influenced their future cooperation, and (2) the forum was not assisted by a qualified moderator as a result of choosing a team member and not an outsider who would be not familiar with the internal relations of the group. Certain prestigious/dominant participants were significantly more active than others, and some participants nearly did not say anything. In a group with such a solid power structure and hierarchy, however, it is interesting to consider whether we want to "intervene" (from outside) into the process (and the power relations) to such an extent, and how legitimate and ethical that would be.

Group Work Dynamics

Cooperation between ESSRG and SGPF can be characterized as a knowledge transfer in both ways. While the actual research actions were conducted by the SGPF (e.g. interviews, organizing and moderating the discussion forums, putting the documents together, etc.), ESSRG continuously helped in methodological decisions at crucial points and also kept putting the project into the conceptual framework of human rights and participatory research. Since researchers are also present in the SGPF itself, the relationship between the two organization was probably more equal in terms of knowledge transfer than in case of a CSO without any research experience. ESSRG provided a necessary critical attitude towards the project and supported the SGPF in the broader context of the PERARES project by opening an international communicative space for a local CSO. ESSRG also put emphasis and facilitated the production of scientific outcomes (publications, presentations) in the collaboration of the two teams.

As the actual day-to-day activity was done by the SGPF, investigation of group dynamics has a real relevance in case of this group. Therefore the following conclusions are presented by focusing on SGPF as the core team of the project.

As one of the characteristics of participatory research, the actual tasks of the group are only defined during the course of the work. Nevertheless, the Hungarian research is organized according to the traditional project approach (detailed planning, measurability, timing, assigning resources to the tasks, planning of resources, etc.) as a part of a large grant. **The characteristics of the participatory research and the project approach together create an interesting hybrid that posed a number of challenges to our Working Group to be** discussed in the following section.

Efficiency and/or participation – the development of organizational culture

In the beginning it was important to engage researchers with Roma descent who would do much of the field work and take the interviews. During the work the participation of Roma members proved to be very important, and greatly contributed to the legitimacy of the group.

The topic of the research, together with its ideological background and methodology made it obvious that the operation of the group should be based on the principle of participation. A democratic, consensual, and proactive attitude of the group members was an important element of the planned working process. The initial approach showed the characteristics of the task culture (Handy 1985). In this culture the organization focuses on the distribution of responsibilities and the tasks to be performed, and assigns the resources accordingly. The influence of the members depends on expertise rather than formal position. During the process of the research so far the initial task culture approach faced various challenges. Decision making and the organization of the working process became more hierarchical, although decisions were made by consensus. This is partially due to the time limitations and the lack of capacity made quick planning and decision making necessary in order to keep the deadlines and come up with results. Therefore, the informal leader often had to undertake these tasks. In addition, the tasks of planning and timing the research were mostly performed by the members with more experience in these areas. If the members entering the group have never participated in such a non-hierarchical working group (and they hardly have a chance to do so during their time spent in the official educational system – primary school, high school, university), they may have different ideas about the organization of work. For instance, they might expect more guidance and a clearer distribution of tasks etc., while a leader with a different background may expect more proactivity from the members. This situation is made more complex by the employer-employee relation because that entails a hierarchical relationship in a group that operates on fundamentally different principles.

As a summary, our experiences show that the context of the project, the time limitations, and the different background of the members significantly moved the original, non-hierarchical approach towards a more hierarchical structure. At the same time, there was a clear demand in the group for an inspiring atmosphere of debates or group discussions.

Resource planning or how to build an airplane while flying?

The context of the project, that defined the Hungarian research as well, raised another question, in addition to the setting up and the operation of the group: the **issue of actual resource planning.** Since the tasks and the related demands only materialize during the working process, we may only think in looser terms during the planning process. In case of group work, the level of competence of certain group members is also revealed only in the course of the work, and the distribution of tasks has to be performed by continuously adapting to the changing circumstances.

Reflections on the science-CSO relationship

According to their traditional roles researchers and CSOs may enter into an action research process with different interests/expectations/goals. It seems sensible to assume that as long as researchers are more interested in understanding and publishing, CSO-s are more interested in social action. This situation is a bit different in our case. Community engagement is such an important goal for ESSRG that they are continuously involved in cooperative fieldwork and also part of an international Science Shop network. On the other hand, the Szeged Group of Protect the Future also has members from the academic sphere (two of them having a PhD degree and one of them used to taking part in PhD education) affecting the perspective of the organization on social issues and action.

Thus the potential difference in interests and goals between research and social activism did not constitute a problem between the two participating teams. However, frustrations in connection with the difference emerging from the different aims of science and activism appear within the CSO itself. The reason for that is – as an act of empowerment – ESSRG involves Szeged Group of Protect the Future in the preparation of scientific publications, attending at national and international conferences, study trips and FP7 project meetings. CSO members do indeed get involved into these activities; however, it causes frustration by taking time away from participatory fieldwork. This means that being a researcher in addition to being an activist is problematic because research takes away a lot of time which could also be used for achieving the action goals of the project.

It is also important to note that through such cooperation it becomes clear that research success and action success are basically two totally different things – even in cooperative research. Getting quite positive feedback on the research part of the project without any proven social benefit (action) being carried out may push the project into the more rewarding scientific-oriented direction instead of an action-oriented one. The action research participants should be aware and reflect therefore continuously on achieving the primary goal of carrying out actions for the benefit of a marginalized social group.

Conclusions

The social **dimension of sustainability** can be considered as a specific manifestation of human rights issues regarding especially the subsistence rights (housing, health, nourishment and livelihood). According to Kates et al. (2005), while earlier sustainable development (SD) literature focused mainly on economic development as a key in improving wealth and fulfilling the needs of current and future generations, more recently "attention has shifted to human development, including an emphasis on values and goals, such as increased life expectancy, education, equity, and opportunity." (p.11). Embracing the intra-generational perspective highlights the unsustainable nature of development leading to growing inequalities in the present. The "losers" in society may include indigenous people drifted from their homeland, local farmers unable to sell their products, and like in our case: slum-dwellers and discriminated groups in wealthy societies. Poverty and marginalization have plenty of faces but it certainly has a strong connection to the lack of basic human rights: rights to appropriate housing, food, healthy environment. In other words, if sustainability is defined as distributional equity in time and space (see Anand & Sen 2000), the equal capability of exercising human rights constitutes a core of it. Moreover, in the last decades the "rights-centred" perspective of poverty has overcome the "needs-centred" approach in the development debates: as in the 1970s, 1980s the poor were seen as bearer of needs, now they are seen as bearer of rights (Sachs 2003). In this perspective, poverty is originated not from the lack of money, but rather from the lack of power (or freedoms in the sense developed by Sen 1999). This means that empowerment of the marginalized community, to take its members as citizens and not as people "waiting for hand-outs," is a political must for every political forces committed to human rights.

Our experiences showed that in this community the rights-centred approach in the discourse regarding Roma issues is not well established yet. The lack of practicing citizenship and the Roma community's lack of power of forming their environment and life is apparent. In this regard, empowerment of the community is a step towards practicing human rights and a more equal and sustainable society.

Furthermore, **organizational sustainability** is also a question in focus. How can we facilitate the positive development of the research process as well as the personal and group performance of the participants? How can we support the organizational sustainability of the research group? Our experiences show that the forming of the group itself should be an important part of the planning process. We should think ahead about the type of activities dominating the project: research or rather organizing and coordinating action, or both. The group should be able to react to changes in the tasks during the research, there should be competent members available for the new task (e.g.: library research after organizing a series of forums in case of tasks related to content analysis).

Before forming the group, the members should clarify whether the available time and resources allow for the group to utilize substantial resources for the empowerment of potentially inexperienced members (e.g.: additional support in field work, or even personal mentoring in order to help the development of the member(s)). In case of marginalized, disadvantaged minority groups, members with some kind of ties to the target group may provide legitimacy for the team. In such cases the composition of the team is itself a source of collaborative learning. We need to continuously communicate the possibility that the team may be restructured in the course of the research. Depending on the new tasks the initial distribution of the work and the tasks may change. In this regard, continuous adaptation is a key factor towards organizational sustainability.

In addition to efficiency, team building is equally essential because in such a work mutual thinking is crucial for a deeper understanding of the research material. It may sound obvious, but this aspect is often neglected due to time pressure and the logic of the project. In the case of such a project the participants need to re-evaluate their prejudices, patterns of thinking, and their ideas about the world. Participatory research, therefore, may be regarded as a process of self-recognition, if the participants are open to mutual learning.

References

Anand, S. & Sen, A.K. 2000, 'Human development and economic sustainability', World Development, vol. 28, no. 12, pp. 2029–2049.

Balázs, B. 2011, 'Structuring PER in Social Sciences Research and Forgotten Citizens of Europe: Local Human Rights', International Journal of Community Based Research No. 9., May.

Bodorkós, B. & Pataki, G. 2009: 'Linking academic and local knowledge: community-based research and service learning for sustainable rural development in Hungary'. Journal of Cleaner Production. 17 (12), 1123–1131.

Bodorkós, B. & Szombati, K. 2009,' "Semmit róluk nélkülük!" projekt eredményei és tanulságai'. Manuscript

Bodorkós, B., Herrmann, P., Gómez González, A. 2011, 'Structuring PER in social sciences research and Forgotten Citizens of Europe: Local human rights', PERARES Milestone document 6.1: Brief report on how partner CSO-s currently use research results in their daily practice (ESSRG Hungary, UC Cork and URV Tarragona).

Boros, L, Hegedűs, G & Pál V 2007, 'A neoliberális településpolitika konfliktusai' in: Települési környezet eds. Z Orosz & I Fazekas, Kossuth Egyetemi Kiadó, Debrecen, pp. 196–204.

Boros, L 2007, 'But some are less equal – spatial exlcusion in Szeged' in: From villages to cyberspace – Falvaktól a kibertérig eds. Cs Kovács, SZTE Gazdaság- és Társadalomföldrajz Tanszék, Szeged, pp. 151–160.

Bruntland, G. (eds) 1987, 'Our common future: The World Commission on Environment and Development', Oxford University Press, Oxford.

Castleden, H, Garvin, T, Huu-ay-aht First Nation 2008, 'Modifying Photovoice for community-based participatory Indigenous research', Social Science & Medicine, vol. 66, pp 1393–1405.

Catalani, C & Minkler, M 2010, 'Photovoice: A Review of the Literature in Health and Public Health', Health Education & Behavior, vol. 37, pp. 424–451.

Chung, K & Lounsbury, DW 2006, 'The role of power, process, and relationships in participatory research for statewide HIV/AIDS programming' Social Science & Medicine, vol.53, pp. 2129–2140.

Cornwall, A & Jewkes, R 1995, 'What is participatory research?' Social Science & Medicine, vol. 61, no. 12, pp. 1667–1676.

Csanádi, G, Csizmady, A & Kőszeghy, L 2010, 'Nyilvánosság és részvétel a településtervezési folyamatban', Tér és Társadalom, vol. 24, no. 1, pp. 15–36.

Daly, HE & Cobb, J 1989, 'For the Common Good', Beacon Press, Boston.

Dennis, SF Jr., Gaulocher, S, Carpiano, RM & Brown, D 2009, 'Participatory photo mapping (PPM): Exploring an integrated method for health and place research with young people' Health & Place, vol. 15, pp. 466–473.

Dupcsik, Cs 2009, 'A magyarországi cigányság története', Osiris Kiadó, Budapest

Egészséges Városok Magyarországi Szövetsége 2004, 'Közösségi részvétel a helyi egészségfejlesztésben és a fenntartható fejlődésben. Megközelítések és módszerek' Európai Fenntartható Fejlődés és Egészség Sorozat, no. 4.

Ekins, P. 2003, 'Identifying critical natural capital: Conclusions about critical natural capital', Ecological Economics, vol. 2–3. pp. 277–292.

Fejes, JB & Szűcs, N 2009, 'Hallgatói Mentorprogram. A szegedi deszegregációt támogató pilot program első évének tapasztalatai.', Új Pedagógiai Szemle, vol.59, no. 2, pp. 61–75.

FRA 2010, 'A romák és travellerek lakáskörülményei az Európai Unióban Összehasonlító jelentés'. Az Európai Közösségek Hivatalos Kiadványainak Hivatala, Luxemburg.

Gómez, A, Puigvert, L & Flecha, R 2011, 'Critical Communicative Methodology: Informing Real Social Transformation Through Research' Qualitative Inquiry, vol.17,pp. 235–245.

Handy, CB 1985, Understanding Organizations, 3rd Edition,. Penguin Books, Harmondsworth.

Hanley, N 2000, 'Macroeconomic measures of sustainability', Journal of Economic Surveys, vol. 14, pp. 1–30.

Hawkins, C 2010, 'Sustainability, Human Rights, and Environmental Justice: Critical Connections for Contemporary Social Work', Critical Social Work, vol. 11, pp. 68-81.

Illge, L & Schwarze, R 2009, 'A matter of opinion—How ecological and neoclassical environmental economists and think about sustainability and economics', Ecological Economics, vol. 68, pp. 594–604.

Kates, RW; Parris, TM & Leiserowitz, AA 2005, 'What is sustainable development? Goals, indicators, values and practices', Environment:Science and Policy for Sustainable Development, vol. 47, no. 3, pp. 8–21

Kóczé, A 2011, Roma Helyzetelemzés. Manuscript. Budapest

Kvale, S 2005, Az interjú. Bevezetés a kvalitatív kutatás interjútechnikáiba, Jószöveg Műhely, Budapest.

Ladányi, J & Szelényi, I 2004, A kirekesztettség változó formái. Közép- és dél-kelet európai romák történeti és összehasonlító szociológiai vizsgálata, Napvilág Kiadó, Budapest

Minkler, M 2004, 'Ethical Challenges for the "Outside" Researcher in Community-Based Participatory Research', Health Education & Behavior, vol. 31, pp. 684–697.

Munté, A; Serradell, O & Sordé, T 2011, 'From Research to Policy: Roma Participation Through Communicative Organization', Qualitative Inquiry, vol. 17, pp. 256–266.

Rátkai, Á & Sümeghy, Z. 2001, 'Szegedi etnikai közösségek területi elhelyezkedése' presented in Földrajzi Konferencia, Szeged.

Rátkai, Á 1997, 'Szeged cigánysága és a Szegedi Cigányprogram. A szegedi cigányság történetéről' Regio. Kisebbség, politika, társadalom, vol. 8, no. 3–4,

Rorke, B. 2011, Beyond Rhetoric: Roma Integration Roadmap for 2020. Priorities for an EU Framework for National Roma Integration Strategies. Open Society Institute, Budapest.

Rostás-Farkas, Gy 2001, A cigányok története, Cigány Tudományos és Művészeti Társaság, Budapest.

Sachs, W 2003, 'Environment and human rights', Wuppertal Papers, No. 137.

Sen, A. 1999. Development as Freedom. Oxford University Press, Oxford

Strack, RW; Magill, C & McDonagh, K 2004, 'Engaging Youth Through Photovoice', Health Promotion Practice, vol 10, no.1, pp. 49–58.

Streng, JM; Rhodes, SD; Ayala, GX; Eng, E; Arceo, R & Phipps, S 2004, 'Realidad Latina: Latino adolescents, their school, and a university use photovoice to examine and address the influence of immigration', Journal of Interprofessional Care, vol 18, no.4, pp. 403–415.

Szuhay, P 1999, A magyarországi cigányság kultúrája: etnikus kultúra vagy a szegénység kultúrája, Medicina, Budapest.

Tanaka, J. (n.d.): Kézikönyv. Részvételen alapuló helyi cselekvési tervezés a szegénység és a romák társadalmi kirekesztettsége elleni küzdelemben.
http://media.cega.bg/Hronika/Narychnik%20za%20syvmestno%20planirane/Hungaria_%20book-FINAL.pdf

UNDP 2010, Human Development Report 2010. 20th Anniversary Edition. The Real Wealth of Nations: Pathways to Human Development.
http://hdr.undp.org/en/media/HDR_2010_EN_Complete_reprint.pdf

Zenkov, K & Harmon, J 2009, 'Picturing a Writing Process: Photovoice and Teaching Writing to Urban Youth' Journal of Adolescent & Adult Literacy, vol. 52, no.7, pp. 575–584.

Participation-Action-Research: a Hungarian Case Study

Vári Anna, Ferencz Zoltán, Bozso Brigitta

Introduction

Since January 2009 the Institute of Sociology of the Hungarian Academy of Sciences (Institute of Sociology) and Energiaklub Climate Policy Institute[48](EK) have been participating in a collaborative action research project entitled Civil Society for Sustainability (CSS) financed by the EU FP7 Programme. The main objective of the CSS project is to establish collaboration between civil society organisations (CSOs) and researchers engaged in sustainable development, on both national and international levels.

The cooperation between civil actors and researchers is aimed at exploring the most important strategic problems of CSOs and implementing pilot projects that are oriented towards the solution of those problems. The CSS project also has joint learning as an objective, primarily in the field of the methods and tools of action research and participatory decision making. The basic issue running through the whole project is how cooperation between CSOs and researchers can be properly structured and organised.

In the project lasting from 2009 to 2011 three research groups and three CSOs have been participating. They form so-called tandems, which are the following: Dialogik gGmbH (Stuttgart) – unw e.V. (Ulm), Mutadis SARL (Paris) – REC Slovenija (Ljubljana), and the Institute of Sociology (Budapest) – EK (Budapest). The three tandems work in parallel by using a jointly elaborated methodology (EU-FP7 Project CSS 2009)[49]. An important component of the collaboration is the regular dialogue both within and among the tandems.

In general, action research begins with the assessment of an initial situation considered problematic; which is followed by developing proposals for interventions and implementing them. Finally, the resulting situation is assessed and potential new problems are defined. Typically, action research projects consist of multiple rounds, as it is assumed that whenever a problem is solved it would generate new problem situations. A further feature of the

---

[48] Before 2010: Energia Klub Environmental Association.
[49] The methodology has been based on a theoretical framework developed by Petschow et al. (2005) and Reichel (2006).

approach is that problem owners are involved in all steps of defining and addressing the problems.

Similarly, the CSS project does not aim at the solution of a predetermined problem, but defining the problem(s) is also part of the project. The project itself consists of three phases (one round). The task of the first phase is to explore the most important strategic problems of the participating CSOs and to plan strategic changes. In the second phase is the elaboration of so-called pilot projects promoting strategic changes. In the third phase the pilot projects, the strategic changes and the emerging situations are assessed. Finally, the CSS project itself – including both tandem-level and international cooperation – is evaluated (meta-research)[50].

The segment of the CSS project implemented by the Institute of Sociology – EK tandem was structured as follows:

Phase 1 (January–June 2009): Definition of the strategic problems of EK

    Analysis of relevant documents

    Semi-structured interviews with associates, partners and clients of EK

    Feedback to EK

Phase 2 (July 2009–March 2011): Implementation of pilot projects

    Elaboration of a climate protection strategy in the town of Gyöngyös

    Laying the foundations of an energy efficiency coalition

Phase 3 (April–December 2011): Final evaluation

    Semi-structured interviews with partners and clients of EK

    Feedback to EK

  Reflection by the tandem

---

[50] The authors wish to express their thanks to a number of individuals participating in the CSS project, particularly to Ada Ámon, Mária Csikai, András Dobák, Márta Dobos, Klára Faragó, Katalin Kápolnai, and an anonymous reviewer.

Definition of strategic problems

The task of the first phase of the project was to define the most important strategic problems of the participating CSOs. The three tandems applied similar empirical methods during this phase. Based on a jointly elaborated guideline, the researchers *analysed key documents and conducted* a series of *semi-structured interviews;* next they fed the results back to the CSO team. The strategic problems obtained their final form during the tandem discussions.

In Hungary the above empirical studies were done by the Institute of Sociology in the spring of 2009 (Vári et al. 2010). The analysis of EK's documents extended over the following:

- Constitution
- Organisational and operational rules
- Plan of Strategy
- Plan of the quality control system
- Code of Ethics
- Strategies of marketing-, HR-, communications-, PR- and resource management
- Strategies of the various divisions.

Interviewees of the semi-structured interviews were selected by the management of EK from three groups, such as: (i) associates of the EK and members of its Board; (ii) allies and cooperating partners of the EK, and (iii) representatives of other organisations in contact with EK, including policy makers, politicians, and high level managers of energy producing companies (21 people in total).

The researchers of the Institute of Sociology discussed the results of the empirical studies with the leaders of EK. Based on these talks the following key strategic problems were outlined:

1. CSO vs. expert organisation

Interviews revealed that the roles and activities of the EK had significantly changed over the years. Initially the greatest emphasis was put on cooperation with and knowledge transfer to other actors of the green movement (networking). Recently, however, networking has been increasingly pushed into the background amidst their activities.

Another important field has been environmental education and "enlightening" of the general public. This has been present continuously in EK's activities, though recently they try to put emphasis on knowledge supply, whereas public information (e.g., campaigns, education) has rather become the task of their partners.

Their third main type of activity has been the implementation of specific projects. These are obtaining growing emphasis, particularly those in which there is need for high-level expertise.

The above changes of roles had been so significant that they affected even the identity of the organisation. The EK has made efforts to become a so-called 'think and do tank' organisation[51] out of a movement actor. This idea has been among their aims ever since 2005. They wish to define themselves as a professional organisation lending great emphasis to environmental values. In 2009–2010 organisational transformation reached its final phase.

2. Choice of topics

Regarding the above changes, it had to be decided upon which topics would be retained, which ones would be eliminated, and which ones should be added. The basic principle was that only such topics should be kept on the agenda that could be financed in the long run.

3. Capacities

The question was how expertise necessary to the think tank role of the EK can be ensured. In the future technical expertise is likely to obtain greater emphasis.

4. Partners and competitors

With moving in the direction of 'think and do tank',EK had to redefine the circle of their main partners and competitors as well. Environmental NGOs

---

[51] Organisations called "think tanks" appeared for the first time in Western democracies in the early 70s. As far as their function is concerned they have three specific features: they offer themes to education, research and public discourse. The contents of the concept has been much disputed but two elements can be found in all the definitions: they are research institutes of public policy that enjoy significant autonomy, in other words they are mostly not under governmental, company or party influence, and participate actively in the disputes on and shaping of policy issues. The so-called "think-and-do thanks" constitute a specific group of think tanks, which go beyond the traditional functions of analysis and recommending. They can be classified under two main headings: part of them actively participate in the elaboration of bills and strategic programs and in making them accepted (mostly through parliamentary and governmental lobbying). Another part of them go beyond these functions and put their ideas into practice through various activities, blending the features of civil society organisations and think tanks.

would be losing their importance as collaborators, while the significance of some other partners (e.g., local governments, enterprises related to energy efficiency and renewable energy sources) would increase.

5. Communications

Based on the interviews it was concluded that the effectiveness of EK's communications needed to be enhanced. Their main target groups are environmental policy makers, decision makers responsible for major energy investments and interested experts. Their messages are usually too complex for the general public; therefore they mostly wish to influence public opinion indirectly.

The Institute of Sociology–EK tandem decided upon the realisation of two pilot projects within the framework of the CSS. These projects, while considering the above aims and transformation of the EK, would promote environmental, social and organisational sustainability (Vári et al. 2011). In the following the pilot projects are presented.

Pilot project 1: Elaboration of a climate protection strategy in the town of Gyöngyös

Climate change is one of the most pressing problems of sustainable development, which has to be managed on national as well as settlement levels. The EK wishes to reach a point where the so-called "climate protection" planning is launched in a number of settlements in Hungary with broad public involvement. The essence of such planning is to prevent the further aggravation of climate change, to reduce its impacts (mitigation) and to compile proposals that would help successful adaptation to these changes. The EK develops methodology for this purpose, prepares publications, and launches pilot projects; it also disseminates the related knowledge at various fora (such as conferences and the media), and calls for the attention of stakeholders to the issue.

In the autumn of 2009 the EK chose the town of Gyöngyös as the location for a climate protection pilot project, because it had learnt about the town's initiatives targeting sustainability. Gyöngyös is a founding member of the Association of Energy Efficient Local Governments (www.ehosz.hu), and possesses adequate political intention (decision by the board of representatives) and experts (energy expert) to the implementation of the strategy.

The EK adapted a methodology used in the international practice of climate protection planning to suit the local conditions. A research team consisting of associates of the Szent István University of Gödöllő developed the renewable energy strategy for the town. The methodology of public involvement was jointly elaborated by the Cromo Foundation and the Institute of Sociology, and the selected tools were revised and refined from time to time on the basis of feedback and the newly emerging demands.

Involvement of local stakeholders

International experience shows that more effective strategies are produced if affected stakeholders are involved in the planning process, and the chances of their implementation are bigger than in case of "traditional" top-down approaches. A further advantage of the participatory approach is that stakeholders would be informed about the planning process and strategy right from the outset, so opportunities would open up for utilizing the knowledge, experiences and ideas of the participants. Mutual exchanges of knowledge would result in better strategy, and the transparent and democratic process of planning would enhance stakeholders' willingness to cooperate.

The development of a climate protection strategy is a complex issue in which a local government may play a leading role, but since it is responsible only for a low percentage of greenhouse gas emissions in the settlement, every local actor has a role and responsibility in it. Therefore, early information and involvement of various stakeholders (such as institutions, enterprises, NGOs, experts and the lay population) is of key importance.

Tools of involving local stakeholders during the pilot project are outlined below.

1. Stakeholder fora

As a first step the project team[52] presented the aim of the project and its expected benefits to the leaders of the town. Next, contact data of organisations and institutions that could be directly affected by the planning and implementation of the strategy were collected. These stakeholders were repeatedly invited to attend planners' fora (altogether four times), and the materials produced by the EK were also placed at their disposal in written form to be commented upon. The themes of the four fora were the following:

　i. *Launching the strategy making project, informing the stakeholders about the process, opening up channels of communication (18 November 2009).* The EK presented the concept and significance of the municipal

---

[52] The project team consisted of experts of the EK, the Cromo Foundation and of the Institute of Sociology.

climate protection strategy, the main elements and the planned process of strategy development. Participants pointed out why and how far they supported the strategy development, and what kind of obstacles they had seen in its way of implementation. While strategy making seemed to have obtained sufficient support, comments indicated possible pitfalls and counter-interests on the part of some stakeholders. Participants also stated their preferences for various channels of communication.

ii. *Beginning of data collection, clarification of the interests and demands of those present (15 April 2010).* The opening presentation of EK focused on results so far achieved (data received, possible conclusions). Participants discussed the aims to be set in the separate sub-areas (e.g., transport, agriculture, energy production, etc.). A number of valuable pieces of information were raised about local specificities (such as what developments would be welcome in the town, what kind of specific problems were recognised, etc.). These points were primarily used by EK at shaping goals and weighting them. For example, the role of education was considered as an outstanding one by the stakeholders, this is why it was assigned major significance in the strategy as well.

iii. *Definition of goals and town-specific priority areas (14 June 2010).* At this forum EK presented the goals set in the strategy as well as the preliminary results of a survey of the renewable energy potential done by researchers of the Szent István University. The participants structured and further specified the goals. It was at this forum that the questionnaires measuring the attitudes and demands of stakeholders were also distributed. The questionnaires filled in and returned later were used by the EK when it determined the individual steps of the strategy.

iv. *Presentation of the draft strategy (26 October 2010).* EK introduced the draft strategy which included the goals, the proposed measures and the possibilities of financing. Members of the Cromo Foundation presented the results of a second questionnaire survey conducted during the summer with the local public. Based on criticisms and comments of the participants, the EK clarified the disputed points (for instance, some new, easily understandable diagrams were made) and modified several points of the strategy. As a result of the forum, some missing data (e.g., energy utilisation data of municipal institutions) were obtained, which were incorporated into the strategy.

Comments made at the fora were recorded, considered and they were included in the documents as far as it was possible. Minutes of each forum were circulated to all invited stakeholders.

2. Eliciting written comments

Stakeholders were invited to send their written comments related to the draft documents in each phase of the work. Prior to the last forum the stakeholders also received the executive summary of the strategy, thus they had the opportunity to comment on it, as well

3. Questionnaire survey of stakeholder views

A detailed questionnaire was prepared for the stakeholders to explore their knowledge, views and attitudes to actions in relation to climate change. An important group of questions aimed at finding out what kind of developments the major actors would like to see in Gyöngyös, and what (sustainable) direction of development they would set for the town in the coming ten years. Unfortunately only 12 questionnaires were returned from the 80-member data base, and this was insufficient for being analysed by statistical means. Nevertheless, information derived from the responses was useful to the development of the strategy.

4. Informing the local public

Several pieces of information were published about the project in the local press (Heves Megyei Hírlap, Gyöngyösi Mozaik), on the homepage of the town, in the local radio (Diórádió), at the national radio programme (Kossuth Rádió), in the local television and other local media (such as the cartoon newspaper read by many). These presented the aim of the pilot project and how it was internationally embedded (CSS project), as well as practical issues affecting the inhabitants (e.g., how far the strategy would affect them, what specific measures were expected, where they could express their opinion, etc.). Information on the pilot project was also provided in some relevant national papers (such as Magyar Polgármester, Bautrend) and on the homepage of EK.

5. Questionnaire survey for the local public

A questionnaire similar to the one elaborated for the stakeholders but in a far shorter version was compiled for the general public. This primarily served for exploring attitudes to the various measures to be taken for sustainable energy economy and climate change mitigation/adaptation.

Altogether 246 questionnaires filled in were collected. The sample was representative: with regard to gender, age, and geographical distribution. It was revealed by the results that the population of the town was rather sensitive to the problem of climate change and they have already taken several steps by themselves that did not require major investments, but rather resulted in savings. All in all, the results offered positive feedback about the need for the strategy and the rightfulness of its direction.

6. Meeting of local CSOs

In order to talk to civil society organisations directly in a more informal atmosphere a so-called civil forum was organised, where interested activists could learn about the draft strategy and get acquainted with further possibilities of joining in. One of the aims of the meeting was that local CSOs should obtain a significant role in the further shaping of climate strategy, in its implementation and monitoring. Unfortunately, there are only few active environmental NGOs in Gyöngyös; hence probably their role would be more limited than expected.

The completed strategy

The climate protection strategy of the town of Gyöngyös presents the *goals of strategy making* (such as adaptation, energy saving and the reduction of emissions) and the *conditions of implementation*. The latter include the elaboration of an action plan as well as the appointment of a person responsible for its implementation (climate or energy officer), among others. Setting up the financial framework of the planned measures, the determination of deadlines and their observance, as well as communicating with the inhabitants are all of great importance.

Next the strategy lists the *energy saving targets* by local government institutions, industrial facilities and private households. Among *measures for reducing emission* energy production stands first but the utilisation of the renewable energy potential can be of equal importance as well. It should be noted that Gyöngyös has extremely good potential concerning renewable energy resources. Finally, the *means of implementation* were summarised.

Dissemination of the practice of climate protection planning

The main aim of the Gyöngyös pilot project was to test participatory methods of planning and decision making, and the dissemination of this practice in Hungary in the field of climate protection. Therefore, in September 2011 the EK organized a training session for local governments in which the presentation of the experiences of the pilot project was an important element.

In order to ensure the further development of the programme, EK will develop a training material for local government experts and CSO activists. In this they wish to publish the methodology of participatory planning for climate protection.

Methodological lessons of pilot project 1

Main lessons derived from the Gyöngyös pilot project are summarised as follows.

(1) It should be an important criterion at selecting the venue of a strategy making project to have a committed representative of the given problem in the local government, possibly with decision-making power. If this precondition is missing the local government cannot become a meaningful catalyst of the processes. In addition, it is important to have a committed local CSO with which it is possible to cooperate in mobilising people and other CSOs and/or communicating about the project.

The interest of participants should be maintained from the very beginning. Local CSOs can be instrumental in this area by providing additional opportunities for the public to get involved in the planning process.

(2) Stakeholder fora were important elements of the project. The first forum had shown the scale of potential interest and the last one showed how important it was to consider the opinion of local people even in minor fields of detail. It was also important to keep in contact with the active participants of fora, so that their interest would not abate.

(3) Questionnaire surveys should be given an important role. The significance of the stakeholder questionnaire should be realised by potential respondents because they can have a better say in shaping the strategy through it. On the other hand, the role of public surveys could be strengthened by raising the interest of the local government, e.g., by suggesting that they could investigate other local issues simultaneously by this method, as well. Some financial contribution by the local government would be needed and local NGOs could also have a role to play in collecting the data.

(4) An important element was missing from the communication due to the scarcity of time and resources: continuity. The existence of the project should be continuously present in the town, on the settlement's homepage, and if possible, in the media as well. The local government and especially the mayor should be given an important role in the communication, since local media pay a lot of attention to them. In addition, local CSOs can keep the project constantly alive in the local media.

Pilot project 2: Laying the foundations of an energy efficiency coalition

The promotion of energy efficient solutions in Hungary is of outstanding importance among the strategic goals of the EK. As there are a large number of organisations in the business, as well as the non-profit and government sectors that are interested in promoting energy efficiency, the EK initiated the establishment of a coalition which is capable of representing this goal more effectively. The Institute of Sociology–EK tandem organised a pilot project in order to lay the foundations of such a coalition.

Empirical research

The first phase of the project included the identification of the potential coalition members, the mapping of their relations, problems and needs, as well as assessing their willingness to cooperate. This research was conducted by Publicus Institute in 2010 (Publicus Research 2010).

At first relevant organisations were identified through *data collection from the internet*. Altogether 220 such organisations were listed, 18% of which belonged to the government, 28% to the non-profit, and 54% to the business sector. These organisations were evaluated on the basis of different hard and soft indicators (such as operational data, lobbying potential, etc.). Based on this evaluation, about 50 organisations were selected from the above list, and their representatives were made to fill in an *online questionnaire*. The questionnaire revealed in detail the inclination of the respondents to act for the formation of an umbrella organisation. The final step of the research was to explore the ideas of the surveyed organisations concerning cooperation. For this purpose *semi-structured interviews* were carried out with the representatives of these organisations.

The results of the interviews

The interviews were trying to map by what means the contacted organisations promoted energy efficiency and if they were willing to participate in a possible newly developed lobby organisation (Publicus Research 2010).

Interviews indicated that all the investigated organisations would welcome such an initiative. A more profound study of the issue, however, brought slightly different positions to the surface. Most of the interviewees agreed that there was a need for a strong lobby organisation, rich in resources, active, communicative, and dynamic. The main dividing line, however, can be drawn at the issue whether this organisation should be a new one, or whether an already existing organisation should be invested with this new function.

Those who would prefer the development of the new initiative as an extension of the function of an already existing organisation were unable to name an organisation that they regarded as a suitable one. Those questioned were somewhat at a loss also about *the content such an organisation should be filled with.*

The majority of the respondents were of the view that what is primarily needed was an initiative of professional interest assertion which could meaningfully participate in shaping the legislative processes and would be a regular partner of the government in offering expert opinion. At this point several respondents suggested conflicts deriving from the possibly divergent interests since the numerous actors placed on a single platform may in some cases represent different business or organisational goals. For example, such situation may emerge in case of technologies or materials almost perfectly replacing each other as possible solutions. While everyone would like to see the spread of energy efficient solutions, there has been competition among a number of business solutions.

Based on the interviews, those actors were identified who could constitute the possible 'core' of an energy efficiency cooperation. Information was gained also about some possible areas and forms of cooperation. All this was, however, characterised by a high degree of uncertainty of the respondents on most issues, as well as the emergence of a number of questions. In order to develop an agreement by the potential participants about the contents and form of cooperation a dialogue was needed for discussing these questions in a face-to-face setting. For this purpose the EK and the Institute of Sociology organised a *decision conference* in November 2010. Representatives of organisations were invited to the conference, which had been classified under the possible 'core' of cooperation.

Decision conference as a group decision support method

Group decision support methods combine techniques developed for problem structuring with group facilitation to improve the efficiency of group decisions. The aim of these methods is to create an opportunity for the realisation of gains deriving from team work, and at the same time moderating wasted time spent on often boundless disputes emerging in group processes.

One broadly used variant of the group decision support methods is the *so-called decision conference* (Phillips & Phillips 1992, Vári & Vecsenyi 1992). A decision conference is a problem-solving meeting lasting for half to three days where the decision makers and the most important stakeholders are present. Participants jointly interpret the problem, agree on its components (e.g., goals, alternative actions, scenarios, evaluation criteria) and generate (qualitative or quantitative) judgments about these components. By integrating judgments, the group has good chances for finding mutually acceptable action(s). Ideally, at the end of the conference participants commit themselves to certain actions.

The ideal size of groups is 7 to 10 people. If the number of participants is more it is worth dividing them to working groups and from time to time, the working groups should be brought together in plenary discussions.

Working groups are assisted by two facilitators. The first facilitator should have skills in group dynamics and problem structuring. This person facilitates the discussions, focuses them, helps finding consensus or compromise, and manages communications problems (such as the participants' passivity or excessive dominance), if any. He/she assists the group to jointly structure the given problem and visually demonstrates ideas emerging in the group discussions (on boards, flip charts). A second person records the discussions of the group or their most important details[53].

Decision conference laying the foundations of an energy efficiency coalition

The main objective of the energy efficiency decision conference was to let the invited participants try and reach a consensus on the following issues:

1. *What could* organisations represented at the meeting *jointly do* for promoting energy efficiency and enlarging the domestic market of energy efficiency?
2. *In what forms* cooperation can be envisaged concerning the above activities?
3. *What should be done* (i) in the longer run and (ii) in the next half year for implementing the preferred form of cooperation?

Representatives of 18 organisations were invited to the decision conference. Ten organisations accepted the invitation. At the meeting on 18 November 2010, ten persons, mostly top managers were representing those organisations. In addition, two leading associates of EK also participated in the meeting.

---

[53] In case of complex problems quantitative models (e.g., decision trees, multi-criteria models) may be applied. In such cases a third facilitator is needed for processing the elicited data on computer and providing feedback to the participants.

The conference focused on discussing the three issues mentioned above. Participants worked on the various issues in two working groups followed by plenary sessions. The so-called Nominal Group Technique (Delbecq et al. 1975) was applied for collecting, discussing and screening ideas and concepts.

Results of the decision conference

A consensus emerged among the participants in relation to question 1. Activities considered as most important were the following:

- Uniform lobby (for legal safety and predictability);
- Raising energy- and environmental consciousness of legislators and politicians;
- Raising energy- and environmental consciousness of the population, elaborating new teaching materials;
- Establishment of a common platform, joining forces, and acting jointly.

Concerning question 2, the results of the two working groups differed. According to one group there was no need for a new organisation for the above joint activities, but a platform (or committee) should be set up. The central actor/engine of the platform (or committee) should be an already existing organisation. The platform would be an open one, and EK was recommended as the central actor.

The second working group proposed two possible forms such as (i) the establishment of a new non-profit organisation, or (ii) the linking of the already existing representative organs and fora into a network. It was suggested here that before a decision was made about the organisational form, foreign formations of similar objective should be investigated.

Participants have made the following proposals in relation to question 3:

- Launching a joint action for the dissemination of energy-efficiency related information with EK as project coordinator. As to its financing, 50% of costs would be covered by LIFE PLUS sources, and 50% would come from the resources of participating organisations. Some of the participants indicated that they would financially support the project.
- To begin setting up a platform under the leadership of EK.

No consensus was reached by the participants about questions 2 and 3. They have committed themselves to continue talks about these and further essential issues (such as the operation of the lobby organisation, its financing, etc.)

Methodological lessons of pilot project 2

The decision conference was organised after major stakeholders of the energy efficiency issue had been identified and their willingness to cooperate had been investigated through empirical surveys. The latter facilitated the selection of participants as well as the formulation of the questions to be responded by the group.

The main aim of the conference was to launch dialogue among the potential members of the coalition, and to bring disputed points, interests and counter-interests to the surface. The meeting has accomplished its main aim, and the outlines of the core of a possible future coalition emerged. Another significant achievement of the meeting was the identification, discussion and ranking of the possible joint activities and organisational forms. The most important achievement was dialogue itself.

The decision conference has proved to be an efficient method: in a short time it has brought a lot of information to the surface and led to the commitment of the majority of participants. Apparently the meeting has induced expectations concerning future joint actions, particularly among the participating business sector representatives.

Some critical remarks:

(1) A lot of efforts were made to ensure the participation at the conference of those invited. For example, those who had given a positive response to the first invitation were later on contacted by phone as well. It would have been useful, however, to invite more organisations than the necessary number, because not everyone turned up even from among those who promised participation in the previous day. If high level managers are invited, this possibility has to be taken into account on other occasions as well.

(2) Decision conferencing is an efficient problem solving approach, therefore it is not expedient to burden the time with long (protocol type) introductory presentations. As in this case the introductory presentations took up too much time insufficient time was left for profoundly discussing question 3.

(3) Slips in time should be taken into account even in the case of stringent time management. If there is no chance for eliminating them it is worth planning the meeting for a longer duration and then lunch should be ensured on the spot. In this case, however, some of the participants may leave during the lunch break.

(4) At the end of the decision conference participants have to agree on whether the meeting and its results would be public or not. In this case this was missing due to the lack of time, which caused some uncertainty later on.

EVALUATION

In the last phase of the CSS project the Institute of Sociology team made a second round of semi-structured interviews with some partners of EK, selected from the academic, business and civil sectors (5 individuals in total). Attempts were made to explore their opinion in relation to the transformation of EK and to its projects. The results were fed back to the EK in the form of a report. The following assessment is drawn from the report as well as from tandem reflections.

EK's problems and the pilot projects

Pilot projects were evaluated from the aspect of what role they had played in mitigating the main strategic problems of the EK.

  i. *Social organisation vs. expert organisation*
  The EK had played the role of expert in both of its pilot projects. The Gyöngyös project, however, had elements of a movement as well. Earlier the EK had called the attention of local governments to the importance of responses to climate change, by various means (e.g., information campaigns, competitions) and had a significant role in that strategy development projects have been launched in some municipalities.
  During the course of the energy efficiency pilot project several participants suggested that EK should be the central actor, organiser and operator of a coalition. This fits into the concept of expert organisation, but raises other issues (such as independence, value commitment). Proper answers to these questions should be given in the future.

  ii. *Choice of topic, financing*
  The EK has obtained experiences and reference in local climate protection planning by the pilot project in Gyöngyös, and proved that it is capable of undertaking similar tasks. The development of local strategies may be one of the new activities of EK which would be financed by its clients. As far as the energy efficiency coalition is concerned its members are expected to finance the services provided by their own lobby organisation, possibly the EK.

iii. *Capacities*
The Gyöngyös project underlines that the EK possesses the proper expertise needed to local climate protection planning. Presumably it will commission contractual partners to do certain activities (e.g., organising public involvement) in the future as well. It should be noted, however, that according to some partners, EK's competitiveness has been significantly reduced by the fact that it does not have a team of technical experts of its own.
Concerning the energy efficiency coalition, it has not yet been outlined for what tasks its central organisation would be set up. Obviously, the human resources to be hired will depend on these tasks.

iv. *Partners, competitors*
The Gyöngyös pilot project confirmed that in local climate strategy making EK's main partners are local governments, energy experts and local NGOs. Developing proper partnership with such organisations has been one of EK's strategic goals. The training course taking place in September 2011 is also aimed mostly at this purpose. It should be noted that the local political and social environment may put the EK into different situations in each settlement, for it is not only the political leadership of the settlement but also the local business and civil actors, their number, involvement and interests that would create different contexts and conditions for cooperation.
In the case of the energy efficiency coalition, the main partners of EK turned out to be the most active companies, professional organisations and CSOs. The pilot project served for the identification of and relationship building with organisations belonging to the core of the coalition. This group is planned to be left open so that others may also join it.
As far as competitors are concerned it was mentioned by several interviewees during the second round of interviews that EK would have to compete with many more and stronger competitors than earlier, including both the researchers of the academic sector and the large capital-strong consulting companies.

v. *Communication*
The Gyöngyös project confirmed that communication among planning experts, municipal government officials, local NGOs and other stakeholders needs to be organised professionally. The EK has acquired important methodological experiences in this field. In case of the energy efficiency coalition there is need not only for a dialogue between the EK and its target groups but a continuous intra-coalition exchange of information is needed too. This is a multi-lateral

communication requiring special means. The internet may be an effective tool but it cannot replace personal meetings. This is why it is highly significant that the EK should learn interactive group procedures like decision conferencing.

Results and experiences of cooperation between CSOs and researchers

In Hungary action research based on the cooperation of CSOs and researchers is not very common, and projects driven by CSOs are rare even among them. The CSS project was one of these, where the civil actors defined the problems awaiting solution and they determined actions (pilot projects) as well. The Institute of Sociology team offered tools related to action research and public involvement, as well as methods of communication and decision making.

The joint research had several successes. It is an important result of the CSS project that the EK had got acquainted with the action research approach, the techniques of semi-structured interviews, questionnaire surveys, and decision conferencing. The observations and comments of the research team helped drawing methodological conclusions and learning.

The findings of the semi-structured interviews with EK's members, partners, competitors and clients were considered highly useful by the EK leadership. These held a 'mirror' to the organisation and helped in their decisions.

What were the most important factors of success? It has been concluded that mutual respect of each other's knowledge and openness to adopt new methods played a crucial role in the successful collaboration of the CSO and the research organisation. Cooperation was also promoted by the fact that both organisations were committed to advancing sustainability and to professional work representing high quality standards. The international research framework (e.g., the possibility of consulting the two other tandems, of discussing the similarities and differences of problems and methods) also facilitated joint work.

Naturally, cooperation was not totally free of tension. It was an unusual situation for the Institute of Sociology team not to direct the research schedule but to adjust both to the timing considerations of the CSO partner and to the time limits of other pilot project participants. They also had to consider that the organisational transformation of the civil partner was in progress during the project which also influenced the timing of the pilot projects.

For the EK it was unusual that the Institute of Sociology team did not fully implement the pilot projects because the projects' volume went beyond their capacities, hence they could undertake merely segments of tasks. During the pilot projects their main task was "methodological monitoring". In some cases this meant that they "discouraged" the EK from applying certain methods whereas they recommended others (public opinion survey, decision conference). It should be noted that the research team did actively participate in the implementation of the latter ones.

The EK as an expert organisation commissioned subcontractors in the various projects. As some of them operated in similar fields as the Institute of Sociology, hence tensions evolved among them, as they did not necessarily agree on professional issues. In some cases the subcontractors did not understand why the researcher team "interfered into" methodological issues, whereas in other cases they wished to implement methods suggested by the Institute of Sociology team according to their own "taste".

In our view most tensions can be traced back to objective reasons, such as the different aims, interests, roles and responsibilities of the various actors. Such tensions can be mitigated only if the parties make themselves aware of and clarify among themselves the above differences right from the outset, and make efforts to push their particular considerations into the background in the interest of the common goals. This requires a lot of self-constraint and mutual respect from all actors of action research projects.

References

Delbecq, AL, Van de Ven, AH, & Gustafson, DH 1975, *Group techniques for program planners*, Scott Foresman and Company, Glenview, Illinois.

EU-FP7 Project CSS 2009, *Civil Society and Sustainability, Kick-off report*. Stuttgart.

Petschow, U., Rosenau, J., von Weizsäcker, E. U. (eds. 2005): *Governance and Sustainability – New Challenges for States, Companies and Civil Society*. Greenleaf-publishing, Sheffield.

Phillips, LD & Phillips, MC 1993, 'Facilitated work groups: theory and practice', *Journal of the Operational Research Society*, no. 44, pp. 533–549.

Publicus Research 2010, *Empirical analysis – network of organizations involved in energy efficiency*, Budapest, Hungary (in Hungarian)

Reichel, A. (2006): *Die Lernarchitektur regionaler Nachhaltigkeitsnetzwerke (Learning architecture of regional sustainability networks)*, Manuscript, Berlin.

Vári, A, Ferencz, Z, Csikai, M & Bozsó, B 2010, 'Civil society for sustainability: experiences of an action research project', *Társadalomkutatás*, vol. 28, no. 1, pp. 109–119. (in Hungarian)

Vári, A, Ferencz, Z & Bozsó, B 2011, 'Civil society for sustainability: experiences of an action research project, 2', *Társadalomkutatás*, vol. 29, no. 2, pp. 269–278. (in Hungarian)

Vári, A & Vecsenyi, J 1992, 'Experiences with decision conferencing in Hungary', *Interfaces*, no. 22, pp. 72–83.

The CSS-Project – new strategies for an established CSO supported by Social Science – A learning process with Dialogik gGmbH and unw e. V.

Joa Bauer, unw, Ulm, Germany and Dialogik, Stuttgart, Germany

Introduction

Within the 7th research program of the EU in the funding scheme "Research for the benefit of CSO" the "Ulmer Initiativkreis nachhaltige Wirtschaftsentwicklung e.V." (unw), a civil society organisation (CSO)[54] based in Ulm, Germany and "Dialogik gGmbH", a social science institute in Stuttgart, Germany started a learning process how to foster the CSO activities for sustainable development with input from social science. This process was based on the research project "Civil Society for Sustainability" (CSS) with two other similar tandems in Hungary and Slovenia/France. The project was designed with three phases:

- Analytical phase with research for research gaps defined by the partners (Phase I)
- Planning and Implementation of a practical pilot project for the CSO (Phase II)
- Evaluation(Phase III)

The overall design of the CSS project is described more detailed in this volume in the articles of Marega et al and Vári et al.

Problem context – unw: a regional based CSO in Germany

The CSO landscape in Germany is manifold. There is a very active scene of different organisations on different levels and topics of influence in governance processes towards sustainable development (Reinert, A. 1998). Most of them target sustainable development in the following main areas of activity, driven by the will to make societal changes:

- Political appointment: gaining influence on political decisions regarding sustainable development by lobbyism, public relations and networking

---

[54] In this paper the wider definition "CSO" is used for unw and similar organisations as it is the term used for the funding scheme. Other concepts with specific and more narrow meanings like "NGO" for Non-Governmental Organisation are seen here as a part of the overall concept "CSO".

- Technical/operational projects: application of defined projects with direct effects for sustainable development

The established and big CSOs do usually both on regional (more technical approaches) as well as on national or international level (more political approaches). One of the most important issues for all CSOs is their reception in media as the most countable indicator regarding their influence on public opinion and legitimation (Altvater, E. and Brunnengräber, A. 2002). The main topics targeted by sustainability-oriented CSOs are environmental protection, human rights and other social themes (Greenpeace 2007). Specific CSOs usually concentrate on one of these specific themes as an expression of their core competences.

The different approaches of the CSOs (areas of activity and topics), their size and spatial orientation between local and global change require different forms of organisation and institutionalisation. Especially big CSOs build on organisational forms that link voluntary action with employed staff that is responsible for organising and planning. Unw is in this context a quite small CSO with orientation on the region of Ulm in the south of Germany, completely based on voluntary action, which is an important difference to the two other CSOs in the CSS project.

The unw was founded in 1993 in the city of Ulm, Germany. A group of scientist and the lord mayor of Ulm came together after a discursive process, initiated by Prof. Dr. Helge Majer, an Ecological Economist, with the idea to foster sustainable development on a practical regional scale on base of societal theory of networking (Majer, H. 1998). It was the idea of establishing a network of regional stakeholders that lead the process of building up this CSO for public benefit. Main targets of unw on the way towards sustainability are

1. Promotion of science and research in sustainability and dissemination of the results

2. Fostering sustainable development with stakeholders in the Ulm region

An emphasis of unw has been laid on close partnerships with local industry and politics involving them directly into the process of change towards sustainable development. For this target, unw aimed for a specific structure of members with entrepreneurs, scientists, citizens and institutions (i.e. the city of Ulm). The organisational activities are based on the executive committee with monthly meetings, a scientific committee (which was not very active recently) and the research group for future questions which is only working on current projects. People responsible for these research projects usually are engaged as employees at unw for the time period of a project. Besides the research projects the main activity of unw was providing Round Tables with different topics and task forces with specific duties and responsibilities. For dissemination and public communication of sustainable topics unw provides regular events like the annual "Town Hall Event" or the "Wednesday Talks", in which recent topics of sustainability are presented and discussed with the public. It is remarkable that the former research projects at unw (target 1) conducted by the research group haven't been linked strongly to the other networking activities of unw aiming for target 2. Research projects for sustainability and regional networking for sustainable development by unw members appeared to be disconnected. Nevertheless unw was successful in both fields of activity. Former results of the unw activities are:

- Different research projects (funded by governmental and beneficial organisations) with regional improvement in sustainable development (Study about traffic and air-pollution in Ulm, Environmental Management for SME with five firms certified after EMAS and/or ISO 9000, the "Network Danube Valley" with co-operations of different SME with common ecological aims, regional industrial ecology with five firms cooperating in waste-management)
- Public activity towards sustainability like the "citizens-report to the mayor of Ulm", a project fostering renewable energy and energy-saving, initiating the planning and construction of an ecological housing-estate and initiating the Agenda 21 process for Ulm

The unw's own perception about its current state at the beginning of the CSS project, more than fifteen years after its foundation, was being at a crossroad: several sustainability issues have been worked on in different "Round Tables" and in action-oriented and funded research projects, but now new issues for unw and its members and activists were needed. Personal and institutional support, the embedding of the unw network into the wider social and political networks of the Ulm region (and on larger scale) seemed to be the most pressing problems unw faced at this time. New knowledge had to be addressed to new segments of the regional population. The discussions with the executive board of unw in the pre-project phase raised awareness of the need for new strategies also regarding the fact, that there has been no new funded project with broad public awareness. As one member of the unw board said: "How can we reach people, companies and other institutions with the same things we are doing for more than fifteen years now? How can we make a sustainability-CSO sustainable itself?" Picking up these questions, the CSS project came in the right moment. In this specific case the research project and the daily activities of unw could be linked directly, the benefit of the project aimed to be for unw itself and not only for the stakeholders or target groups. This induced a new situation for the relation of the scientist and the active members of unw: How can this project (and especially the scientists) provide a useful benefit for unw? This was the first opportunity for a long time to take a project as a chance for reflexivity. Former funded research projects have always targeted external target groups like SMEs or public administration but not the performance of unw itself.

Tools, Methods, concepts used

<u>First Step – building an internal working group for CSS</u>

For unw it was after 16 years of sustainability action a new situation to be evaluated by an external institution. As activities usually are planned by the executive board of unw, methods and questions of analysis had to be discussed in this operational unit of unw before the analysis phase could start. This lead to the decision of building a new operational unit within unw, the "Working Group CSS" in order to provide a permanent collaboration of the activists with the scientists. The parallel analysis of unw was based on verbal interviews, a questionnaire review, document analysis and workshops on different levels of the unw network. For this process DIALOGIK provided a simplified network model, distinguishing different spheres of connectivity and commitment of stakeholders to the aims of unw, the "onion model". In this model one distinguishes four different states of connectivity to the aims of unw which are characterised by increasing distance to the core of the network like onionskins. Group A, the inner circle of active members, which is at the same time the executive board. Group B with the different unw members, stating their commitment by membership. Group C with interesting stakeholders with a weak connection to unw and group D with possible networking partners, which have not been involved directly in unw's activities. For the analysis representatives of each group have been interviewed.

Phase I – Analysis

The activities of the researchers have been discussed within the Working Group-CSS, which was an important learning process for all sides, the scientists as well as the activists. Different approaches of how to handle such a process and different ideas how to translate analytical results into daily practice of a CSO lead to iterative back loops which took more time as expected (especially by the practitioners). The role of social science in the unw case was questioned on different levels by some of the activists who were strongly focused on the benefit for the CSO and who questioned the efficiency of the process within the CSS project. The first and second phases were partly dominated by discussions about goals, methods and efforts and the use of the research activities for unw. Finding a common base for cooperation was a question of finding a common language and mutual understanding was the prerequisite for finding research gaps and for defining the role of the scientists in a CSO where activists "already know what's going on".

After some fine tuning between science and the CSO in several workshops of the Working Group-CSS results of research were balanced between the needs and requirements of unw, the theoretical demand of DIALOGIK and the overall requirements of the CSS project. Especially the role of the scientist within this process was a balancing act between different roles of a consultant on the one hand and a neutral observer of the ongoing processes with the focus on generalisability on the other hand. Alternating between these two roles as stylized positional extremes, means a specific demand to the scientists. Acting like a consultant might imply to interpret the role of science as a simple service provider for the aims of the CSO, which is interested in usable results. In this (extremely oversubscribed) role, taking the mission of science serious as producer of "truth", the truth will not remain scientific as it will be shaped and optimised for the use of the CSO. "What you want is what you get" is the hidden headline behind this scenario of using the possibilities of science to find new approaches and insights like a musical request programme of the participating activists. This might be the agenda of the research programme "Research for the benefit of CSOs" but it is far away from the theoretical standard of science that leads to the imperative of playing the consultant.

On the other hand there is the real assignment and the political will to provide benefit for the participating CSOs, making science immediately useful for them and not only from an indirect position of producing knowledge about civil society and sustainable development. This is a pressing approach to the scientists but it is legitimate from the CSOs point of view. Most CSOs do not need rocket science and infinite reflected monuments of theory for their daily work. They need applicable knowledge of different quality and see the science in responsibility to deliver this in a useful and coherent manner. There's no need to reflect or know the scientific methods, there is a need of results which influence and improve the activities. This might lead to "informative entertainment", especially in the case of unw, where all activities are provided by voluntary activists who have jobs and businesses which need usually all their power. Taking this extreme position, science will deliver easy understandable results, using comprehensible methods. Giving up this service oriented position and taking the role of the neutral scientist sometimes lead to the dialectic positioning as an "evil genius" who has to tell the "truth" no matter if it is useful for the CSO or not. The role of unw in this context was between asking for the real benefit and "doing things for the sake of science". The latter was an often used expression by the activists, transporting their hidden resistance against an exclusive scientific position with theory based approaches. Within this process of finding the track for the CSS project trust grew up slowly between the partners and the main results of the analytical phase satisfied both at the end, being useful for the CSO as well as being a scientific base for further development of the pilot project to be applied within CSS. Out of a broad field of questions and findings five leading questions were developed:

1. **What's the mission?** New environment(s) and the need for adaptation
2. **(New) role of unw** Educator-Networker-Implementer: What activities to choose?
3. **Connecting to other Stakeholders** Using unw's credibility with the economy to connect to others, especially from (civil) society and as special target group young people
4. **Sustainability Impact** How to improve and measure unw's effect on Sustainability in Ulm
5. **Communication with Stakeholders** Professionalising unw's communication strategy

Additionally the researchers developed a strategy map for unw which should help to find a feasible pilot project in order to meet the research gaps found in the analysis phase.

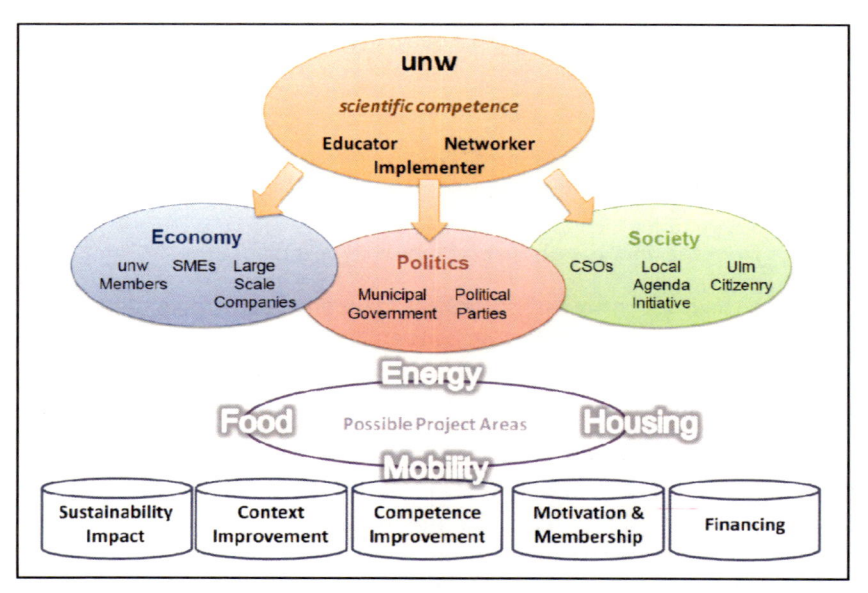

Picture 1: Strategy Map for unw, graphic by André Reichel, Dialogik

The map shows the analytical frame in which all unw activities are embedded regarding the five leading questions. Top-down it stresses the different possible roles of unw to which a new pilot project should fit, asks for the target group(s) which should be reached with a project and structures possible project areas as specific topics. In the end the possible success of an activity has to be assessed with the following criteria: Which impact on regional SD will the activity reach? Does it lead to a context improvement of unw in Ulm, regarding its connectivity within the regional networks of stakeholders? Will it improve the competence for sustainable solutions within the membership and the network of unw? Will it improve the motivation of activists and lead to an increase of members? Which influence will the project have on the financial situation of unw?

After the development of this strategic map, the scientific analysis could start on the base of this first experience of working together. The analysis was based on different analytical instruments:

- Document analysis of all available documents that describe the activities of unw since the beginning, qualitative and quantitative examination of all activities by year
- Questionnaire based survey with the members of unw and the different circles from the "onion model"

- Strategic discussions with the board of unw, reflecting the findings of the analysis
- Workshops with the Working Group CSS
- Interviews with persons from the different Scales of the unw network (members, persons from associated institutions, stakeholder)

Findings from the analysis phase and their usefulness for unw

Regarding the roles unw was a successful "networker" and "enlightener" for the last 15 years. Unw was and is very strong in these both roles and decided to keep them within the process of implementing CSS and not to try to change this. Implementing activities in the sense of a "technical NGO" usually need stronger involvement by the CSO and this is hardly being provided by a CSO solely based on voluntary work. There was a strategic discussion with more than 20 members, held on a weekend, where these issues were discussed with the result, that an approach with more emphasis on implementation strategies would require a completely new basis of professionalisation and a strong change in the strategy. This change seemed to be too ambitious for the restricted working force of the volunteers and the decision was taken to keep the successful roles of a networker and enlightener.

The historical analysis showed a quick increase of activities and number of members from the beginning until 1998. Afterwards one can state decreasing activity and a stationary number of members of unw. There seems to be a link between low activity and stopped growth that was not intended by the members. For unw it was a pressing question, how to handle this situation in order to keep the development on-going.

Another finding of scientific analysis in the first phase was a lack of (voluntary) activities within the membership of unw. The most active people inside unw are the members of the board, or the other way round: members who want to become more active have to join the board (which is "officially" only possible once a year at the members meeting). There was no other unit established for activities within unw. On the other hand activities within the board are not very transparent for members and there have not been many measures in order to get more members involved in (or motivated for) unw activities.

Knowledge and activity of interested members is the most important resource of unw. So there is a gap between things that should be done and the capacity of the board organising the activities of unw. Meetings are dominated by decision making in order to do an efficient job. There is only small room for further discussions about sustainability as a new concept and approaches to motivate members. An interesting point is that the researchers of all tandems within the CSS project discussed this point in a similar way, asking for the creative potential within the CSOs. In a common workshop of all tandems one called that concept the "Third Room", in which more conceptual thinking would be possible.

One specific research question came out of this for unw: How can members be activated? Sustainable development has entered the mainstream and is widely discussed across the media in Germany, but the wider public, and also some enterprises, still do not know too much about how to behave "sustainable" (except one should save energy and use resources efficiently). Sustainability has become a "one size fits all" phenomenon without *real* implementation in daily practice. Everybody is talking about it, but there are many different understandings of the implications, even within unw (and the executive board) itself. But these issues have not been discussed in unw for years and activities have remained the same. From the outside the reception of unw was on the one hand that of a trustworthy institution that fosters sustainable development, on the other hand that of an elitist organisation, appearing to be a closed shop.

Research and analysis of the unw network showed, that for unw it is important to find new approaches after being a successful "networker" and "enlightener" for the last 15 years. Unw was and is very strong in these roles and decided to keep them within the process of implementing CSS. Now the question was how these roles could be filled with new ideas and activities in order to reach a "higher level" of sustainable activities with new and – if possible – younger members. The Working Group-CSS called this approach *"Action Platform for Sustainability" (APS)*.

Phase II: Decision for a pilot project: Action Platform for Sustainability (APS)

In an iterative loop the Working Group-CSS discussed these findings again and searched for an adequate pilot project which had to provide measurable benefit for unw while targeting the research gaps from the first phase. The learning process went into a new dimension. In different sessions more than twenty project ideas were developed but only one or two could be realized. This was the crucial phase within the CSS project as the Working Group-CSS itself was an unexpected success in the beginning of the project. After years in which just the executive board of unw had been active and responsible for unw activities, there was a new unit now with up to 15 participants, working on ideas for unw. For a small CSO like unw this was an essential change.

Dialogik guided the preparation and decision finding process within the team. All project ideas run through an assessment process with a criteria analysis. Criteria from the "Strategy Map" had to be rated on a seven-points-scale by all participants of the Working Group-CSS after all project ideas had been discussed in several workshops. After this multistage selection process based on a decision tool, developed on base of the "Strategy Map", the team decided to implement the APS.

The APS was thought as an internal think (and "do") tank and an additional active unit besides the executive board, which was responsible for unw activities until then. It was sought to attract new activists and especially younger people, as the age structure of unw was dominated by 50+, which have been labelled by an interviewee in the analysis phase as an "elitist club of old men." As a first task for the APS the group decided to develop first steps of a Social Marketing Concept for unw whereas market research for different and partly new target groups of unw was seen as the ideal start for this new unit. An important decision in this phase was to replace the Working Group-CSS by the APS in order to keep the active participants in the process. In this phase the role of the scientists was to deliver more practical input like the framework for a Social Marketing concept and methods for the market research, in this case "Focus Groups" (Kitzinger, J. 1994)[55]. This part of the project was mainly driven by science and there were only few discussions within the APS if this is an adequate approach. There was a mood of trust the participants showed to the scientists that this is the right thing to do regarding the research gaps identified in the first phase of the project. For unw this was an additional learning process on a new level, participating with the members of the APS within the different phases of the application of Focus Groups. New network partners should be approached and a new level of activities by unw members was one of the most important effects of CSS, which has to prove its sustainability after the project. One in a first glance trivial effect was the increasing number of members. Watching this effect more precisely it was the consequence of the new activities, public information and a higher level of public awareness, which shows a regional context improvement.

After the successful Round Tables in the past, the approach of Focus Groups could on the one hand be adapted to the tradition of Round Tables, on the other hand unw learned an innovative form of networking in order to gain

---

[55] Focus Groups are a specific method of group discussion for the collection of qualitative data in Social Science or market research. The group is focused on a specific topic involving common activity regarding specific issues of the topic in order to explore the experiences and perceptions of the participants.

knowledge about the reception of sustainable development by different stakeholders in the region of Ulm. Focus Groups have been chosen as a specific analytical instrument for guiding a selected group of persons through a structured workshop process in order to gain qualitative information about their reception of sustainable development in the region of Ulm (Henseling, C., Hahn, T. and Nolting, K. 2006).

Action Platform for Sustainability meets "Business Juniors"

After several meetings of the APS the group has formed a common understanding of what sustainable development is (for the participants) or might be in different contexts. This is an important basis for external communication with the target groups in order to make clear, which ideas and goals are on the agenda of the APS. The first envisaged group for cooperative activity were young entrepreneurs in Ulm, organized in the association "Business Juniors Ulm" (Wirtschaftsjunioren Ulm) which is based at the chamber of industry and commerce. First contacts were made on their annual "Town Hall Talk" in February 2010, an event quite similar to unw's annual "Town Hall Event". The latter was an occasion for the next step. Unw invited a representative of the "Business Juniors" to participate in the discussion plenum at the "Town Hall Event" of unw, which was the first step to build up trust in the ideas and activities of unw. Contacts have been intensified over the next months and the development of a trustful relation seemed to be still the main issue. As this target group is an organised and institutionalised association, contacts have even in this phase been regulated by indirect ways over the executive board of the group. One of the participants of the APS even joined the "Business Juniors" as new member in order to intensify personal contacts. Networking theory rules that trust is one of the most important values in networking and practice showed in this case, that it is a long way to go after the first contact with the requested networking partner. The APS and also the scientists hadn't expected that it would be such a long way to the first event with the Economic Juniors. After repeated processes of tuning a date the "Focus Group" with the young entrepreneurs was scheduled later than planned. The event itself was arranged by Dialogik attended by selected activists of the APS. The result was a clarification of the perception of sustainable development by young entrepreneurs which opened the space for further cooperation like participation at the events of the "Business Juniors."

Action Platform and local public administration

The second target group for a Focus Group was regional public administration. Again the APS could tie in this event with former unw activities. In the mid Ninetieth there was a Round Table for administration, offered by unw. In this specific case, former networking of unw showed a surprising effect. A former member of the public administration of Ulm who had recently retired joined the APS for the phase of preparing the Focus Group. The new concept of a "part time volunteer" was found for unw, which brought additional flexibility into the activities. The improvement of unw's social network in mind, scientists and activists collaborated in this phase with profit for both sides. Competences in networking from the activists' side and competences in providing the analytical framework for the activities from the researchers provided the humus for a collective learning process. In the same time it was approved, that the old networking rule was also valid in this collaborative project: networking requires the right persons in the right place. A network is not just a theoretical system, it has to be stimulated by real persons. The networking agent for this Focus Group was trusted by the representatives of the city of Ulm and New-Ulm. Eight members from different departments participated at the event and showed a very broad view on the questions of sustainability. While it was a very vivid discussion driven by the different worldviews of representatives from the different departments, the scientific moderator had to control the process accurately in order to lead the group to final conclusions. One can state, that there is much knowledge about different topics of sustainable development, distributed to the different departments. For unw the conclusion was that there are options for further networking with the public administration, for example in establishing a Sustainability Report for Ulm. Contents for further activities are not fixed yet.

Action Platform and college students

Another new and important target group was identified with college students because there was a lack of young members at unw since the beginning. As the APS was originally planned as a unit for younger members there were already students engaged in the activities. In this case these new members of unw got the opportunity to train themselves in new ways of networking in order to make students interested in the topic of sustainability and attending the planned event. While this duty was clear, the APS discussed about the fitting format for the event with the students, moderated by the scientists. The students were seen as a difficult target group, confronted with many opportunities for their free time they would have to spend for this event. The approach of a Focus Group was quit in order to make it more interesting for the students. In this phase, the scientists went into an attitude of activists, targeting mainly the success of the event which was dependent on the participation of enough interested students. In several sessions the APS developed a workshop concept that seemed to be adequate for the requirements of the students, providing more "action". A group of twelve students attended the event with the specific finding that the students are the most solution oriented target group the APS has met within the CSS project. This result was valuable for the activists as well as from a scientific viewpoint. The students appeared to be the most interesting target group regarding the aim of developing common activities. Within the workshop three potential projects for collaboration were developed. One of them might be adapted by the APS. In this case, the scientific input was productive in preparing the event and moderating the discussions by giving a stringent structure on the topics of SD that have been discussed. In this case client orientation was crucial for the success of the project. Further cooperation is planned with a group of students who organise an annual event called "eco social university day". So contact to younger activists will remain also in the future.

Phase III: evaluation and results – Discussion of results and Conclusions

There are different conclusions to be drawn from the CSS project in general and for the collaboration of the CSO unw with the scientific partner Dialogik. The following topics were the most important from the scientists' viewpoint. This singular point of view is due to the fact, that the evaluation of the activists' perception of CSS was not finished.

Provide discursive culture

An important task was to research on civil society and science cooperation. Some remarks can be made here. The role of the scientists in such cooperation is to ensure "discursive rationality" (if this is really possible) by highlighting dominant themes and discussants, thus aiding self-reflexivity in the group and avoiding one-sided monologues or only bi-directional discussions. In the best case a professional moderator is running the process of collaboration because this will help the scientist to concentrate on the main issues. If it is not feasible to provide this moderation role by a third (non-scientific) person, the involved scientist has to integrate these managerial functions within his neutral position of a companion of the process. What is also important from the science side of life: to provide structure after and before discussions. Activists in general feel uneasy with the principal openness of a scientific research project and need assistance to overcome this. Also, within discussion, nothing can be structured "on the go", least decided. This will be a permanent tension: aiding reflexivity, ensuring "power-free" discussion, providing structure – without pushing or pulling the working group into an overtly science-oriented direction. The scientists need also to be aware that there is a general background feeling that science is too far-off the ground and that there is a severe theory-praxis gap. To avoid frustration for both activists and scientists, two simple rules apply:

(1) **Results first**: Scientists should evade discussions before presenting their results. Activists are interested in results, not scientific puzzles, although they like to discuss them if they are presented in a manner that makes sense (and is of relevance) to them.

(2) **Go where it hurts when it hurts**: If there is a group dynamic starting, address it as soon as you notice it. Most of all break power structures of dominant actors, bearing in mind that they do not execute their dominance deliberately, but have it just happening to them as well as on the group.

And most important: As the responsible person for the process itself, the scientist should keep a neutral position and should also try to solve difficult situations with a good sense of humour about himself, it softens situations and breaks any ice that is about to freeze. In the best case a neutral moderator is involved in the process in order to handle frictions.

Be careful with implicit control

The main approach of the CSS project was to support the activities of CSOs by scientific supervision. Within the collaboration research gaps were identified by the tandem with a leading role of the CSO. Dealing with these gaps was also teamwork lead by the scientists then. The team of scientists had specific ideas in mind how to improve the "performance" of the CSO already before the analysis phase of the project started. Regarding these ideas as possible scenarios for future development of the CSO partner, some of these ideas got a dominant role within the internal discussions of the participating researchers and lead to a kind of "implicit control". Important decisions went usually in the direction the scientists had favoured. Challenging these effects on the background of the program "research for the benefit of CSOs" one could ask whose benefit was dominant in the project. "You want it also, I feel that." As feelings are not the main topic for scientists, this seemed to be a variety of this phenomenon like the scientists "knew" what's the best for the CSO as they have the analytical skills and have the free point of view without organisational blindness on the questions which had to be solved within the project. Although all decisions for specific topics and the pilot project were made in democratic processes with adequate tools like voting for the different pilot project suggestions, especially in the pilot phase the scientific approach seemed to be dominating in important phases. This lead to a quite scientific approach regarding the activities of the APS. It also indicated an effect like an internal border between unw and the executive board on the one hand and the scientist, responsible for the implementation of the CSS project on the other hand, which went so far that some of the board members talked about "your project" and not about an unw project. Communication between the partners in such a collaboration is crucial to find and keep a common understanding of aims and ways to reach them. There is a need to take enough time for this internal communication and tuning in order to develop and cultivate a common understanding. Without this effort the activities within the collaboration will not reach adequate progress. Results of such a collaboration will be integrated in the daily activities when they are understood and covered by the activists who will work on after the project.

In the beginning CSS initiated a learning process especially for the CSO participants how to discuss and find decisions in workshops and especially in learning about the tool "Focus Groups" on the one hand and the formulation of a Social Marketing approach for a CSO on the other hand. But as Focus Groups are limited in the number of possible participants, only few CSO activists could attend the events besides the scientists. This was one of the main problems in the important activity phase of the project. Persons who were involved in the preparation and discussion of the Focus Groups were involved just until it got interesting with the events in practice. With the benefit of hindsight it is to state, that this approach was not ideal for the long-term activation of CSO members because this seems to be one reason for the decreasing interest in activities of the APS by the members. Another point was the missing link to the organisational basis of unw. Members of the APS did not feel really involved and didn't feel as equal partners within the organisation, which seems to be an important point for motivation (Knowledge Development Centre 2005). For some of the members the approach with Focus Groups was too theoretical and results were not concrete enough so some of them lost interest in the APS. Nevertheless Focus Groups are a very interesting tool for CSOs in order to get a deeper understanding of the surrounding conditions within the field of activity. But it was not the appropriate tool to keep the new forum alive with participation of the target groups. For this aim (to attract young activists) other activities with scientific approaches seem to be adequate like the planned participation at a "Science Slam" with a presentation about sustainability or educational programmes for an interesting target group like pupils (the so called "T-Shirt project" which was developed in the event with the students). The latter will be the program of the APS for the next time. So scientist should be able to get out of their usual role for such a specific approach as in a voluntary driven CSO like unw and add practical strategies how to attract volunteers (DHHS 2005).

Provide a "Third room" for reflexive discussion

Though time used for the project by the participants from inside unw and its wider network was discussed heavily within the WG-CSS, sometimes even apostrophised as "waste of time", establishing this new unit within unw was one of the main effects for unw. Before CSS the executive board was the only active unit within unw. There was not much opportunity to engage actively for sustainability for the other members or fellow travellers of unw. For some members the board appeared to be an elitist closed shop, which was working very well but without transparency even for the members and not each member was satisfied with this situation. So one of the open research questions was, how to provide and run a "Third Room" for self-reflection of unw and its activities. This appeared as a universal question which arose also on the CSS project level and seemed to be a key to the understanding of the processes within different CSOs. How are decisions taken? How effective and efficient are all the unw activities regarding sustainable results? Which "new" approaches and activities towards sustainable development are feasible facing limited personal resources? What's our common understanding of sustainability? It was discussed heavily in the different CSOs and especially in the unw case, if such a room for "free from daily agenda discussions" could be useful and which additional benefit this approach could provide regarding the time needed for extra discussion about topics which seemed to be clear by the time. Interesting in this case was the quite different reception of this idea by the scientists and the activists not just in the unw case. Scientists with their "meta-viewpoint" interested in the understanding of processes guiding the networking activities saw the opportunities of reflecting the criteria which navigate the CSOs towards common goals, the activists with their inside knowledge of the history and usual measures of the CSOs seemed to be reserved. Challenging what have been good for a long time and reflection of mission(s), goals, measures and results hasn't been on the agenda and there were complaints regarding the benefit for unw. Nevertheless discussions with a meta perspective came up within the process of CSS regularly in the different phases. On the one hand this was induced by the questions posed by the scientists, on the other hand the willingness to reflect on the common sense of the activities of the CSO increased with the collaboration of activists with scientists. Without providing this "Third Room" for thinking out of the box apart from using management tools for the decision making process there would not have been much reflection about the organisation unw from the inside. Concentration on daily business sometimes blocked creativity. In this case the scientists and the CSO expert in the project had to keep in mind, that also demanding on this intellectual playing field was part of the service which has not been asked for by the CSO directly. Challenging routines of a grown team was also in the case of this CSO an important approach in order to develop new ideas.

But do not build a "parallel project world"

All new activity within unw would not have been possible without CSS from an organisational viewpoint. Research and questions posed in the first phase within CSS lead to additional activities within unw, driven by the overarching concept of mutual learning. This seems to be one of the most important aspects of CSS in the case of unw. In a first glance simple questions like "where do we come from?", "where and who are we?" and "where do we want to go to?" became an important driving force while implementing CSS within unw.

The risk of constructing a "parallel CSS universe" within unw had to be considered while the process of finding a common base for CSS within unw and with the European partners was going on. Quote from a meeting of the unw board: *"If the EU wants to have it like this, you (the CSO-expert and the RTD-performer) seem to have to do it ..."*. So finding a common ground of understanding the benefit and constraints of CSS for unw was an important part of storming and norming within the working group we established within unw as an unw unit and not only as an organisational bracket for the CSS-project. This was an important aim: to make CSS a serious unw project and not an event exclusive for the sake of science. Nevertheless there appeared constraints to link all CSS activities to the existing activities of unw because it was a totally new concept to have this new working unit with the WG-CSS and later the APS. One link was given by the regular attendance of the CSO-expert at the meetings of the executive board of unw. Activities and results were discussed and decisions of how to act and which target groups should be incorporated had to be taken by the board members. On the one hand this cut the competences and freedom of the APS, on the other hand this was the only regular link to the organisation. This weak tie was the minimum of connection such a project needs in order to be integrated in the organisation as a whole. Some of the members of the APS felt the need of even a stronger connection to the rest of the CSO but the response was that the way the project run was right for the unw board, in order to keep complexity low. So for unw, this kind of balance between loose and strong coupling seemed to be an ideal construction without loosing the track of the overall goals and to keep the process integrated.

Second order thinking is not the original way of doing things at unw, so it was an important role of Dialogik, to convince the participating unw members of the necessity of a scientific position with an overarching view on unw and CSS activities in one go. Being a "scientific driven" CSO in the self-perception of most unw-members, it was not easy to be an object of scientific observance in the same time, because the common understanding of the benefit of science for unw was provisioning useful knowledge about sustainable development and its implications and not self-reflexivity.

Take your time (despite the latter paragraph)

In such a collaboration project two quite different worlds meet on the basis of usually different ideas and ends of the project. In this case, the initiative and the idea was developed by Dialogik. There have already been contacts between the scientists of Dialogik and the activists of unw before and also experiences with former research projects which lead to the idea to choose unw as partner for the project. Differently to the planned CSS project these former projects focused solely on external target groups of unw (like entrepreneurs), while the idea of the programme "Research for the benefit of CSO" required an approach that targets the activities and properties of unw itself. As the process for the project was designed absolutely open regarding the contents and questions to be dealt with, there was the need for a long phase of finding the common ground of the project. The board of unw is used to a stringent and efficient working style because time of the active persons is restricted due to their voluntary commitments, which have to be managed besides their full-time jobs. Time of the board members (and of other active persons within unw) is the most scarce and at the same time most important resource of such a CSO. In this context taking decisions quickly is crucial for the unw board. The CSS project did not change this situation. In opposite CSS induced new situations in which decisions had to be taken in order to keep the project running. The engagement of members into the new activities induced by CSS actually intensified this problem (which also is a restriction for the amount of unw activities). Nevertheless it was obvious (mainly for the researchers), that particularly searching for a common ground within the project needed an intensive and time consuming process of finding mutual understanding and trust. From the researchers point of view this was a necessary approach, while the activists' point of view, focused on the benefit for unw, was driven by the will to start as early as possible with "real" activity (starting the pilot project). In this constellation friction between these two different approaches to CSS came up in several meetings of the working group. Regarding the fact, that there was no common understanding of sustainable development within unw while the mission of reaching sustainability as a goal seemed to be clear within the board, there was a hidden antagonism that appeared in the workshops of the Working Group-CSS. Challenging this belief into the own knowledge base (which was seen as a natural truth within unw) was an approach, some of the members of the Working Group-CSS did not support. They called the discussion about sustainable development as a general principle and the meaning for the participants "a waste of time". Furthermore the methods of moderating the workshops and managing the process were challenged by some activists. The process of discussing the discussions in the sense of an unintended meta- perspective, lead to a discursive vicious circle nearly similar to a "double bind". There was the need to discuss formally the process itself in following circles, which needed sometimes half the time of a meeting while the main topic of discussion was the scarcity of time for the volunteers. The only way to come out of this dilemma was to take these discussions as an opportunity to reflect also the whole process within CSS. The question of how sustainable development was and is perceived within the active membership of unw remained the dominating sub text which appeared again for several times without direct impetus by the scientists. There was also the consciousness of the necessity to keep this reflection about the basis of all unw activities running. It was an important effect of CSS to provide the space and time for reflexivity and trying to cut this process in order to come to results more efficiently would have been counterproductive.

References:

Altvater, E. and Brunnengräber, A. (2002), NGOs im Spannungsfeld von Lobbyarbeit und öffentlichem Protest, *Aus Politik und Zeitgeschichte*, no. B6–7, 2002, pp. 6–14

Calließ, J. (Ed. 1998), Barfuß auf diplomatischem Parkett – Die Nichtregierungsorganisationen in der Weltpolitik, Loccum

DHHS-U.S. Department of Health and Human Services (2005), Successful Strategies for Recruiting, Training, and Utilizing Volunteers – A Guide for Faith- and Community-Based Service Providers, DHHS Publication No. (SMA) 05–4005, Rockville, Maryland

Greenpeace (Ed. 2007), Das NGO Handbuch, Hamburg 2007

Henseling, C., Hahn, T. and Nolting, K. (2006), Die Fokusgruppen-Methode als Instrument in der Umwelt- und Nachhaltigkeitsforschung, IZT Werkstatt Bericht Nr. 82, Berlin

Kitzinger, J. (1994), The methodology of Focus Groups: the importance of interaction between research participants, *Sociology of Health & Illness*, Vol. 16, no. 1, pp. 104–121

Knowledge Development Centre (2005), Attracting and Keeping Youth Volunteers Creating a Governance Culture that Nurtures and Values Youth, Toronto, Ontario

Majer, H. (1998), Pflastersteine – Ulmer Wege zur Nachhaltigkeit, Sternenfels

Reinert, A. (1998), Welche Erfahrungen haben Nichtregierungsorganisationen gemacht? Und wie haben sie sich bewährt?, in: Calließ (Ed. 1998), p. 65

Civil Society Involvement towards Sustainable Energy Development in Africa: Expectations, Challenges and Perspectives

Angela Meyer, Gregor Giersch

Over the last twenty years, the role of civil society in sustainable development has been widely acknowledged by governments, international institutions and development agencies. Recognizing and strengthening the involvement of non-governmental non-profit movements in view of establishing an integrated approach towards sustainable development has been included among the guiding principles of many international agreements and multinational programmes of the last years.

Already the UN Action Plan on Sustainable Development, Agenda 21, which has been adopted in 1992, devoted its entire chapter 27 to the role of non-governmental organisations (NGO) as genuine partners for sustainable development. It emphasised in particular on the independence of these actors, as well as their "experience, expertise and capacity in fields which will be of particular importance to the implementation and review of environmentally sound and socially responsible sustainable development" (UN 1992, §27.3). Also the Rio Declaration, based on the goal of "establishing a new and equitable global partnership through the creation of new levels of cooperation among States, key sectors of societies and people", specifies in its Principle 10 that "environmental issues are best handled with participation of all concerned citizens, at the relevant level", through their access to information and involvement in decision-making processes (UN 1992a).

In a similar way, the European Union has made the involvement of the civil society a key element of its approach to governance and promotion of Sustainable Development. The 2001 White Paper on European Governance, emphasizes that changes require concerted action including the civil society who plays "an important role in giving voice to the concerns of citizens and delivering services that meet people's needs" (EC 2001). In a similar notion the European Commission's reviewed Sustainable Development Strategy welcomes initiatives "which aim at creating more ownership for sustainable development". It moreover expresses its commitment for more intensified dialogue with relevant organisations and platforms and calls for an increased involvement of civil society in sustainable development matters (EC 2006).

Despite these statements and a growing global awareness, the potential of Civil Society Organisations (CSO) in contributing towards sustainable development, and especially the development and implementation of appropriate energy solutions is insufficiently specified and only partly realised. This becomes more evident when looking at specific sustainable development challenges in specific countries and world regions.

Especially regarding the energy sector in low income countries, the role of civil society to reconcile growing demand and ecological sustainability has long been neglected.

Initially missing as specific issue in the Millennium Development Goals (MDGs), the access to clean, safe and affordable energy is finally receiving growing attention within the MDG review process. In April 2010, UN Secretary General Ban Ki-Moon emphasised that "decisions we take today on how we produce, consume and distribute energy will profoundly influence our ability to eradicate poverty and respond effectively to climate change". Stressing that "these challenges [are] beyond the reach of governments alone", he concluded that "the active engagement of all sectors of society: the private sector; local communities and civil society; international organizations and the world of academia and research" is required (AGECC 2010, p.2). However it remains largely unclear how such active engagement of all sectors of society – especially CSOs – could effectively be realised within the heterogeneous context of Africa's low income countries.

This article provides some analytical reflections concerning the role of CSOs in selected African states in the field of sustainable energy development. Its aim is to present and discuss where and how these organisations effectively and potentially contribute towards sustainable energy production and consumption on the continent. It hereby recalls major observations and findings from the two-year European project SustainergyNet. Based hereon, the article discusses the lack and challenge of multi-stakeholder cooperation as regards the development and implementation of sustainable and appropriate energy technologies and strategies. It elaborates what factors appear to be critical for a successful collaboration between these actors and RTD and policy stakeholders.

Africa's Energy Challenge and CSO Involvement

Given the heterogeneous and complex challenges in African energy development, exploring the potential of CSO contributions on the continent appears to be both, crucial and difficult at the same time.

In most African countries, and especially since the 1990's, civil society organisations have emerged as an ever more significant social pillar. Many of these non-governmental organisations, associations, people's movements, faith-based communities and other institutions are committed towards contributing to the continent's development in a sustainable way that matches the population's needs and concerns. Individual motivation and personal initiative have helped them to partly become a substitute for defunct state services and insufficient provision of public goods. Where central government for a variety of reasons is failing to effectively achieve development goals, the active engagement of CSOs has partly helped to raise the living standards, protect the rights and interests of citizens, communities or specific social groups and contributed to the conservation of natural livelihoods.

However, despite the key importance of access to energy for socio-economic development, civil society still plays a relatively marginal role in the field of energy development in Africa and the cooperation with other stakeholders is limited. Collaboration with the research and technology development (RTD) sector is weak and exchange with the policy domain remains sporadic or bound to individual efforts. This is particularly problematic given the complex interdependencies of sustainability, socio-economic development and the issues of environmental protection and the energy sector. Economic and social development can only be achieved with a safe, reliable and affordable access to energy. This clearly cannot be done by relying on traditional forms of energy production and use that already lead to serious environmental costs. Therefore efficient and sustainable energy provision also plays an essential role for environmental conservation.

In most African developing countries, the energy sector at large suffers from enormous inefficiencies of production, provision and consumption with serious implications for the environment and the climate. As in these countries energy demand is growing fastest, solutions have to be found that respond to the current economic, social and demographic developments while allowing for the preservation of the environment and responding to the need to mitigate Climate Change.

Statistical data, as well as comparative concepts like the Ecological Footprint reveal that Africa's energy consumption is far below world averages. According to the Ecological Footprint Atlas 2010, "Africa's average per person Ecological Footprint of consumption is 1.4 gha [global hectares], substantially lower than the global average Footprint of 2.7 gha per person." (GFN 2010, p. 40). However Africa's insufficient and inefficient energy infrastructures leaving hundreds of million people literally out in the dark, already comes at enormous ecological and social costs. With no access to clean, safe and efficiently produced energy, the majority of Africa's 1 billion people has to resort to firewood or charcoal, leading to irreversible deforestation and subsequent aggravation of poverty.

While rapidly growing urbanisation will inevitably require some large scale centralised efforts, a step by step modernization based on local bottom up initiatives appears to be the most feasible way for rural and peri-urban communities that are otherwise left without any alternative to the unsustainable overuse of traditional energy sources. Technologies developed to produce energy from renewable sources – like solar, wind and biomass – will only help tackling this challenge if they are adapted to the situation where they are implemented, i.e. if they correspond to local capacities, needs and demand.

Although CSOs appear to be best placed and suited to act as an interlocutor between the society and RTD performing institutions, their effective participation in RTD processes remains rather limited today. In light of the necessity to 'translate' both, societal needs and circumstances to the scientific community and technological improvements to the local population, CSO involvement appears a key approach to ensure social acceptance and prevent potential social conflicts arising from technological modernization. Despite this promising role of civil society organisations, their effective participation in RTD cooperation is still struggling with a variety of shortcomings.

The SustainergyNet Project

Assessing, exploring and supporting the potential of CSOs in the context of African sustainable energy development has been the main objective of the two-year European project SustainergyNet[56]. SustainergyNet has been implemented between August 2008 and July 2010 under the 7th European Research Framework Programme (FP7). Its activities have been focused on the issue of CSO involvement in Research and Technology Development (RTD) processes for the development of African sustainable energy solutions. The consortium[57] has assessed and discussed achievements and shortcomings regarding CSO participation in the development, implementation and maintenance of sustainable energy technologies.

---

[56] SustainergyNet – Integrating civil, scientific and stakeholder knowledge towards African sustainable energy policy. Project 211662, funded under the 7th European Research Framework Programme (FP7), web: www.sustainergynet.eu.

[57] The project consortium was composed of research organisations and universities in Europe, Kenya and Egypt and has worked in close cooperation with actors from the civil society in Europe, Northern and Sub-Saharan Africa.

The project has collected information and experiences from concerned stakeholders in order to identify, in a first step, major problems and barriers that can more accurately explain why multi-stakeholder approaches still remain rather limited today and studied best practices that nevertheless exist. A series of over 80 stakeholder and expert interviews have been conducted in Egypt, Kenya and Europe. These have gathered on the one hand, the experience and opinions of stakeholders representing civil society, the research community and the policy making level of several Northern African and Sub-Saharan countries mainly focussing on East Africa. On the other hand, interviews have provided expert testimony and opinion, as well as comparative data on the situation in Europe. Interview partners were selected by the project partners, mainly based on already established contacts and networks, and in view of reflecting a variety of backgrounds and experiences. Moreover, it was tried to ensure a balanced representation of members from the civil society, the research community and policy related actors. Interviews were either conducted face-to-face or by telephone, using a semi-open questionnaire. The interviews' findings were first presented and discussed on a 2 days internal project meeting. This allowed the partners to compare the collected data and to draw first conclusions on assessed perceptions regarding multi-stakeholder cooperation, major challenges, problems and obstacles, and possible ways for improvement addressed by some of the interviewees. Additional insight was gained through workshops bringing together the SustainergyNet project partners and stakeholders with different backgrounds in the field of renewable energy, a number of visits and on-site meetings with local CSO initiatives, as well as the studying of examples of best and failed practices of multi-stakeholder cooperation. Information, data and opinions thereby collected were subject to discussion on a conference in Nairobi, gathering representatives from the three concerned stakeholder groups. The conference's results were additionally enriched by a concurrent online conference with forums in English, French and Arabic that allowed a wider range of participants mainly from Africa and Europe to share their ideas and comments. This e-conference also summarized and presented the major findings from the conference during and after the event, and thereby enabled interested users to respond and comment on them. By the end of the e-conference, a total of 87 users had registered although participation in the forums was also possible without registration. A total of 132 comments were contributed in the different forums: 69 in English, 32 in French and 31 in Arabic.

Given the large variety within each stakeholder group, especially within the group of CSOs involved in interviews, workshops, field visits and the conference, empirical quantitative conclusions were impossible and would have required research activities beyond the coordinating and networking scope of the project's funding scheme. However the qualitative analysis of the collected data indicated some typical issues and notions that allowed formulating a set of conclusions.

The Potential of CSOs to support and apply sustainable energy solutions in Africa

Benefiting from CSOs' proximity to local populations and end-users

According to the opinions assessed, a major strength of civil society organisations lies in their proximity to local communities. This makes these groups appear as interesting partners for accessing, gathering and interpreting data and information on needs and concerns of specific social groups and potential end-users. Not only for RTD but also for policy stakeholders a participatory approach involving local civil society therefore presents a promising option for ensuring that technological developments correspond to circumstances and livelihood patterns in particular target regions. Most respondents mentioned their positive role in effectively preventing any harmful or unequal effects on specific social groups that technological changes on energy production and consumption could unintendedly bring about. Similarly, their participation is seen to be effective for increasing the social relevance of research results, for promoting the acceptance and acceptability of new technologies and hence mitigating social conflicts and tensions that a merely technological focus ignoring local interests might cause. Neglecting the impact of technological solutions on local communities, especially when they are not directly benefiting from the implementation might extinguish any associated progress. Changing the socio-technical system of rural or peri-urban communities in African low income countries always comes at the risk of undermining the livelihood of local populations or forcing them to adapt their living in a way that may contradict their interests. Consequently it may also force people to resort to strategies and practices that are not compatible with sustainable development. Assessed opinions reflected the widely shared view that CSOs often present a source of practical know-how, traditional knowledge and problem-relevant experiences that can additionally enrich research activities, and introduce different and complementary perspectives. CSOs can offer the contact to the "reality on the ground" that researchers and engineers often lack. In this regard, these movements can act as important bridges between the research sector and the society, between researchers and local communities, between needs and solutions. They can contribute towards closing the gap that often hinders technological developments from effectively contributing to better living of local communities and underprivileged poor.

CSO-RTD cooperation towards innovation

Recent literature exploring the way in which innovative ideas for sustainable development emerge emphasises the link between social and technological changes within socio-technical systems. Smith (Smith & Voß & Grin 2010) for instance advocates a "multi-level perspective" of macro, meso and micro processes, in order to conceptualise more accurately how socio-technical systems innovate and change at different societal levels. Innovation in this perspective is not reduced to technology alone, but includes changes in the socio-technical system as a whole.

Another aspect of innovation in the context of socio-technical systems is the incremental evolutionary nature of changes resulting from cooperation processes. Progress towards affordability, applicability and acceptability are key factors for appropriate technologies.

Interviews conducted with Northern and Eastern African scientists and RTD performers within SustainergyNet have moreover revealed that CSOs are considered by some respondents to present flexible and hence rapidly available partners that can quickly respond to research needs and opportunities. They appear less bureaucratic and do less depend on long lasting procurement processes. Cooperating with CSOs is therefore often seen as uncomplicated and smooth and can even be arranged on an ad-hoc basis. Some practical examples studied suggest however, that these expectations are not always met, especially if the terms of cooperation and commitment are not entirely made clear.

Disseminating solutions and ensuring local ownership

Acting as a bridge between the population and the RTD sector, CSOs are widely considered to be appropriate to communicate scientific findings and promote behavioural changes and move away from unsustainable forms of energy production and use. As the assessment conducted within SustainergyNet has revealed, many researchers and RTD performers, for instance in Egypt and Kenya, already rely on actors from the civil society to raise awareness about new technologies and products. CSOs are seen as "having the ability to popularise science."[58] This role of CSOs is again mainly based on their proximity to local communities but also on the fact that due to their non-scientific backgrounds, members "speak the same language" and can hence communicate findings and results in an easy understandable way.[59]

CSOs can also play a critical role for the application and decentralised maintenance of technologies. Especially if they have already been involved in early stages of research processes, CSOs can encourage a sense of responsibility and ownership among the communities the results are eventually applied to. As has been illustrated by several cases in Northern, Eastern and Western Africa studied during the project, new energy technologies have often not been successful and long lasting in African communities if their application has not sufficiently involved local stakeholders and concerned populations. Plenty examples can demonstrate failure, where renewable energy facilities have been implemented without being properly explained to end-users in terms of their benefits, functioning and maintenance. CSOs are able to play here a key role in raising local awareness on innovations and their benefits and promoting the end users' acceptance. As notably in rural areas in Africa mouth-to-mouth propaganda presents an important way for communicating information and raising awareness and trust, CSOs can take a central position, notably by sharing experiences already obtained in other communities with similar solutions. As a result locally owned initiatives with few financial resources often outperform donor driven prestigious show cases.

Craftsman with (Jiko-) stoves, Nairobi

---

[58] Interviews conducted in SustainergyNet, between January and April 2009.
[59] Interviews conducted in SustainergyNet, between January and April 2009.

BOX 1: Appropriate technologies and the role of CSOs: The example of energy-saving improved cook stoves

In most African countries, families, as well as small institutions such as hospitals or schools traditionally rely on biomass as main fuel of cooking. The use of fire wood in basic traditional stoves (based on coal pot or tripod) or open hearth fire is not only high energy consuming, inefficient and unsustainable from an ecological point of view. Indoor pollution also presents a significant health risk. According to the International Energy Agency (IEA), the number of people likely to die by 2030 from smoke from biomass due to highly-polluting traditional ways of cooking will be higher than that estimated by the World Health Organisation (WHO) for malaria and HIV/AIDS combined. (OECD/ IEA 2011).

CSOs are important and mainly well-positioned actors for raising awareness on the harmful effects of traditional cooking methods and promoting more efficient, cleaner and energy-saving approaches. A very illustrative example is given by the improved energy saving cook stoves that are developed and distributed in Africa under different local names, such as Jiko (Kenya), Mitsitzi or Dago (Madagascar) or Roumdé (Burkina Faso). These stoves use a special ceramic inlay that improves their efficiency compared to metal stoves or open fire by 30% to 60%. Many CSOs are already active in raising awareness and disseminating these cooking devices. Some for instance play an intermediate role in training local craftsmen, informing families about the advantages of the improved stoves and assisting with their use. They propose trainings and workshops or offer public cooking shows on markets and fairs. Through their direct contact to the local population and communities, CSOs thus present a crucial partner for RTD producers as they can collect feedback that can be useful for further improving and adapting the stoves according to the different needs. The bridging role of CSOs can especially be seen in their efforts to align the interests of end-users - cooks on the family and small scale institutional level (in schools, hospitals, etc.) –, local producers and retailers, with the researchers' interests that are mainly focused on improvements in the field of energy-efficiency, resource-saving, pollution-reduction and economic relevance.

Where CSO Involvement matters most

It is important to figure out where and when particular benefits from civil society involvement can best be achieved within RTD processes. Research activities differ widely and so do the options for CSO involvement. Obviously it makes a difference whether the focus is on basic research or applied development.[60] Interviews conducted by consortium partners revealed that RTD performers estimate the participation of CSOs – and in particular of grass root movements with no scientific background – in basic research more difficult to realize and less interesting than involving civil society in applied research and technology development. Given the nature and questions of basic research this is not surprising. However, even if the contribution of CSOs to basic research is less evident and relevant, it could nevertheless be of some value for instance to stimulate new research questions and refocusing the research agenda.

Contributions of CSOs to applied and more product-oriented research activities focussing on particular practical challenges from design to implementation are generally considered more promising for the CSO and the RTD side. CSOs can help adapting new technologies to local needs and requirements and contribute practical experiences.

In a more general way, the potential of involving CSOs in research activities can vary according to the different research stages, as the following table, based on SustainergyNet findings illustrates.

---

[60] According to the OECD, basic research is "experimental or theoretical work undertaken primarily to acquire new knowledge of the underlying foundations of phenomena and observable facts, without any particular application or use in view." Applied research, in contrast, is research also undertaken "to acquire new knowledge" but "directed primarily towards a specific practical aim or objective". See: OECD

Research Stage	Potential Benefits from CSO Involvement in RTD
Research Agenda Setting	Emphasise and explain end-user perspectives in the definition and prioritisation of RTD topics; Pool, represent and translate concerns of otherwise neglected end-user groups, such as local rural or peri-urban communities; Raise awareness of hardly accessible end-user groups with limited purchasing power, such as rural or remote communities, as potential market for environmental RTD solutions.
Problem Definition	Ensure that expected results will improve a situation, without neglecting or harming interests of local communities; Emphasise the societal dimension and relevance of research; Introduce alternative perspectives, creative ideas and innovative approaches.
Data Collection	Access data reflecting the situation in a particular setting; Bring in specific experiences, practical know-how, lessons learned and best practices.
Technological Development/ Engineering, Demonstration	Provide information on behaviour patterns, abilities and capacities and expectations of targeted end-users; Help to ensure that solutions match the situation on the ground and contribute to improvements.
Application / Implementation Production / Maintenance	Raise end-users' awareness on new technologies and their application; Create a sense of local ownership; Collect feedbacks from end-users, to further adapt and improve technologies; Facilitate the maintenance of products on the local level by defining training needs, accompanying training and supporting community-based management.
Dissemination of Results, Multiplication	Help disseminate solutions, especially through mouth-to-mouth propagation; Stimulate replications of best practices.

Table 1: Potential Benefits of CSO Involvement at different Research Stages

Problems, obstacles and barriers

As illustrated by assessment activities carried out within SustainergyNet in Northern and Sub Saharan Africa, the effective involvement of CSOs in building a renewable energy perspective for Africa faces several obstacles. Although on the global level, civil society has been widely acknowledged as a committed partner for sustainable development, this engagement is far from being realised. In the countries studied, the active participation of CSOs in RTD processes focussing on sustainable energy remains largely elusive and uneven and poses a challenge.

To some extent, this challenge is linked to the heterogenic nature of the civil society itself. As no evident definition exists, it encompasses very diverse groupings, ranging from transnational non-governmental organisations with considerable budgets, international networks and complex structures to small, loose and issue-based social movements on the grass root level with highly limited resources, access to information and capacities. In general, the former can more easily interact with other stakeholder groups and are more visible, especially for international partners. Grass root movements, in return, have usually more difficulties in expressing the concerns and interests they represent.

Several examples, notably in Egypt and Kenya, analysed as part of SustainergyNet have revealed that multi-stakeholder cooperation and meetings dealing with sustainable and renewable energy mainly concern representatives from larger and more established organisations. They are often considered easier to cooperate with, than smaller less organised local groups. However resulting partnerships in some cases also appear to mainly serve demonstrating the willingness for CSO involvement and legitimize activities a posteriori. In a similar vein, contacting already well-established and integrated networks is often seen as a promising way to open up potential channels to external partners, projects and international funding.

Weak CSOs – weak partners?

Community based civil society movements, especially if not supported by a donor or other third party, often have very limited available capacities. Some even have no institutionalised organisational structures at all. This reduces their attractiveness as potential partners for a variety of reasons: First, it may be difficult for other stakeholders to figure out who is the contact person and how to conclude binding agreements. Second, lacking institutional structures on the CSO side poses problems in financing any form of cooperation since accountancy of the use of resources is often a prerequisite to take part in research programmes as a beneficiary. Consequently, especially research organisations and technological development performers again either favour larger, more established think tank style organisations instead of grass root movements. Or they may completely refrain from CSO involvement.

Due to their limited capacities and local interests, grass root CSOs often focus on narrow objectives that do not consider sustainable development in a wider context. Beyond this scope, their commitment may be rather limited, which may generate some divergences when it comes to multi-stakeholder cooperation. RTD performers often acknowledge local particularities but only if it helps to demonstrate particular advantages of their technology and suggests the appropriateness of their solutions compared to alternatives.

Finally, although promising more flexibility and spontaneity, insufficient institutional structures nourish many researchers' fear that especially small civil society groups are not able to efficiently perform desired tasks and meet high formal scientific standards and administrative deadlines. Also very personality-based structures are sometimes seen as an obstacle for cooperation, as objectives and hence commitment may depend on one or few lead persons and may, consequently, easily change. For long-term arrangements, too much flexibility is indeed problematic and jeopardizes confidence building measures. It can be considered as incompatible with the idea of cooperation that is intended to rely on a long-term partnership and reliable structures and agreements.

Constrains for multi-stakeholder partnerships

The exchange with African stakeholders in Kenya and Egypt active in the field of sustainable energy production and management has revealed that cooperation between the RTD level and the civil society may also fail because of neglected common interests on both sides, as well as limited awareness of the potential benefits resulting from multi-stakeholder networking. Often incentives and structures that would further encourage such cooperation are too weak or even completely missing.

Researchers working on sustainable energy technologies often do simply not consider civil society actors as project partners. This may be related to the difficulty of especially small organisations to make themselves sufficiently known. CSOs in rural areas most often do not have the necessary capacities to express in a far-reaching manner what experiences and skills they could offer. Lacking visibility and transparency is a problem that many NGOs in many parts of Africa have to face, especially those without external funding sources. Also the difficulty to get in contact with them discourages many stakeholders that would otherwise be willing to collaborate with small organisations. In addition, without professionalized public appearance, CSOs often do not earn the credibility and confidence from potential partners. In a similar way, limited representation may also generate the impression that these groups have no clear objective and goal and are not well organised. They are viewed by some actors as not presenting a trustworthy partner. As the exchange with stakeholders has shown, some researchers may even fear to have more troubles than advantages if involving them into their activities.

But even if considered and known, CSOs are likely to fail to be invited to participate in RTD activities if they do not respond to specific expectations or even simply are not trusted to do so. Either the contributions they could make – in terms of information and data supply, contacts to local end-users or integration of more practical and result-oriented experiences – are not sufficiently evaluated. Or CSOs are viewed as having not enough capacities, expertise and qualified staff to present a competent partner. These perceptions – or non-perception – of CSOs may be linked to limited information, lacking or bad experience and insufficient exchange between the different stakeholder groups. The result may be either pure neglect of CSOs in RTD processes or a climate of distrust among different stakeholders.

As the SustainergyNet assessment has revealed, distrust regarding CSOs can also be linked to these groups' need to resort to third-party funding sources. Several interviewed researchers therefore defined them as mouthpieces of their mainly international sponsors, such as international associations, churches or foundations. They are considered as sharing at least some of their donors' positions and ideologies in order to ensure financial contributions. This may create a dilemma for some small CSOs: Whereas contacts to foreign donors often present for them the only way to afford the costs of their activities and build up some organisational and institutional structures, they may also give them a dubious and ambiguous character in the eyes of researchers or the industry. In addition it may distance them from local communities. But also larger CSOs in Africa witness similar problems. As they often are partners or even field offices of non-governmental organisations based in Europe, the United States or other non-African countries, it is likely that they too are perceived – with or without cause – as being opportunistic and influenced by interests that are foreign and difficult to assess.

The reason for multi–stakeholder cooperation to fail can also be a lack of trust and interest on the civil society side. As pointed out during the assessments, many CSOs perceive scientists as sitting in their "ivory tower" and being too far from reality and the non-scientific world. At the same time, civil society representatives may have a feeling of inferiority. They assume that they do not speak "the same language" as scientists and lack the scientific background needed to express their concerns and interests. Some fear that their own knowledge would be dismissed, as it cannot compare with academic expertise.

Hence, in Africa, but also in some cases in Europe, the different forms of knowledge and know-how – practical oriented versus theoretically founded – brought in by partners with different backgrounds is rather considered as barrier for cooperation instead of being used as complementary pillars to base collaboration on. As a result, especially small CSOs often do not see why and how they should invest their limited human and financial capacities in partnerships with other stakeholder groups they are not familiar with. They consider their mainly practical goals and objectives better achieved through campaigns and events, than through their participation in RTD activities.

Contact and communication problems

Lacking capacities also negatively affect the possibilities of stakeholders to get in contact and find a common ground for cooperation. Internet of course is playing an increasing role in easing the communication between different stakeholder groups. In European countries internet has long become the means of choice for multi-stakeholder communication. Its use is rapidly growing in most parts of Africa. However, as has been noted during the assessment activities, especially elder persons or people in rural areas still often refrain from using this means of communication. On the one hand, the reason is limited availability and accessibility of internet services. On the other hand, especially in rural communities a culture of face-to-face meetings is often favoured as written communication de facto excludes a large number of people. These limits to the use of modern communication means hinders and complicates the interaction with partners located in other parts of the country or internationally. In return, it encourages the consolidation of already established partnerships.

Also the important role of international meetings and conferences for getting in touch with other stakeholder groups bears especially for smaller groups a number of problems. Having only limited resources at their disposal, travelling and attending relevant events is usually rather difficult for civil society representatives. In many parts of Africa, international travel costs are relatively high and prohibitive to the budgetary constraints of most local CSOs. In addition, appropriate local meeting opportunities that gather members from different stakeholder groups are still considerably limited throughout Africa. As has been complained by many experts involved in SustainergyNet activities, conferences and workshops organised by universities, research centres or government agencies in the field of sustainable energy are rarely open to members from the civil society, or only few selected CSOs are invited to participate. As Kenyan Ministry officials explained during the assessment activities, cooperation is easiest for them with large scale organisations to which relations have been established for long. These are regularly invited to exchanges and network events. But even in cases where meetings are open for actors from the civil society, information about them, their venue and registration is generally difficult to access.

The lack of appropriate incentives, supporting instruments and frameworks

Multi-stakeholder cooperation may also fail because of an inappropriate policy context. Research frameworks are often not suited for participatory approaches, and there are only few programmes and policies that target on supporting and encouraging this kind of interaction.

Besides the lack of suitable programmes, the relatively limited participation of CSOs in scientific research and RTD projects is also linked to the amount of bureaucracy that comes with the preparation of project proposals and the management of their implementation. Also, several civil society members interviewed and consulted during SustainergyNet criticised that their access to information on calls and relevant opportunities is considerably limited compared to other stakeholder groups who are more easily made aware of new and upcoming project funding programmes.

Without proposing appropriate and simple mechanisms (practices) and instruments (funding), the mere call to put more emphasis on the social dimension and relevance of research will be insufficient to give the involvement of civil society in environmental RTD projects and activities an increased importance and value.

Also regarding the involvement of small scale CSOs in research related agenda setting processes remains very low. Compared to the EU, the situation in Africa is even more alarming. These groups' influence on research programmes and policies is considerable limited or even not existent. This hinders local knowledge and know-how from being considered within the scope of research agenda setting. This is in stark contrast to policy statements calling for increased influence of civil society on sustainable development programmes and activities.

Whereas European institutionalised approaches of multi-stakeholder research policy making can be found in form of research forums, platforms or national research councils, including members from the civil society, comparable structures are currently still very weak or even non-existing in most African states. Here, the only way for CSOs to influence the research agenda is through mainly personal contacts to either larger civil society movements, research or policy related stakeholders who accept to lobby for their cause.

Promoting CSO contributions to sustainable energy development in Africa – The way ahead

Summarizing the SustainergyNet findings, there are a number of major barriers that currently hinder and limit CSOs from contributing to RTD activities related to sustainable development and energy in Africa:

- Most African CSOs suffer from weak and insufficient institutional and organisational capacities. This reduces the likelihood for them to be considered as potential cooperation partners by scientists and RTD performers.
- There are not enough appropriate measures and programmes to encourage and support CSOs and members from the scientific and RTD community to get in contact with each other and cooperate.
- Information, especially on local African CSOs in remote areas is scarce as these organisations only have limited ability to enhance the transparency and visibility of their scope, goals and activities.
- Limited knowledge about their activities and few possibilities to meet and exchange with them, make it often hard for researchers and RTD performers to imagine the benefits CSOs could bring about, notably in terms of data collection and practical experiences. These contributions are often not acknowledged, underestimated or even deliberatively discarded.
- If involved in RTD processes focussed on sustainable energy solutions, the role of CSOs is mainly seen in disseminating and implementing results. Whereas CSOs are indeed important partners for awareness raising, they are likely to encounter difficulties in explaining and promoting new technologies if they have not also accompanied the entire RTD process.
- A vicious circle of insufficient trust, mutual understanding and unsatisfactory cooperation experiences often undermines efforts towards future multi-stakeholder cooperation.

Overcoming these obstacles requires efforts and commitments from all concerned groups. In several conferences and workshops, stakeholders with different backgrounds, mainly from Egypt, Kenya and other Northern and Eastern African countries have expressed and discussed ideas on how to address these barriers. This has led to the formulation of a set of generalised recommendations for the way ahead.

Visibility and specialisation of CSO actors

In order to be recognized by other stakeholder groups as vital partner, CSOs have to make known and evident what contributions they are able to make. Regular publications, such as brochures or articles in newsletters, as well as the participation in public events can help CSOs to enhance their visibility and provide a clearer picture about their structure, aims, agenda and background. This however requires sufficient financial and human resources, or at least access to other publishers. With its growing and expanding influence in Africa, the internet offers many promising and cost efficient possibilities, notably through the use of websites and web forums or blogs.

In addition, specialisation can also present a means for raising general awareness. Concentrating on a fine-tuned goal can help a CSO to set itself apart from others working in similar fields and be able to offer and increase specific expertise and experiences.

Joining capacities

Whereas a more and more common approach in Europe, institutionalised networks of civil society organisations are still rather rare in Africa. The major potential behind umbrella organisations and other forms of alliances lies in opening the way for synergies to their members: starting with shared technical, material, personal and financial resources, to an increased attractiveness for RTD performers and policy makers because of the pooled know how and experiences these alliances can offer. Especially for small CSOs a joint approach may be helpful to have a stronger voice and enhance their appearance. The success of umbrella organisations is however closely linked to the questions whether appropriate policy and administrative conditions are available, how tensions between either too diverse or too similar members can be avoided and if especially small organisations are supported and encouraged to join.

CSO involvement in different ways and at different steps

In order to increase the effectiveness, relevance and usefulness of results, stakeholders involved in SustainergyNet recommended that CSO involvement should be taken into consideration at every step of a RTD process. Consulting them already at the beginning could notably help to better focus the research scope on particular needs and demands. Having them take part in the testing and demonstration of products is a good way to evaluate whether these correspond to the expectations and abilities of end-users and to eventually adapt them to the available capacities and skills. Due to their proximity and linkage to local communities, CSOs may be suitable partners for raising general awareness on novel technologies and ensuring their implementation on the local level. In a similar way, it may also be beneficial to consider different ways and approaches to rely on CSOs as partners. These may range from more spontaneous and isolated events to long-term agreements, projects and programmes. As CSO involvement often fails because of lacking experience, the consulted stakeholders underlined the importance of researchers to share and exchange best practices.

Creation of new partnerships

As often mentioned in the interviews, long-standing relationships based on personal ties and previous cooperation are favoured by many stakeholders: they are considered as bringing higher levels of trust and commitment between the partners and allowing for more efficient collaboration. Selecting and involving CSOs on a case-by-case basis may however allow to find partners that best fit the scope and nature of the concerned research or RTD project, bring in target-specific experiences and thereby optimize the effective contribution of research solutions and outcomes.

Encouraging inter- and transdisciplinary partnerships

Research agendas and programmes are often not appropriate for promoting interdisciplinary and transdisciplinary approaches that research on sustainable development requires. Many of the available funding instruments primarily address scientists and RTD performers and thereby neglect the involvement of partners with other backgrounds. The participation of the civil society could well be promoted by encouraging precisely the building of multi-stakeholder consortia, covering topics of concern for CSOs or that require focusing on the societal dimension of technological innovation, lowering administrative hurdles and adapting the composition of juries and evaluation committees.

Concluding Remarks

The involvement of civil society in research, development and implementation of energy technologies and systems in view of a sustainable modernization of the African energy sector remains a promising but complex challenge. While the advantages of cooperation between stakeholders from research, policy and civil society receives growing acknowledgement from different sides, concrete results and achievements are still struggling with a variety of obstacles. Following our assessment some of these obstacles can be highlighted and formulated in general terms. Moreover, as has been attempted within this article some fairly vague recommendations can generally be suggested. However it is necessary to point to the fact that despite any similarities between many of the cases studied, simple copying of best practices is likely set to fail. Not only the conditions are defined by such a diverse set of circumstances but also the stakeholder groups themselves are far from being a homogenous type of actor. Especially civil society organisations remain weakly defined, diversely motivated and hard to describe in quantifiable terms that would allow reliable statistical characterization.

References

AGECC [The UN Secretary-General's Advisory Group on Energy and Climate Change] 2010, Summary Report. Energy for a sustainable future (Foreword by the Secretary General), New York, United Nations, April, 28

EC [Commission of the European Communities] 2001, European Governance. A White Paper, Brussels, Belgium, July

EC [Commission of the European Communities] 2006, Review of the EU Sustainable Development Strategy (EU SDS) – Renewed Strategy, Brussels, Belgium

GFN [Global Footprint Network] 2010, Ecological Footprint Atlas, Oakland (CA)

IEA [International Energy Agency] 2011, Energy for All. Financing access for the poor, Paris, France, October

OECD [Organisation for Economic Cooperation and Development], Glossary of Statistical Terms, http://stats.oecd.org/glossary/index.htm (accessed July 22, 2011)

Smith, A., & Voβ, J-P. & and Grin, J. 2010, 'Innovation Studies And Sustainability Transitions: The allure of the multi-level perspective and its challenges', Research Policy, vol. 39, no. 4, pp. 435–448

UN [United Nations] 1992, Agenda 21, Documents of the United Nations Conference for Environment and Development (UNCED), Rio de Janeiro, Brazil, June

UN [United Nations] 1992a, Earth Summit – Rio Declaration & Forest Principles. United Nations Conference on Environment and Development (UNCED), Rio de Janeiro, Brazil, June

Social Acceptance in Quantitative Low Carbon Scenarios

Eva Schmid, Brigitte Knopf, Stéphane La Branche, Meike Fink

Introduction

Significant reductions of global greenhouse gas emissions play a key role in addressing the problem of dangerous anthropogenic climate change. In order to achieve low-stabilization targets, emissions have to peak before 2020 (UNEP 2010). Yet, greenhouse gas mitigation is a challenge for which no simple and single recipe exists, as exemplified by the abortive developments of international negotiations and limited mitigation success since the ratification of the Kyoto protocol. The dominant source of greenhouse gas emissions, especially CO_2, is the anthropogenic use of fossil resources for energy supply. Consequently, mitigation requires a long-term transformation towards low carbon energy systems. To date, the majority of research efforts on how to achieve this have concentrated on identifying innovative technological solutions and assessing optimal deployment pathways, as well as suitable policies in the different sectors of the energy system. This tendency manifests itself in the predominantly model-based low carbon energy roadmaps published recently, e.g. the "Lead Study" in Germany (Nitsch et al. 2010) or on the European level the EU Roadmap 2050 (European Commission 2011a). Central topics are aggregate assumptions on the developments of energy demand, energy efficiency, investment costs of future technologies, technical potentials, demographic structures, etc., that serve as an input or are an output of the respective quantitative energy system model frameworks. However, sociological and normative dimensions, in particular the social acceptance of implications of the suggested energy futures, are rarely addressed. This is a serious shortcoming, as the transformation of national energy systems represents a profound and long-term change process involving society as a whole. Moreover, a high level of unacceptability could result in group's refusal of climate measures or in avoidance strategies that would then decrease its potential efficiency; the question of "social acceptability" is also one of relative unacceptability and its consequences.

In the context of energy system strategies, social acceptance has three dimensions (Wüstenhagen 2007): (i) socio-political acceptance, referring to the acceptance of technologies and policies by the public, key stakeholders and policy makers, (ii) community acceptance of site-specific local projects and (iii) market acceptance, referring to the process of consumers' and investors' adoption of innovative low-emission products. For addressing these dimensions in the context of energy system transformation scenarios, it is necessary to extend the engineering/economics toolbox of research methods towards truly interdisciplinary approaches by combining them with methodology developed in other strands of social science and the humanities. One implication is to not only rely on quantitative methods, but also on qualitative methods, that are useful when the specific individual perspective of the research subject is focused upon, the research subject has been poorly investigated so far and verbal data is to be interpreted (Bortz & Döring 1995); all of these issues apply in the present context.

One approach to address social acceptance in low carbon scenarios to is to include well-managed and repetitive stakeholder consultations as an integrative part of an energy system model scenario definition process. The parameters and input variables of the aggregated model are carefully translated into tangible, real-life, implications for the public and then evaluated by civil society representatives with respect to their social acceptance. The normative considerations emerging from these stakeholder consultations are translated back into configurations of technical model parameters, i.e. political framework conditions, and result in different low carbon energy system scenarios. These integrated scenarios are calculated by the quantitative models and the results are again translated into tangible meaning and presented to the civil society stakeholders, emphasizing at least the first of the three dimensions of social acceptance in energy system strategies. Such a collaborative scenario definition process has been undertaken together by non-governmental organizations (NGOs) and research institutes within the EU-project ENCI LowCarb (Engaging Civil Society in Low Carbon Scenarios) for France and Germany. Based on the ENCI LowCarb experience, this paper proposes a pragmatic project design blueprint, intending to foster repetitive collaboration between civil society and science for introducing dimensions of social acceptance into model-based, low carbon energy system scenarios. Whereas the approach is described in detail here, the results are presented in Schmid and Knopf (2012).

Section 2 presents barriers to interdisciplinary research and collaboration processes between science and civil society in the context of energy system scenarios. Section 3 introduces a conceptual project design blueprint intended to overcome these difficulties. It describes four distinct phases of a collaborative scenario definition process. Section 4 elaborates on the specific experiences from the ENCI LowCarb project and problems encountered during the process. Section 5 reflects on limitations and compares to other scenario projects involving stakeholders. Section 6 concludes.

Barriers to Collaboration

In order to derive a project design that encourages collaboration between engineering, economics and other strands of social science as well as civil society, it is worthwhile to step back and analyse why comprehensive collaborative projects between scientific disciplines and civil society are to date rare, especially in the field of energy system scenarios. Three general observations are helpful. First, one has to acknowledge that "science" and "civil society" are umbrella terms for communities that again consist of a large variety of distinct sub-communities. Second, these communities and sub-communities are distinct with respect to their raison d'être, objectives and culture, i.e. values, norms and language. Third, they have a tendency to coexist, in the sense that there are few institutional intersections per se; collaborative projects across communities are often preceded by proactive, innovative, and open-minded individuals.

Civil Society and Non-Governmental Organizations

Civil society is a rather vague umbrella term, Reverter-Bañón (2006) argues that her understanding of civil society is three-fold: as associational life (Putnam, cited in Reverter-Bañón 2006), as good society, and as public sphere (Habermas, cited in Reverter-Bañón 2006). In more concrete terms, the World Bank (2004) defines the notion as follows: "The term civil society refers to the wide array of non-governmental and not-for-profit organizations that have a presence in public life, expressing the interests and values of their members or others, based on ethical, cultural, political, scientific, religious or philanthropic considerations. Civil society organizations (CSOs) therefore refer to a wide array of organizations: community groups, non-governmental organizations (NGOs), labor unions, indigenous groups, charitable organizations, faith-based organizations, professional associations, and foundations". CSOs are formed as people with similar interests organize themselves and represent a certain set of claims, beliefs, norms and values. Often, the term CSO and NGO are conflated. Willets (2002) defines the term NGO as an independent voluntary association of people acting together on a continuous basis and for some common purpose. In this paper, CSO is used as the umbrella term and NGOs are considered as a subset of CSOs.

Many CSOs intend to change the status quo of a certain affair; environmental NGOs lobby for reducing pollution, churches preach humanitarian values and citizens' initiatives fight for local projects. Often,

CSO activists operate at the grass-roots level and are ideal-driven. In terms of climate change mitigation, environmental NGOs have played a visible role with projects focused on greenhouse gas emission reduction involving lobbying, campaigning or protesting against specific local affairs. With the intention to scientifically back up their lobbying work, NGOs have increasingly been seeking contact to the scientific communities. Moreover, many environmental NGOs have shifted from constituting an activist movement towards more mature organizations employing scientists that did not want to continue a purely academic career. NGOs have published comprehensive scientific studies to underpin their claims and objectives with research results, e.g. WWF (2008; 2009) and Greenpeace (2007). However, these studies were largely commissioned to research institutions and prepared in principal-agent relationships rather than in iterative collaboration processes. In sum, it appears natural to foster collaboration between NGOs, rooted in the civil society community, and scientists as a starting point for incorporating social acceptance into energy system scenarios. In later steps, CSO representatives are included in the collaboration process.

Scientific Cultures and Mitigation

In terms of public attention and academic outreach visibility, the mitigation problem has mainly spurred natural scientists and engineers to develop and assess low-emission technologies, system scientists to perform integrated analyses of optimal deployment paths, and economists to analyse energy market forces and suitable policies. Politically prominent theoretical research results on long-term mitigation strategies have been obtained by engineering or economic methods: mathematical modelling, optimization, game theory, statistics and econometrics, i.e. quantitative methods. Maybe this is due to the seductive charm of hard numbers and associated "scientific facts". Yet, a recent publication of the German Academies of Sciences strongly encourages collaborations between engineers, natural and cultural scientists, as they consider this a prerequisite for achieving ambitious climate policy targets in Germany (Renn 2011). Within the social science literature, the refusal, acceptance, or avoidance strategies of actors regarding mitigation measures is less investigated. There are efforts to understand the public and local acceptance of renewable energies by means of specific case studies, e.g. Zoellner, Schweizer-Ries and Wemheuer (2008), Musall and Kuik (2011) and Nadaï (2007), involving qualitative interviews and questionnaire-based survey analysis. However, there are to date no visible efforts to combining these findings with purely quantitative energy/

economics models. One possible explanation is the coexistence of the different scientific sub-communities.

Even within different scientific disciplines, there are many coexisting and often conflicting strands of research. Many of the conflicts root from methodological issues. Albeit scholars of both the quantitative and the qualitative tradition share the overarching goal of producing valid descriptive and causal inferences (Brady & Collier, cited in Mahoney & Goertz 2006), there are substantial discrepancies in basic assumptions and practices. Schrodt (cited in Mahoney & Goertz 2006) observes that the dynamics of the debate between quantitative and qualitative scholars on the validity of their methods are best understood by comparing it to one about religion, with deep cleavages between the two. Mahoney and Goertz (2006) provide an excellent discussion on how the two research traditions are to be understood as alternative cultures with proprietary values, beliefs, norms and language that may lead to severe "cross-cultural" communication problems when "forced" to work with each other. Thinking of different research traditions in terms of ethnocentric, coexisting and potentially conflicting cultures helps for explaining and mastering the challenges of collaborative research projects. One can draw on the large body of literature on culture in other academic disciplines, e.g. organizational behaviour and cultural studies. Clearly, parallels exist between methodological, organizational and ethnological culture. Considering the effective cultural barriers to collaboration even within science, it is not surprising that the barriers towards collaboration between science and NGOs or CSOs are even higher.

The Collaborative Scenario Definition Process

The collaborative scenario definition process proposed in the following[61] is a pragmatic interdisciplinary approach that aims at producing quantitative engineering/economics model scenarios in collaboration with civil society stakeholders. It is organized in four distinct phases. Phase 1 is concerned with establishing a fully functional project team and Phase 2 with establishing the technological framework conditions for the scenarios. The normative political framework conditions are elaborated with civil society stakeholders during Phase 3, resulting in scenarios that differ with respect to their degree of social acceptance. Phase 4 synthesizes.

---

[61] It is based on the experience from ENCI LowCarb, but presented on a meta level. It is applicable to projects involving the definition of scenarios with both technological and political framework conditions.

Core Project Partners

To accommodate the interdisciplinary requirements of the objective to include social dimensions in quantitative mitigation scenarios, core project partners come from both the scientific and the civil society communities. From the latter, NGOs constitute good candidates, as they form a continuously working formal entity, which cannot necessarily be generalized to all CSOs. Additionally, one can expect that NGOs are well embedded within the CSO landscape and act as facilitators between scientists and other CSOs. From the scientific communities, it is on the one hand necessary to have project partners from one or more research institutions that operate an engineering/economic type of quantitative model (here an energy system model), termed quantitative modelers, hereafter. On the other hand it is necessary to have project partners from the social sciences or humanities that are proficient in both quantitative and qualitative research methods of their discipline, termed social scientists hereafter[62]. Due to the distinct professional cultures of the project partners, it is decisive to stimulate their awareness for cultural issues in general and cultural differences in particular. A trivial, but effective means to achieve this is to define a core project team with each a research institution and NGO from at least two countries that do not share the same language. There are several practical advantages of combining the three different *professional cultures* with two or more different *national cultures*. Project partners communicate in a non-mother language, which fosters the awareness for unfamiliar terms and alleviates barriers to clarification requests during conversations. Furthermore, as the problem of climate change mitigation presents itself and is addressed very differently in individual countries, the transnational perspective helps to reframe and to challenge the purely domestic point of view.

Phase 1: Intra-Group Development

Albeit the intra-group development of project teams is a fairly standard procedure, a conscious group-formation process is of particular importance for collaboration across project partners from different communities. A suitable organizational structure is proposed in Figure 1. It resembles a matrix structure and enables vigorous communication flows between all

---

[62] In the following, it is assumed that both modelers and social scientists are from one research institution and the representative terms research institution, quantitative modeler, social scientist and NGO will be used in singular for simplicity; more than one project partner may be included from each community.

project partners; the colour codes visualize the different communities and countries. Tuckman (1965) observed that groups generally develop by passing through four distinct stages: forming, storming, norming and performing. Given project partners from different communities, with their respective cultural backgrounds, the first three stages need special attention for being successful in the fourth.

The forming stage of group development is characterized by uncertainty: project partners from the different communities are "testing the waters" and get acquainted to each other by exchanging ideas, expectations and world views; one gathers information and impressions of each other, but avoids open controversies or conflicts (Tuckman 1965). It is very likely that during this stage, many of the others' positions are not immediately obvious and even beyond clear assessment to the individual project partner. During the storming phase of group development, which is characterized by intra-group conflict and requires tolerance and patience, project partners express opinions and views more openly, including criticism (Tuckman 1965). One can expect that substantial cultural distance (Triandis 1994) exists between each the social scientist, the quantitative modeler and the NGO member. To overcome these, and enable the group to develop interdisciplinary approaches with regard to the specific research question of the project, conscious intercultural communication is advantageous. McDaniel, Samovar and Porter (2009, p. 13) argue that five aspects of culture are especially relevant to intercultural communication: perception, cognitive thinking patterns, verbal behaviours, nonverbal behaviours and the influence of context.

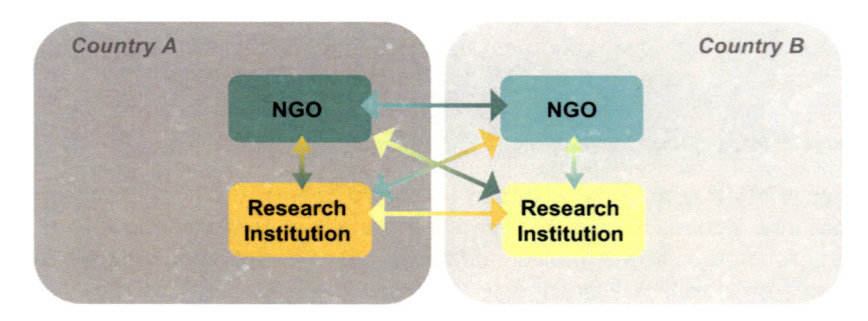

Figure 1. Organizational structure during Phase 1 of the collaborative scenario definition process.

A promising format to foster viable cross-cultural communication is to employ formal "wish-lists". The quantitative modeler receives model features that the others would like to see in the model and what kind of results they expect. The social scientist receives ideas on how social acceptance is defined and will be explored, interpreted and measured. The NGO member receives considerations on what kind of stakeholders to consult. Such a process allows project partners to get a good understanding on how the others *perceive* their discipline. In a meeting, they present what they originally planned to contribute in the project and relates it to the "wish-list" items. Such an exercise will reveal their *cognitive thinking patterns*. After each presentation, sometime is reserved for clarifying terms, so project partners have a chance to realize potential *verbal* and *nonverbal* barriers to communication. Finally, in thematic sessions, the history and status quo of the domestic energy system can be presented, so one learns facts and *context* of the other country's challenges. During the "wish-list" process, the project partners have a chance to develop a common language and gain realistic expectations of the abilities of the quantitative model, the concept of social acceptance and the stakeholder landscape. In repetitive exchange, project partners develop a joint idea of the research methods they will employ. Finally, they pass the norming stage of group development, characterized by cohesiveness and in-group feeling, on to the performing stage, during which group energy is channelled into the task (Tuckman 1965).

Phase 2: Technological Framework Conditions

Phase 2 of the scenario definition process is concerned with model development and the technological framework conditions of the scenarios by involving external experts. The task is to refine the national quantitative models and bring them to a stage, in which they are applicable to stakeholder consultations, fulfilling as many "wish-list" items as feasible, driven by the overarching question of "What is technically possible in the future?". Thus, the social science issues regarding social acceptability do not yet enter the stage, they will be integrated in the next phase. Figure 2 proposes an organizational structure during Phase 2; with the core structure prevailing, but now the national sub-teams, indicated in green, have formed a tighter entity. This ideally results from the intense communication flows during Phase 1. The yellow shading of the consulted experts symbolizes the notion that they will most likely be closer to the researchers in terms of "professional culture" than to NGO members.

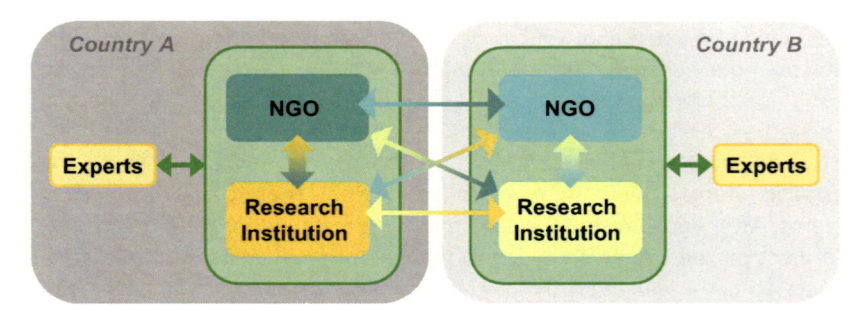

Figure 2. Organizational structure during Phase 2 of the collaborative scenario definition process.

Expert workshops are organized in each country, for the national sub-teams to engage in focus group discussions with experts for obtaining state-of the art knowledge on technical details. Thereby, the experts can assess the validity of the quantitative model and have a control function on the scientific quality. In the end of Phase 2, a finalized version of the energy system model exists, along with a detailed documentation that is also understandable to the non-technical reader. It is necessary to provide such a document during the stakeholder consultations in order to create transparency and alleviate the frequent black-box accusation when it comes to quantitative scenario building. Central to the model description are detailed translation rules, from "model parameters" to "real-world implications" and vice versa, that serve as a basis for taking into account political framework conditions explicitly.

Phase 3: Political Framework Conditions and Corresponding Scenarios

A central issue in Phase 3 of the collaborative scenario definition process is to elaborate different and potentially controversial political framework conditions with relevant CSO stakeholders, involving normative considerations. The political framework conditions relate to the quantitative model by applying the aforementioned translation rules from model parameters to "real-world implications". Coherent sets of political framework conditions form one scenario, differing with respect to the articulated level of social (un-)acceptability of mitigation options. The integrated scenarios are again evaluated by the CSO stakeholders. Figure 3 proposes an organizational structure for Phase 3. The blue shading of the CSO Stakeholders indicate that they are culturally close to the NGO project members, these indeed serve as facilitators in a two-step interaction in workshop format.

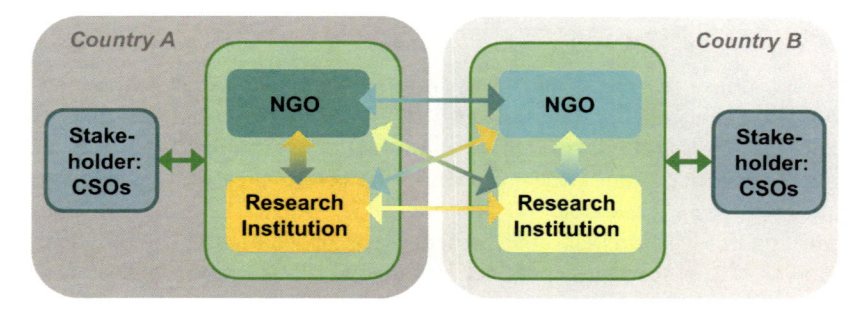

Figure 3. Organizational structure during Phase 3 of the collaborative scenario definition process.

Before inviting CSO stakeholders, the sub-national project teams identify sectors of the domestic energy system that are of particular interest or controversy regarding social acceptance. Together with a professional and neutral moderator, the national sub-teams develop concrete workshop agendas. The social scientist selects suitable methods for capturing stakeholder's assessments during the workshops. A practical format is a questionnaire with Likert scales (Likert 1932), measuring the level of agreement or disagreement of the respondent towards specific statements. The specific statements are the translated "real-world implications" and postulate particular and tangible developments[63]. Per item, two Likert scales are employed: Stakeholders are once asked to indicate whether they find the proposed developments *likely* and once whether they find it *desirable* from the point of view of their organization. Stakeholders are unlikely to express a uniform opinion, so several different sectoral "scenario building-bricks" in terms of political framework conditions will emerge from the workshops. The national sub-teams combine them into coherent scenarios for the fully integrated energy system, which serve as an input to the quantitative model. During the second sectoral stakeholder workshops, ideally attended by the same CSO representatives, the developed scenarios are presented, discussed, and evaluated. The feedback loop ensures that the social acceptance considerations are actually realized and gives the CSO representatives a chance to indicate their assessment of social (un-)acceptance of the integrated scenarios. At this stage, one possible outcome of the scenario definition process may be that the CSO representatives judge one or more integrated scenarios socially unacceptable as a whole, even though individual building bricks can be in line with their preferences.

---

[63] An example from the transport sector workshop of the ENCI LowCarb project is "Cycling and Walking will contribute substantially to the Modal Split. Please indicate your perception whether this is likely and, seperately, desirable from the point of view of your organization on a 7-point scale from Yes to No.".

Phase 4: Synthesis

The last phase is concerned with the synthesis of results obtained throughout the collaborative process, formalizing the outcomes of the stakeholder consultations as well as an evaluation of the final scenarios in terms of social acceptance. Ideally, a workshop communicates the scenarios to policy makers, stakeholders, and the wider public. Possibly valuable extensions for the collaborative process are to elaborate the political feasibility of the scenarios' political framework conditions as well as the reasons for social (un-)acceptance of specific mitigation options in more detail. Here, one could extend the socio-political point of view adopted during the collaborative scenario definition process, and analyse market and community acceptance.

The ENCI LowCarb Experience

The ENCI LowCarb project is financed in the 7th Framework of the EU Commission and constitutes a rather novel format involving both research institutes and NGOs. The core project partners are the Potsdam Institute for Climate Impact Research (PIK), Germanwatch, the Centre International de Recherche sur l'Environnement et le Développement (CIRED), and Reseau Action Climat France; the project phases, identified ex post, are summarized in Table 1.

ENCI LowCarb had two main project objectives: developing a reproducible methodology for engaging civil society, and preparing the German and French integrated energy system scenarios. The following reports on specific experiences made during the project on a more abstract level, with the intention to deliver beneficial input for future projects that involve collaboration between science and civil society, additive to the blueprint outline in Section 3. The German and French domestic energy system scenarios are accessible on the project website[64] upon publication.

---

[64] http://www.lowcarbon-societies.eu

	Phase 1	Phase 2	Phase 3	Phase 4
Objective	Intra-group development of the project team	Model building "What is technologically possible?"	Stakeholder workshops "What is socially desired?"	Synthesis, communication of scenarios
Leadership	Fragmented	Research Institution for sub-team in each country	NGO for sub-team in each country	Joint responsibility
Events	Kick-off meeting, Planning workshop	Expert workshops, Planning workshop	Repetitive CSO stakeholder workshops	Synthesis workshop, Communication Workshop
Deliverables / Output	"Wish-Lists" and feedback	Workshop summaries, model with description	Workshop summaries, national scenarios	Country reports, Comparative report
Time Horizon	6 months	12 months	12 months	6 months

Table 1. *Overview of the phases in the collaborative scenario definition process within the ENCI LowCarb project.*

Attitudes and Politics

In the beginning of the project, the different professional cultures and different intrinsic objectives of NGO members and scientists became tangible. NGOs are generally interested in developing scientific (counter-)expertise that can be used for proper lobbying activities, corresponding to their fundamental values. Especially, if the NGO is a network composed by several NGOs (like RAC-France), with individual future energy visions, there can be a strong internal pressure for obtaining politically relevant outcomes. Scientists have an interest in producing coherent, technically sound and objective research and tend to care less about the politics. These potentially conflicting attitudes were made explicit early in the project. In later stages, many conflicts could be avoided due to project partners pointing out that the argument or problem at hand actually had to do with our different attitudes and perceptions, resulting in more productive discussions. Raising awareness for such issues proved to be crucial, especially during the definition of the integrated scenarios, as these were based on the stakeholders' assessments of *political* framework conditions.

Joint Understanding of Quantitative Models

Large and complex quantitative models are a very powerful tool for pursuing integrated system analyses; however, the models and their output are often meaningful only to the expert or insider. Outsiders are not enabled to judge the quality and validity of model results, and either have to believe the modelers, or not. During the ENCI LowCarb project, it was very important for the NGO members to learn more about quantitative models in general, and the models of the project partners in particular, so that modeling results can be put into perspective. It was a rather time-intensive process for the quantitative modelers to explain the models and was perceived as a real cross-cultural communication effort. During this process, it was very enlightening for the modelers to learn about the requirements from an NGO perspective, which sometimes differs substantially from academic peer group discussions.

For the NGOs, it was important to distinguish between means and measures in the energy system models: technical solutions, e.g. offshore wind turbines, and political measures to foster them, e.g. feed-in-tariffs. Whereas energy system models contain a whole range of technical solutions, it is not possible to integrate the full impact of political measures. NGOs are interested in a mixture of both, so it is helpful to differentiate and focus on what is feasible in the model during the project. The joint effort of clarifying the capabilities of the energy system models turned out to be a crucial success factor for the ENCI LowCarb project. The "wish-lists" introduced earlier were invented during the explanation process and turned out to be an extremely useful tool. The modeling teams were forced to think about the "real-world implications" of the aggregate model results and develop concrete translation rules on how parameters and variables may be expressed in tangible meaning. During the preparation and post processing of the stakeholder workshops these translation rules served as a helpful structuring element for the quantitative modelers.

From the perspective of the quantitative modelers, the expert meetings in Phase 2 were very helpful and stimulating. The modeling teams learned a lot and sometimes revised the models according to the experts' opinions. Expert meetings are much more interactive than research conferences, where models are compared with other models, but not scrutinized in detail. For the NGOs, it was important to point out the sometimes double faced nature of experts, who are in fact also stakeholders, e.g. technical subjects like the necessary length of new transmission lines are a politically critical subject and even experts are not able to exclude this dimension from their opinions. For the NGOs, it was destabilizing sometimes that the modelers continuously improved their models, until the final scenarios were calculated. From the point of view of the researcher, this was natural to do, but it resulted in a situation in which the NGOs and became rather impatient as they wanted to see the model finished and ready to use. This should be anticipated and accompanied by setting and enforcing deadlines, sounding trivial, but proved to be a major source of conflict and dissatisfaction within the project team.

Stakeholder Workshops and Scenario Definition

The stakeholder workshops were the focal point toward which all efforts in the ENCI LowCarb projects were directed to. However, it was absolutely necessary to go through the first two phases of intra-group and model development for reaching a stage in which the project team was enabled to understand the stakeholders' requirements and translate them into coherent quantitative model scenarios. The preparation of the first stakeholder workshop was very demanding, as the agenda set here would determine the success of the collaborative procedure. The translation rules, from "the model" to "the real-world" and vice versa, had to be thematically summarized to determine those energy sectors (e.g. transport, electricity, heat) for which a feedback process was technically possible. For developing the agendas of the first sectoral CSO stakeholder workshops, the project team had to strike a balance between anticipating the areas in which social acceptance is problematic, and being prescriptive in the selection of topics. Furthermore, it was challenging to decide on how the stakeholder assessments would be collected, formalized, and grouped for constructing the integrated scenarios.

The stakeholder workshops on different energy sectors were stimulating and successful events. The instructions on the "scenario building bricks" in terms of political framework conditions were very valuable to the modelers. The workshops helped the project partners to understand which political scenario assumptions are socially more or less accepted, and specifically *why*. Due to the sector specific stakeholder workshops, particular attention had to be paid to assure inter-sectoral coherence without neglecting the statements of the stakeholders for defining the final scenarios. A basic problem is that regarding energy system futures, there are many problematic technologies or developments in terms of social acceptance. However, it is not possible to define one scenario for each issue. This implies that the different options have to be combined into "worlds" that are structurally different, but still coherently reflect the stakeholder's assessments. Without the lengthy preparation of the translation rules from model to reality the project would have failed at this point. The synthesis phase can under certain circumstances be disappointing for the NGO partners. The final outcomes can be opposing to the principles of the NGO, which then hinders their communication on project results or even challenges the overall NGO strategy.

Limitations and Comparison

Limitations to the presented conceptual approach relate mainly to the reduction of complexity during the collaborative scenario definition process. One practical limit of the project's intention to develop socially acceptable scenarios is the necessity to find a compromise concerning the representation of stakeholder opinions. The national sub-teams select and invite stakeholders, thereby consciously limiting the wide range of opinions to a manageable number. It is an important task for the social scientist to ensure the representativeness of stakeholders. Furthermore, stakeholders that are invited to express their assessment and opinions during the workshop are situated in an artificial situation with rules established by the project partners, which may bias the discussion.

The focus of the ENCI LowCarb project was on socio-political acceptance; a representation of market and community acceptance were beyond the scope. One could, however, extend this in future projects and include more case-studies or field research for the social scientists to investigate and elaborate on these issues. It would also be interesting to include more than one model of each country, to overcome the risk of model bias. Another aspiration could be to include also industry and policy makers in the collaborative procedure, or, in a supplementary phase, one that would try to take into account the political feasibility of the measures generated by the previous process. Generally speaking, one should be careful about including too many core project partners, as this may be detrimental to Phase 1 of the process.

For putting these limitations into context, it is helpful to consider the methods and setup of other scenario processes that involved civil society and/or stakeholder assessments and how they compare to ENCI LowCarb. However, there is to our knowledge no comparable project that was as transparent about the civil society stakeholders' roles. For example, Friends of the Earth Europe (FOEE) and the Stockholm Environment Institute (SEI) formally describe themselves as partners in a project aiming at developing an ambitious European mitigation scenario. The roles between FOEE and the SEI, however, were close to a traditional client agent relationship. FOEE fixed in advance technical assumptions on the availability of certain technologies in line with their internal strategy and SEI delivered the technical modeling knowledge. Nevertheless, several national FOEE associations were included in the initiative and a continuous exchange was established. It is interesting that the project partners decided to publish one publication each, supporting different communication strategies: FOEE (2009) and Heaps et al. (2009).

Another example is the European Climate Foundation (ECF) "Roadmap 2050" (ECF 2010), which outlines technically feasible pathways to achieve an 80% emission reduction target in 2050. Representatives of the EU institutions have been consulted periodically throughout the course of the project and a wide range of stakeholders (companies, consultancy firms, research centers and NGOs) have counselled ECF in the preparation of this report. Their names are mentioned, but not the method of how opinions were weighted, neither the rhythm of meetings. The hierarchy varied between project partners (a group of consultancies and research centers), core working group participants (European utilities, transmission system operators, clean tech manufacturers and CSOs) and further outreach (40 more companies, NGOs and research institutes). ECF tried to follow the recommendations in the scenarios, but claims to be solely responsible for the choices.

Then, the "Roadmap 2050" for a low carbon economy published in March 2011 by the European Commission (EC) (European Commission 2011a) comes with an impact assessment (European Commission 2011b) of three DGs, evaluating a set of possible future decarbonisation scenarios. The EC consulted individuals and stakeholders on their vision and opinion regarding an EU low carbon economy by 2050 through an online questionnaire "Roadmap for a low carbon economy by 2050"; 281 responses have been submitted. In its impact assessment, the EC declares that the wide range of views on how the EU can decarbonize its economy have been taken into account. However, the robustness of such an online questionnaire may be questioned. The core difference between these scenario processes and the ENCI LowCarb project is that here, domestic mitigation scenarios are one outcome, embedded in a project foster cooperation between science and CSOs.

Conclusion

Quantitative low carbon scenarios, developed in response to the problem of climate change, clearly benefit from an introduction of sociological dimensions, in particular social acceptance. Addressing the social acceptance of mitigation options can by definition not be a one-way process from science to the public. In this paper, we propose a project design intending to foster collaboration between science and civil society for that purpose. One distinct feature is a conscious emphasis on intra-group development, accounting for the issue that collaboration partners come from significantly different and potentially conflicting professional cultures; a situation that may give rise to severe communication barriers. NGOs and researchers can learn substantially of each other and create a mutual understanding of appropriate methods and perspectives. This enables the development of interdisciplinary research methodologies, intertwining both qualitative and quantitative tools of the different scientific disciplines.

In order to structure a collaborative scenario definition process, it is helpful to differentiate between technological and political framework conditions that serve as an input to the quantitative models. Experts are invited to define the technological framework conditions. The normative considerations of political framework decisions are guided and evaluated by relevant CSO stakeholders. A necessary prerequisite is that aggregate model input and output data are translated into tangible meaning. However, the methodology and organization of such a process is to date not well studied and should be developed formally for empowering more collaborative scenario definition processes in the future. In the end, this process can lead to the conceptualization of innovative low carbon scenarios that take into account social dimensions, in particular the social (un-)acceptance of mitigation options.

Meaningful energy system scenarios and policy roadmaps can only be developed if such organizational setups become more mainstream. Civil society has to be involved in solutions of climate change mitigation; purely academic solutions will not be successful. Climate change is not an isolated environmental problem like the ozone-hole, where there is one clear cause and one clear solution, but it is a problem whose solution will affect the entire economy and therefore the whole global society.

Acknowledgements

This research was funded by the project ENCI LowCarb (213106) within the 7th Framework Programme for Research of the European Commission. We thank the tree anonymous reviewers from the International Conference "Connecting Civil Society and Science – A Key Challenge for Change towards Sustainable Development" in Stuttgart, Germany on 20/21 October 2011 for valuable suggestions.

References

CAT, Centre for Alternative Technologies 2010, *'ZERO CARBON BRITAIN 2030 A new energy strategy'*, Available from: http://www.zerocarbonbritain.com/zcb-home/downloads [4 April 2011]

ECF, European Climate Foundation 2010, *'Roadmap 2050 A practical guide to a prosperous, low carbon Europe'*, Study commissioned by the European Climate Foundation (ECF), Contractors: McKinsey & Company, KEMA, Energy Futures Lab at Imperial College London, Oxford Economics, E3G, Energy Research Centre of the Netherlands, Regulatory Assistance Project and the Office for Metropolitan Architecture, Available from: http://www.roadmap2050.eu/ [14 July 2011]

European Commission 2011a, *'A Roadmap for moving to a competitive low carbon economy in 2050'*, Communication of the European Commission to the European Parliament, the Council, the European Economic and Social Committee and the Committee of the Regions, Available from: http://ec.europa.eu/clima/documentation/roadmap/docs/com_2011_112_en.pdf [8 August 2011]

European Commission 2011b, *'Impact Assessment'*, Accompanying document to European Commission 2011a, Available from: http://ec.europa.eu/clima/documentation/roadmap/docs/sec_2011_288_en.pdf [8 August 2011]

FOEE, Friends of the Earth Europe 2009, *'The 40% Study. Mobilizing Europe to achieve Climate Justice'*, Available from: http://www.climateshareeurope.org/Studysummary.pdf [8 August 2011]

Greenpeace 2007, *'Klimaschutz: Plan B Nationales Energiekonzept bis 2020'*, Study commissioned by Greenpeace Germany, Contractor: EUtech Energie und Management, Authors: Barzantny, K, Achner, S, Böhling, A, Schuring, S, Available from http://www.greenpeace.de/fileadmin/gpd/user_upload/themen/klima/Klimaschutz_PlanB.pdf [8 August 2011]

Heaps, C.; Erickson, S.; Kartha, S. & Kemp-Benedict, E. 2009, *'Europe's Share of the Climate Challenge. Domestic Actions and International Obligations to Protect the Planet'*, Stockholm Environment Institute, Available from: http://www.climateshareeurope.org/EU27%20LowRes.pdf [8 August 2011]

Likert, R. 1932, 'A Technique for the Measurement of Attitudes', *Archives of Psychology*, vol. 140, pp. 1–55.

Mahoney, J. & Goertz, G. 2006, 'A Tale of Two Cultures: Contrasting Quantitative and Qualitative Research', *Political Analysis*, vol. 14, no.3; pp. 227–249.

McDaniel, E. R.; Samovar, L. A. & Porter, R. E. 2009, 'Using Intercultural Communication: The Building Blocks' in *Intercultural Communication, A Reader*, (eds.) Samovar, L. A.; Porter, R. E. & McDaniel, E. R., Wadsworth, Boston.

Musall, F. D. & Kuik, O. 2011, 'Local acceptance of renewable energy – A case study from southeast Germany', *Energy Policy*, vol. 39, no. 6, pp. 3252–3260.

Nadaï, N. 2007, '"Planning", "siting" and the local acceptance of wind power: Some lessons from the French case ', *Energy Policy*, vol. 35, no. 5, pp. 2715–2726.

Nitsch, J.; Pregger, T.; Scholz, Y.; Naegler, T.; Sterner, M.; Gerhardt, N.; von Oehsen, A.; Pape, C.; Saint-Drenan, Y.-M. & Wenzel, B. 2010, 'Langfristszenarien und Strategien für den Ausbau der erneuerbaren Energien in Deutschland bei Berücksichtigung der Entwicklung in Europa und global „Leitstudie 2010"', Federal Ministry for the Environment, Nature Conservation and Reactor Safety, German Government, Avilable from:
http://www.bmu.de/files/pdfs/allgemein/application/pdf/leitstudie2010_bf.pdf [5 March 2011]

Renn, O. (ed.) 2011, 'Die Bedeutung der Gesellschafts- und Kulturwissenschaften für eine integrierte und systemisch ausgerichtete Energieforschung', Available from:
http://www.pik-potsdam.de/members/edenh/publications-1/Rennetal.2011DieBedeutung derGesellschaftsundKulturwissenschaftenfreineintegrierteundsystemischausgerichtet eEnergieforschung.pdf [1 August 2011]

Schmid, E. & Knopf, B. 2012, 'Ambitious Mitigation Scenarios for Germany: A Participatory Approach', *Energy Policy*, under revision.

Triandis, H. C. 1994, *Culture and social behavior*, McGraw-Hill, New York.

Tuckman, B. 1965, 'Developmental sequence in small groups', *Psychological Bulletin*, vol. 63, no. 6, p. 384–99. doi:10.1037/h0022100

UNEP, United Nation Environment Environment Program 2010, 'The Emissions Gap Report. Are the Copenhagen Pledges Sufficient to Limit Global Warming to 2°C or 1.5°C? A Preliminary Assessment', Available from:
ttp://www.unep.org/publications/ebooks/emissionsgapreport/pdfs/EMISSIONS_GAP_TECHNICAL_SUMMARY.pdf [8 August 2011]

Wüstenhagen, R, Wolsink, M. & Bürer, M. J. 2007, 'Social acceptance of renewable energy innovation: An introduction to the concept', *Energy Policy*, vol. 35, no. 5, pp. 2683–2691.

Willets, P. 2002, '*What is a Non-Governmental Organization? Article 1.44.3.7: Non-Governmental Organizations*', UNESCO Encyclopedia of Life Support Systems, Available from:
http://www.staff.city.ac.uk/p.willetts/CS-NTWKS/NGO-ART.HTM#Part11
[1 August 2011]

World Bank 2004, '*Defining Civil Society*', Available from:
http://web.worldbank.org/WBSITE/EXTERNAL/TOPICS/CSO/0,,contentMDK:20101499~menuPK:244752~pagePK:220503~piPK:220476~theSitePK:228717,00.html
[1 August 2011]

World Wildlife Fund (WWF) 2008, '*-30% de CO2 = +684000 emplois L'équation gagnante pour la France*', Study commissioned by WWF France, Contractor: CIRED/CNRS, Authors: Philippe, Q & Demailly, D, Available from
http://www.wwf.fr/pdf/Rapport_WWF_REDUCTION_GES.pdf [8 August 2011]

World Wildlife Fund (WWF) 2009, *Modell Deutschland Klimaschutz bis 2050: Vom Ziel her denken'*, Study comissioned by WWF Germany, Contractors: PrognosAG & Öko-Institut, Authors: Kirchner, A , Matthes, F C & Ziesing, H-J, Available from: http://www.wwf.de/fileadmin/fm-wwf/pdf_neu/WWF_Modell_Dutschland_ Endbericht.pdf [8 August 2011]

Zoellner, J.; Schweizer-Ries, P. & Wemheuer, C. 2008, 'Public acceptance of renewable energies: results from case studies in Germany', *Energy Policy*, vol. 36, no. 11, pp. 4136–4141.

AUTHOR INFORMATION

Baudé, Stréphane
stephane.baude@mutadis.fr

Stéphane Baudé is an engineer (Ecole Polytechnique) with complementary education in political sciences (Institute for Political Studies of Paris). Since 2004, he is a researcher and head of projects at MUTADIS. Stéphane Baudé has been involved in several European research projects in the fields of governance of activities or situations entailing risks for people and the environment (TRUSTNET IN ACTION, COWAM 2, COWAM IN PRACTICE, EURANOS, NERIS-TP European research projects) and has been a member of the CSS research team. He has also carried out field missions aiming to build democratic governance frameworks for tackling complex issues with the concerned citizens and actors (long-term response to long-lasting contamination of a territory by pesticides or radioactive elements, new technologies, territorial development).

Bauer, Joa
Joa.bauer@unw-ulm.de

Joa Bauer, who is a member of unw e. V. executive board has long-standing experience with unw activities, a CSO based in Ulm, Germany. He participated in different research projects in sustainable development with the "research group for future questions" of unw. Topics were regional concepts of sustainable development, networking and innovation and Industrial Ecology, which was also the topic of his doctoral thesis. He holds a master's degree in (technical oriented) Management and a doctoral degree in Economics and Social Sciences from University of Stuttgart. Mr. Bauer served as the CSO-researcher for the unw in the CSS project, building the project tandem with Dr. Reichel from Dialogik.

Balázs, Bálint
balazs.balint@essrg.hu

Bálint Balázs is a member of the Environmental Social Science Research Group (ESSRG), Hungary. He holds a master's degree in history from Central European University, Budapest and in sociology from EötvösLóránd University, Budapest. He lectures on environmental sociology at the Institute of Environmental and Landscape Management, Szent István University, Gödöllő, Hungary. His main research interest focuses on the socioeconomic conditions of local food systems and alternative agri-food networks in Hungary.

Von Blanckenburg, Christine
Blanckenburg@nexusinstitut.de

Christine von Blanckenburg is a Senior Researcher at the nexus Institute for Cooperation Management and Interdisciplinary studies. Within the institute she is the coordinator of project area "Civil society, globalization and identity". Her professional focus lies on Participatory Methods. She currently works for the Project "City of Solidarity", that analyses special opportunities of cooperatives in Climate Change. For further information on this TU-Berlin Project ,please: visit http://www.solidarischestadt.de.

Bozso, Brigitta
bozso@energiaklub.hu

Brigitta Bozso is a Project manager at Energiaklub Climate Policy Institute and Applied Communications. She graduated from Corvinus University as a landscape and garden architect, and after practicing landscape architecture for a year she went on to CEU and studied at the department of Environmental Sciences. She has been in the civil sphere for 6 years. She worked for WWF Hungary as a Natura 2000 program officer. During these years she got involved in international spaces and species conservation work with special focus to sustainable land use. She has been a member of the ENERGIAKLUB team since 2008. She started to work in the field of climate politics: supporting and convincing decision-makers and informing the public. She took part in the international climate talks in Poznan and Copenhagen and also in the social consultation process of the Hungarian national climate change strategy and program. She is responsible for FP7 CSS project since the beginning as CSO expert.

Dubreuil Gilles Hériard
g.heriard-dubreuil@wanadoo.fr

Gilles Hériard Dubreuil is director of MUTADIS since 1990. MUTADIS is a research group on sustainable development & governance activities entailing risks for people or the environment. He mathematician by education and graduated from Université Jussieu Paris-VI. He has developed governance expertise on socio-political dimensions of hazardous activities. He has a long standing experience since 1985 in various fields of research, methodological expertise and facilitation of deliberative processes involving civil society in the context of hazardous activities in the EU and in the international context.

He is also Chair of the Fund for Democratic Culture, Chairman of the regional cooperative "Landes Bois Energie" in the south west of France and member of the Consultative Committee of the French Federation of Local Commission of Information attached to nuclear facilities (ANCCLI).

Ellersiek, Annekathrin
Ellersiek@unrisd.org

Annekathrin Ellersiek is a Research Analyst at the United Nations Research Institute for Social Development in Geneva, Switzerland. She holds a master's degree in Work and Industrial Psychology from the University of Leipzig, Germany, and a doctoral degree in Organization Studies and Social Sciences from Tilburg University, The Netherlands. Her main research interests are the governance of inter-organizational networks in service-delivery and advocacy with a special emphasis on the area of development cooperation. Annekathrin currently works together with civil society in designing and governing such networks to bring about and implement transformative social policies in various development contexts.

Ferencz, Zoltan
ferencz@socio.mta.hu

Zoltan Ferencz is an economist and political scientist, working as research fellow in the Institute of Sociology at Hungarian Academy of Sciences. His main research topics are: Environmental sociology (floods, radioactive waste, food safety, sustainability; etc.); R&D policy; Social vision for the future; Lifelong learning. In the last 8 years he was involved in several international projects (NATO CCMS; FP6 (SAFEFOODS, COWAM2, TLM-NET); FP7 (CSS; PROSUITE; INSOTEC)).

Fink, Meike
meike@rac-f.org

Meike Fink works as "Climate and Energy campaigner" at the Climate Action Network – France, a French CSO network focusing on climate change policy. Her actual work covers the coordination of a European FP7 research project aiming at the development of ambitious energy scenarios for Germany and France. She also works on European climate and energy policies and the analysis of French energy scenarios.

Griesch, Gregor
gregor.giersch@idialog.eu

Gregor Giersch (Mag.) is co-founder and Financial Director of the Organisation for International Dialogue and Conflict Management (IDC), a Vienna-based interdisciplinary research association. He holds a master's degree in Political Sciences from the University of Vienna and is currently completing a Ph.D. on Monetary Theories. Gregor Giersch works with IDC in the management and implementation of research activities and projects, funded by European and national programmes. From 2008 to 2010, he was involved in the coordination of the European project *SustainergyNet* (FP7) on integrating civil society, scientific and policy knowledge towards sustainable energy policy in Africa. Since October 2011, he is participating in the European project *CiVi.net* (FP7) analysing the role of civil society organisations in Ecosystem Service management in Brazil and Costa Rica.

Klemenc, Andrej
Andrej.klemenc@rec-lj.si

Andrej Klemenc is a project manager at Ljubljana Office of the Regional Environmental Centre for Central and Eastern Europe. He holds Bachelor of Arts degree in political science at the Faculty of Social Sciences of the University of Ljubljana. He was actively engaged in the environmental movement Slovenia during 1980ies, establishment of the political party of The Greens of Slovenia at the turning point to parliamentary democracy in Slovenia and afterwards in fundation of new civil society organisations in Slovenia. As freelance researcher and editor he contributed to social science and humanist editions on ecology, environmental discourse, public participation, energy and environmental policy and waste management. As project manager, he has been particularly engaged in projects related to capacity building on climate mitigation, energy efficiency and renewable energy and most recently also in sustainable mobility. His theoretical background is in critical theory of society (Adorno, Habermas) and political sociology of Claus Offe.

Knopf, Brigitte
knopf@pik-potsdam.de

Brigitte Knopf holds a PhD in physics and is head of the group Energy Strategies Europe and Germany at the Potsdam Institute for Climate Impact Research. Her scientific work focuses on low concentration pathways of CO_2 emissions for mitigating climate change. Her main interest is the transformation towards a low carbon economy and the economic consequences and technological requirements for mitigation. She coordinated a model comparison within the EU project ADAM and is head of the group Mitigation Scenarios at

PIK on the assessment of low stabilization scenarios. In a recent project she is developing long-term scenarios for the energy system in Germany within the EU project Engaging civil society in low carbon scenarios.

La Branche, Stéphane
asosan95@hotmail.com

Stéphane La Branche is a Research Fellow at Grenoble's Institute of Political Studies where he heads the research chair "Planet, Energy, Climate". His main research interest is on the limits of participatory democracy and sustainable development in the fight against climate change, and its adaptation. He has worked on daily refusal and obstacles to modal reports, on the climate responsibility of firms, on the institutional obstacles to climate governance and he participates to the efforts of several cities in their efforts against climate change. He now specializes on adaptation strategies.

Marega, Milena

After graduation on the Faculty of Architecture in Ljubljana, Milena Marega worked for ten years as a freelance architect on several architectural, spatial planning and design projects. She established Center for Advanced Living Culture, a non-governmental organisation in 1998. Her interest on environmental issues led her to get involved in several research projects dealing with environmental protection and sustainable development. She coordinated the team of experts working on environmental education, sustainable consumption and ecologically-sound architecture.

Since 1993, Milena Marega has been the director of the REC – Regional Environmental Center for Central and Eastern Europe, Country Office Slovenia. She coordinates the REC Country Office's work and manages projects dealing with the following thematic areas: environmental protection, sustainable mobility, spatial planning, protected area management, project cycle management and evaluation, management of grant schemes, sustainable production and consumption and education. Her special interest is in public participation in decision-making processes and participative governance. She has been involved in several national and international projects that aim to strengthen the involvement of stakeholders and citizens in preparation, implementation, monitoring and evaluation of policies, programs and projects.

Málovics, György
malovics.gyorgy@eco.u-szeged.hu

György Málovics is an associate professor at the University of Szeged, Hungary. He holds a master's degree in economics from the University of Szeged and a doctoral degree in economics from the University of Pécs. He is a lecturer of environmental economics, environmental policy and valuation at the faculty of Economics and Business Administration in the University of Szeged. His main research interest is focused on the economics of sustainability with a special emphasis on the community level (e.g. cities). His theoretical background is ecological economics.

Mihók, Barbara
barbaramihok@gmail.com

Barbara Mihók works for the Environmental Social Science Research Group (ESSRG) and is also the co-ordinator of the Society for Conservation Biology – Europe Section (www.conbio.org). She holds an Advanced Diploma in Environmental Conservation from the University of Oxford, an MSc degree in Biology and a PhD in Ecology and

Evolutionary Biology from Eötvös Loránd University, Budapest. Her research activities have covered botanical and vegetation surveys, forest ecology and interdisciplinary studies of ecosystem services valuation. Currently her main interest is focused on the science-society interface, especially with regard to environment and conservation.

Meyer, Angela

angela.meyer@idialog.eu

Dr. Angela Meyer is co-founder and Board Director of the Organisation for International Dialogue and Conflict Management (IDC), a Vienna-based interdisciplinary research association. She holds a Ph.D. in Political Sciences/ International Relations from Sciences Po-Paris and the University of Vienna (co-tutelle). With IDC, she conducts project and research activities on sustainable development, sustainable resource management and civil society involvement as well as the prevention of social conflicts related to new and converging technologies. From 2008 to 2010, she coordinated the European project *SustainergyNet* (FP7) on integrating civil society, scientific and policy knowledge towards sustainable energy policy in Africa. Since October 2011, she is involved as partner and investigator in the European project *CiVi.net* (FP7), coordinated by the Leibniz-Centre for Agricultural Landscape Research (ZALF), where she analyses the role of civil society organisations in Ecosystem Service management in Brazil and Costa Rica.

Ollagnon, Matthieu

matthieu.ollagnon@affress.fr

Matthieu Ollagnon is a French sociologist and holds a PhD in Economics and Social Sciences from the Catholic Institute of Paris. He joined MUTADIS (France) in 2006, where he worked on research projects as well as public participation processes in governance of activities involving risks and impact on health and environment. He manages the French Association for Research and Teaching in Social Sciences (AFFRESS) and is the director of the electronic review *Incursions.fr*. He fosters researches on the relationships between quality of life, religious community and social ecosystem.

Pataki, György

gyorgy.pataki@uni-corvinus.hu

György Pataki is an associate professor at the Department of Environmental Economics and Technology, Corvinus University of Budapest (CUB), Hungary and a senior research fellow of the Environmental Social Science Research Group (ESSRG), Hungary. He holds a master's degree in economics and a PhD in management and organization studies. He lectures ecological economics at the Human Ecology master programme at the Eötvös Loránd University, Budapest. He also lectures a social entrepreneurship and social economy master course at the Faculty of Business Administration in Corvinus University of Budapest, postgraduate courses in ecological economics at the Environmental Sciences Doctoral School in Szent István University, Gödöllő and in corporate sustainability management at the Business Administration Doctoral School of Corvinus University of Budapest. His main research interest is focused on social-ecological change, biodiversity governance, participatory action research, and science-society interface.

Reichel, André
andre.reichel@zeppelin-university.de

André Reichel is a Senior Researcher at the European Centre for Sustainability Research at the Zeppelin University in Friedrichshafen Germany. He holds a master's degree in Management and a doctoral degree in Economics and Social Sciences from the University of Stuttgart. His main research interest is on degrowth (décroissance in French, Postwachstum in German) with a special focus on the firm level (e.g. company size, business model, legal form). He is also leading the CSS project on civil society involvement in sustainable development which is funded by the 7th framework program of the European Union. His theoretical background is in social systems theory (Niklas Luhmann) and its extensions towards studies on the next society (Dirk Baecker).

Renn, Ortwin
ortwin.renn@sowi.uni-stuttgart.de

Ortwin Renn serves as full professor and Chair of Environmental Sociology and Technology Assessment at Stuttgart University (Germany). He directs the Interdisciplinary Research Unit for Risk Governance and Sustainable Technology Development (ZIRN) at Stuttgart University and the non-profit company DIALOGIK, a research institute for the investigation of communication and participation processes in environmental policy making. Renn also serves as Adjunct Professor for "Integrated Risk Analysis" at Stavanger University (Norway) and as Affiliate Professor at the Harbin Institute of Technology and Beijing Normal University. Ortwin Renn has a doctoral degree in sociology and social psychology from the University of Cologne. His career included teaching and research positions at the Juelich Nuclear Research Center, Clark University (Worcester, USA), the Swiss Institute of Technology (Zuerich) and the Center of Technology Assessment (Stuttgart). His honours include an honorary doctorate from the Swiss Institute of Technology (ETH Zurich), an honorary affiliate professorship at the Technical University Munich and the "Distinguished Achievement Award" of the Society for Risk Analysis (SRA). Among his many political advisory activities the chairmanship of the State Commission for Sustainable Development (German State of Baden-Württemberg) is most prominent. Renn is primarily interested in risk governance, political participation and technology assessment. His has published more than 30 books and 250 articles, most prominently the monograph "Risk Governance" (Earthscan: London 2008).

Schmid, Eva
eva.schmid@pik-potsdam.de

Eva Schmid is a PhD candidate at the Potsdam Institute for Climate Impact Research. She holds an MSc in Econometrics and a BSc in International Business from Maastricht University. During her PhD project, she developed an energy system model for Germany. Her research focus lies on the development and analysis of long term domestic mitigation scenarios for achieving a significant reduction of CO_2 emissions in Germany by 2050.

Šepec Jeršič, Mateja
Mateja.Sepec@rec-lj.si

Mateja Šepec Jeršič is a Project Manager at the Regional Environmental Center, Country Office Slovenija in Ljubljana. She holds a bachelor's degree in Landscape Architecture from the University of Ljubljana. The bulk of her work is focused on support to NGO sector and on promotion of public participation in environmental decision making. She is involved in several environmental projects at EU level, mainly dealing with spatial planning, sustainable mobility and protected areas. At national level she is involved in providing technical assistance to national authorities in management of grant schemes for NGOs. Within the CSS project she was engaged as a CSO partner in the REC – Mutadis tandem.

Spangenberg H. Joachim

Joachim.Spangenberg@BUND.net; http://seri.academia.edu/JoachimHSpangenberg

Joachim studied biology, mathematics, ecology, and economics. Professionally, he is a senior researcher at the Helmholtz Centre for Environment Research UFZ and an affiliate with the Sustainable Europe Research Institute. As a scientist, he serves in science-policy interface institutions like the European Commission's expert group on the economics of environment and resource use, the IPCC and the IUCN Commission on Ecosystem Management. As a volunteer, he chairs the BUND/FoE Germany expert group on economic policy. In the past, he has among others. represented the European Environment Bureau at the OECD and FoE Germany in the environmental statistics and green accounting expert group of the German Statistical Office, was chairman of FoE Europe, Deputy Chair of the FoE Germany Scientific Council, European NGO spokesperson on biotechnology. He was also board/executive committee member of the International Network of Scientists and Engineers for Global Responsibility INES, the German Environmental Citizens Groups BBU, the German Peace Movement Coordination, the GenEthic Network, and the German Forum for Environment & Development, etc.

Stehr Nico

Nico Stehr is a Karl Mannheim Professor of Cultural Studies at the Zeppelin University, Friedrichshafen, Germany. His research interests center on the transformation of modern societies into knowledge societies and on developments associated with this transformation in different major social institutions of modern society (e.g. science, politics, governance, the economy, inequality and globalization); in addition, his research interests concern the societal consequences of climate change. He is one of the authors of the Hartwell Paper on climate policy.

(http://www2.lse.ac.uk/researchAndExpertise/units/mackinder/theHartwellPaper/Home.aspx). Among his recent book publications are: Biotechnology: Between Commerce and Civil Society (Transaction Books, 2004); Knowledge (with Reiner Grundmann, Routledge, 2005), Moral Markets (Paradigm Publishers, 2008), Who owns Knowledge: Knowledge and the Law (with Bernd Weiler, Transaction Books, 2008), Knowledge and Democracy (Transaction Publishers, 2008), Society (with Reiner Grundmann, Routledge, 2009) and Climate and Society (with Hans von Storch, World Scientific Publishers, 2010). His monograph on Experts: The Knowledge and Power of Expertise (with Reiner Grundmann) has just been published by Routledge. The monograph The Power of Scientific Knowledge (with Reiner Grundmann) is scheduled for publication by Cambridge University Press in 2012.

Szentistványi, István

szentistvanyi@gmail.com

István Szentistványi is currently a member of the local city council in Szeged, Hungary as the representative of the green party LMP. He holds a master's degree in humanities from the Eötvös Lóránd University, Budapest. He used to teach on the secondary school level, and specialized on marginalized students. His main research interest is critical and transformative education. His theoretical background is critical literacy (Paulo Freire), critical eco-pedagogy (Richard Kahn), in relation with contemporary literary theories – e.g. literary hermeneutics (Hans-Georg Gadamer).

Vári, Anna
anna.vari@socio.mta.hu

Anna Vári is Senior Researcher at the Institute of Sociology in the Hungarian Academy of Sciences and a Professor at the Budapest University of Technical and Economic Sciences. She holds a Ph.D. in Economics from the Budapest University of Economics. Her main fields of interest include health and environmental policy, risk analysis, conflict management, public participation and decision support. She has been principal investigator in a number of Hungarian and international research projects sponsored by various funding organisations including – among others – the European Union, the U.S. National Science Foundation, the International Institute for Applied Systems Analysis, the Regional Environmental Center for Central and Eastern Europe, and the United Nations Development Program. She has been author or editor of 9 books and about 140 chapters/articles in professional journals and scholarly books.